W9-AGN-501

FABULOUS

MEXICO

Where Everything Costs Less

by Norman D. Ford

Eighth Revised Edition
Copyright © 1967
HARIAN PUBLICATIONS, GREENLAWN, NEW YORK
Trade Distributor: Crown Publishers, Inc.

TABLE OF CONTENTS

THIS BOOK CONTAINS NO ADVERTISING WHATSOEVER, PAID OR UNPAID. EVERY ESTABLISHMENT OR ORGANIZATION HAS BEEN RECOMMENDED WITHOUT BIAS ON ITS MERITS ALONE.

RELIEF MAP

OF

MEXICO

Figure 1. Relief map of Mexico.

A Bargain Paradise At Your Backdoor

EVERY DAY, almost 4,000 Americans retire on fixed incomes. Every week, several thousand newly retired couples move south in search of sunshine, warmth and lower living costs. The majority settle in Florida, Arizona or California. A smaller proportion move farther afield to Mexico. Today, over 40,000 Americans have retired south of the border. At least six popular Mexican resorts are home to large American retirement colonies and on the plateau of Mexico, hardly a single colonial town or village is without at least the nucleus of a colony-in-the-making.

Barring the perennial dissatisfied, and the maladjusted who took their problems with them and realigned their values in terms of Bacardi at $4.50 a gallon, the majority appear eminently satisfied. Almost without exception, those with the capacity to adjust to Mexico and to capitalize on what Mexico offers are living on a grander scale than they could have north of the border. Most have discovered a life rich in values not seen in many years in the United States.

To mention a few: full time domestic help at $16 a month or less and gardeners at $1 a day; modern home construction at $4-$5 per square foot; modern private hospital rooms at $6-$8 a day; king sized filter cigarettes for as little as 8¢ a pack; a haircut, shave and shoeshine for 56¢; high grade investments yielding on the average a tax-free eight per cent and running up to twelve per cent; custom made clothes, shoes and furniture for less than their machine made counterparts in the United States.

With this new found freedom from household and garden chores, they have discovered a maximum of time in which to enjoy the leisure years. To this challenge of time, Mexico offers a unique opportunity to discover one's latent talents and an entirely new life of stimulating hobbies, sports and pastimes.

Understandably, since the fare to Mexico is often less than one third the fare to Europe, Mexico has outdrawn such bargain paradises as Spain, Mallorca and the Canary Islands. From most parts of the United States, Mexico is easier and cheaper to reach than is California from New York. You can load up the family car and over good highways, drive from your front door to almost any retirement town or resort in Mexico. *Thus this land of bargains lies literally at America's back door.*

Not all Americans have retired successfully in Mexico. Every year, thousands of first time tourists whose travel is confined to the Mexico City-Cuernavaca-Taxco-Acapulco circuit return convinced that Mexico is just as expensive as the United States. Others who read glowing accounts in magazines and other literature return disillusioned after fleeting visits. Still others find the adjustment too severe and leave. For those successful-minded people who have—just as they would have anywhere else—planned their retirement ahead and adjusted themselves to life south of the border, Mexico has proved to be the Utopia they sought.

Most people either love Mexico or hate it. There is seldom any middle road. Those who love Mexico find it a land of overwhelming spectrums of color and pageantry, a seductive mistress with charm and character and qualities of honest beauty which they cannot find at home. Within the great diversity of Mexico, they discover the ideal compromise between modern progress and the slow manana rhythm of yesterday. For in this paradoxical, many dimensioned land, the ancient and modern coexist side by side. Those who love Mexico find charm in the sharply defined contrasts of poverty and progress, in biblical scenes of goatherds who also chew bubble gum, in the oxcarts and the streamlined buses, the cobbled streets and the country clubs, the pagan idols behind Christian altars and the alien moods and colors. Whereas, others see in Mexico only a picturesque mantle of decay with villages and towns that resemble inhabited ruins.

What these people fail to realize is that Mexico has one foot in the past and the other in the future. Modern technology is constantly bringing yesterday closer to today. The knowledgeable, well oriented American is, therefore, able to combine the charm, luxuries, liesure and lower costs of 19th century living with many of the conveniences of the 20th century. Whereas on his quick dash through Ajijic, the tourist fails entirely to see that behind the noncommittal adobe walls are homes and apartments as luxurious as those in Park Avenue or Hollywood.

It is true that retiring in Mexico is not exactly like retiring in the United States. Living in Mexico calls for more adjustment than does living in Florida or Arizona. Mexico lacks some things that we take for granted. By contrast, it offers many comforts and luxuries out of reach in the United States. The principal aim of this book is to present the pros and cons so that you can decide for yourself whether Mexico is meant for you.

Much the same can be said if you plan to vacation in Mexico. In the great variety of this sun-loved land are some of the world's outstanding beach and desert resorts and spas. In many ways, Mexico offers more variety than Europe and is certainly more foreign and exotic. In the entire western hemisphere, no other country can boast such a wealth of history and ancient culture. It has beaches superior to any in Bermuda, Nassau or Jamaica. It has night life as gay as Havana's once was and inns as fascinating as those of England. It has the world's finest salt water fishing and hunting far superior to ours. It has Aztec pyramids and palaces, cathedrals, vivid markets, hoary churches and amazingly civilized cities that were old when Columbus arrived. It has some of the world's greatest bargains in hand-hammered silver jewelry, glassware and pottery, leather and lacquer, baskets, furniture, textiles and tinware. Considering the fare and utilizing the lore in this book, nowhere else will your vacation dollar go as far. Nor, anywhere else, can you spend such a unique vacation while looking over Mexico as a place to retire.

But this is not a travel guide for tourists. Rather, this book begins where the average guidebook leaves off. The purpose of this book is, first and foremost, to bring you up to date on Mexico, to give you an old timer's first hand knowledge of this fascinating land, its customs, traditions and peoples. Then in terms of climate, costs and conditions, this book covers the entire field of sports and vacationing in Mexico and of investing and retiring throughout the republic.

WITHIN THESE PAGES you will find most of the knowledge possessed by veterans who have lived or vacationed in Mexico for years. This book will bring you up to date on Mexico to the copyright date. After that, no book can foresee the future. Changes of one sort or another are bound to occur after publication date. All prices and conditions are subject to change. Although this book is revised at regular intervals with all data carefully checked beforehand, it must of necessity be assembled prior to publication. The aim of this book is, therefore, to give you an old timer's knowledge of Mexico *updated to our copyright date*. No book can do more.

Unless otherwise stated, all prices quoted in dollars and cents refer to U.S. dollars and cents. As previously mentioned, the book does not duplicate the basic data on touring and transportation found in travel guides. Undoubtedly, when you are ready to plan your visit to Mexico, you will find a guidebook useful. And since for some years, Harian has published one of the most complete and up-to-date guides to Mexico and Central America, we feel you cannot do better than to invest in a copy of *Mexico and Guatemala by Car* by this same author and available for $1.50 postpaid from Harian Publications, Greenlawn, New York.

SOURCES OF FURTHER INFORMATION

General tourist literature and information: Mexican Government Tourist Department, 630 Fifth Ave., Rockefeller Center, New York 20, also at Reforma y Lafruaga, Mexico 1, D.F.; Pemex Travel Club, Avenida Juarez 89, Mexico City.

Free monthly travel magazine: Pemex Travel Club Bulletin, PO Box 55 bis, Mexico 1, D.F.

Daily newspaper—six months subscription $24: The News, Balderas 8713, Mexico City.

Monthly magazine—$4 a year: Mexico This Month, Calle Atenas 42-601, Mexico 6, D.F. *$3 a year:* Mexican Life, Uruguay 3, Mexico City.

Non-tourist and cultural subjects: Instituto Mexicano-Norteamericano de Relaciones Culturales, Hamburgo 115, Mexico City; Comite Norteamericano Pro-Mexico A.C., Atenas 42-602, Mexico 6, D.F., sends free booklets "It's the custom, señor" and "Thumbnail history of Mexico."

Current highway and tourist information: Sanborn's, McAllen, Texas.

Railroads: National Railways of Mexico, 2016 Transit Tower, San Antonio 5, Texas.

Americans in Mexico: Anglo-American Directory, $4.50, Aptdo Postal 27-210, Mexico 7, D.F.

Free highways maps (some require application by postcard obtainable at local gas stations; do not send credit cards): Gulf Tourguide Bureau, 1375 Peachtree St. N.E., Atlanta 9, Ga.; Humble Touring Service, Box 2180, Houston 1, Texas; Ohio Oil Co., Marathon Travel Bureau, 539 S. Main St., Findlay, Ohio; Sinclair Auto Tour Service, Sinclair Oil Bldg., 600 Fifth Ave., New York 20; Chevron Standard Information Service, 225 Bush St., San Francisco 20; the AAA has maps for its members.

Summer Schools in Mexico

Open to both American residents of Mexico and to summer school vacationers are courses at the following Mexican institutions, many accedited in the United States and counting toward degrees. Many retirees also enjoy taking these inexpensive courses. Write to the addresses given for a prospectus and further information. (For a more complete list, look up the UNESCO publications *Vacations Abroad* and *Study Abroad* in any public library.)

Instituto Allende, San Miguel de Allende, Gto. Summertime cultural extension courses in all the fine arts, accredited in U.S.

Instituto Tecnologico Monterrey, Sucursal de Correos J, Monterrey, N.L. Summertime cultural extension courses in wide range of subjects, accredited in U.S.

University of the Americas, Aptdo 968, Mexico 1, D.F. Cooperative courses in Spanish and Latin American subjects, especially anthropology; summer workshop, accredited in U.S.

University of Guadalajara, Guadalajara, Jal. Summer sessions in fine arts and Spanish.

University of Guanajuato, Guanajuato, Gto. General college curriculum in Spanish,

University of Mexico, Ciudad Universitario, Mexico 20, D.F. Full all year curriculum for foreign students.

University of Vera Cruz, Juarez 23, Jalapa, Ver. English and Spanish summer sessions in a choice of subjects.

Some others are: Mexican-North American Institute of Cultural Relations, Hamburgo 115, Mexico City (summer Spanish language classes); Cento de Escritores Mexicanos, Valle Arizpe 23, Mexico City (writing); University of Morelos, Humboldt 306, Cuernavaca, Morelos. (summer arts and crafts school); Universidad Michoacana de San Nicolas de Hidalgo, Morelia, Mich. (summer cultural courses); State Teachers College, Aptdo 164, Satillo, Coah. (summer school in almost all college subjects); Universidad de Campeche, Campeche, Camps. (summer Spanish language courses); Universidad Iboamericana, Cerro de Las Torres 395, Campestre Churubusco, Mexico 21, D.F. (social sciences).

Most of Mexico's summer schools are operated as branches of famous American colleges and universities, are accredited by U.S. standards and approved by the V.A., and teachers attending the courses may deduct expenses from their federal income tax. The general range of subjects includes history, the performing arts, technical subjects, all the fine arts, folklore and archeology, and anthropology, in which subject Mexican schools rank among the world's highest rated. Tuition fees range from $50, room and board from $60 a month with total fees for tuition, room and board, fees and books seldom above $200-$300.

7

Part I

Inside Mexico – A Complete Introduction To Vacationing, Investing and Retiring

Chapter I

This Is Mexico

AEONS AGO, when North and South America were separated, a heaving volcanic peninsula rose from the sea below the North American continent. During later periods, more land was heaved up, linking the American continents together. Other land sank, leaving Cuba and Jamaica as islands. By the Pliocene Period, Mexico had assumed its present horn-shaped configuration. The center remained a skyline of volcanoes spewing masses of lava into the valleys below. Down through the geologic ages volcanic activity diminished. Erosion rounded off the sharp volcanic profiles and Mexico began to look more as it does today—a checkerboard of mountains, valleys, bowls and plateaus framed by azure seas and tropic beaches.

As a glance at Figure 1 reveals, mountains dominate the Mexican scene. Y-shaped, the main Andean cordillera runs north from Guatemala as a single range—the Sierra Madre de Chiapas—until south of Mexico City (marked Mexico on map) it runs into a sea of jumbled volcanoes that reach westward almost to the Pacific Coast. The state of Michoacan alone still boasts 80 rounded dormant volcanoes plus Paricutin, a now dead cone that in 1943 rose in a pyrotechnic cloud from a cornfield to a height of several hundred feet in a matter of days. Steeply slanted Popocatepetl (17,761') still occasionally puffs smoke within sight of Mexico City though her twin Ixtaccihuatl (17,343') has slumbered for centuries. To the northwest rise the 15,036' cone of Toluca peak and to the west, the symmetrical Fuji-like peak of Orizaba, at 18,800' Mexico's highest mountain. Subterranean fires, still primordially alive, smolder beneath this great central cross-section as occasional rumblings and the numerous hot springs testify.

At the fork of the Y the mountains split. The lower eastern range, the Sierra Madre Oriental, parallels the Gulf Coast to the Texas border. The western range, the Sierra Madre Occidental, runs west to the Pacific in a series of wild precipitous peaks, then towers steeply above the coast all the way to California. Between the two ranges lies a broad plateau. Known as the Mesa del Norte in the north, this is a land of stark desert landscapes cut by deep serrated *barrancas* or canyons and crossed by ranges of rocky eroded mountains. Dry and zestful with an average elevation of 3,500'-4,000', this vast sparsely populated tableland shares with the United States an unguarded frontier of over 1,500 miles. It is essentially a frontier country, receptive to new ideas and nowadays highly Americanized. Today, the six huge states bordering the U.S.A. comprise almost half the entire territory of Mexico.

Farther south the plateau rises to an elevation of 4,500'-8,000' and is known as the Mesa Central or Central Plateau. Here, in a series of wide rolling valleys ringed by mountains, the Spaniards discovered Mexico's fabled climate of perpetual springtime. Here, around a rich, loamy, lake-dotted plain called the Bajio, they built their colonial cities which later became the cradle of Mexico's independence movement. Together, the two mesas form the world's third largest plateau. One half of Mexico lies at an altitude above 3,280' and at this elevation or higher, lives 70% of the country's population.

Below the Sierras, the coast curves around the Gulf of Mexico in a tropical facsimile of our own Gulf shores. Apart from an outcrop of mountains in Vera Cruz, the entire 1,774-mile sweep of shore is low and flat and marshy. Gray or brown beaches rim a coast dotted with delightful hideaway resorts and fishing ports. Caribbean overtones are strongly evident and in the south, luxuriant rain forests crowd the shore. Forming the mouthpiece of the Mexican horn is the low Yucatan Peninsula, a shallow plain on a limestone foundation, scrub covered in the north and richly forested in the south.

But Mexico's true tropical beauty is found along the Pacific Coast. For 4,437 miles, the Pacific laps at coral white beaches, some of which have yet to know a white man's tread. Thrusting south for 1,000 miles is the immense peninsula of Baja California—arid, mountainous, inaccessible, beautiful and relatively unexplored. Between this peninsula and the mainland lies the shimmering Sea of Cortes (known in English as the Gulf of California). Cradled by the desert, this warm, limpid sea is incredibly rich in plankton and forms a *cul de sac* for equally incredible swarms of oversized game fish. From the multi-towered Sierras, the mainland coast drops abruptly to fecund tropical shores as like the South Seas as the South Seas themselves.

Along this incomparable coast flocks of parakeets flit through luxuriant jungles of banyan and feathery bamboo. Giant *coquito* palms line great blue bays and in between are spectacular vistas of sea cliffs and headlands. On the entire sweep of mainland shore lie only two modern resorts. Elsewhere, primitive banana ports are interspersed with fishing villages, most linked to civilization only by irregular coastal freighters. Coconuts, bananas, pineapples, and mango flourish in the rich coastal valleys and the transparent sea is the scene of the finest bill-fishing on this planet.

South of the Mesa Central, the Sierras meet in a sea of ancient volcanoes and trail south to the Guatemala border in a jumbled backbone of mountain ranges. This is Mexico's Deep South, a back country studded with potential Shangri-Las and Edens and broken midway by the low Isthmus of Tehuantepec, a bare 140 miles across. From Zenpoaltepec's 12,000' peak you may view both the Gulf of Mexico and the Pacific and until the Panama Canal was built, there were ambitious plans for a canal across this isthmus instead. South of the Rio Balsas (see Fig. 1) lies the Mesa del Sur, a dissected flat land with an average elevation of 5,000' on which stands the city of Oaxaca.

Its vertical topography has made of Mexico a masterpiece of geographical condensation. Within an hour you can drive from the torrid tropics to alpine mountain tops and en route, pass through every intervening temperature zone. Short summer rains keep the countryside green but for 8 months of the year, the skies are crystal clear, the country dry and brown and dusty. As a result, a cosmic cloud of dust remains suspended over Mexico giving rise to the fiery sunsets of the Pacific Coast and to the old saying that, "once the dust of Mexico has settled on your heart, you cannot then find peace in any other land."

The whole of Mexico is one vast museum with pyramids that rival those of ancient Egypt and with colonial cities as grand as those of Spain. But the face of Mexico is merely a background. A country is its people. And Mexico today has some 37,000,000 people. To understand Mexico you must understand its people. Despite the ease

9

with which you can drive across the border, we know far less about the Mexicans than we do about the Greeks or even the Egyptians. And Mexico is far more foreign than either Greece or Eygypt. Every year, countless Americans spoil their trip to Mexico through their lack of knowledge of Mexico and its customs.

If you hope to live successfully in Mexico, you must *understand* the Mexicans. Who are they? Not one American in ten—even among those heading south to retire —has the haziest idea. Of those Americans who return from Mexico disillusioned with retirement, almost all belong in this uninformed category. You must grasp the Mexican's basic outlook or you may find yourself bewildered, out of your depth and disappointed. By contrast, the informed retiree who realigns his values to conform with the Mexican's basic patterns of behavior and customs will discover rich dividends, a new enjoyment of life. For above all, Mexico has one vital attraction which we lack at home—its undeniable charm. Understand the Mexican's history, aspirations and achievement and you will enjoy life in one of the world's most charming countries.

The customs, standards, values and habits of Mexico are as foreign to us as those of China or India. For one thing, the pursuit of leisure is valued more highly than the pursuit of money. As a person of leisure, this puts you high on the scale of Mexican achievements right from the start. But many Americans simply stop there. Lacking the necessary knowledge, most American tourists live in the sterilized isolation of expensive luxury hotels which are so like home they might not be in Mexico at all. They discover none of Mexico's charm and go home convinced Mexico is no longer inexpensive.

The knowledgeable traveler, by contrast, shuns the impersonal service of the tourist palaces for Mexico's older and far less expensive colonial hotels, converted *haciendas* and *posadas* or inns. In them, he discovers not only charm but character. Knowing Mexico, he is able to thrust aside the tourist facade and enter into the fun of *charriadas, serenatas, fiestas* and markets. He discovers an eminently enjoyable, leisurely, low cost way of life rich in unsuspected values. This he is able to do because he knows who the Mexicans are. He knows their background, how they think, how they live. Mexico is his. And the same knowledge can make Mexico yours.

THE MEXICAN BACKGROUND. The Mexican is largely the result of his geography. For centuries, the mountains isolated the people, keeping them pure in culture and race. Even today, large groups exist in remote mountain valleys, cut off from modern culture and living almost as they did in primitive Aztec times.

Possibly about 30,000 years ago successive waves of a Mongol people crossed the Bering Straits from Asia and spread south to Mexico and beyond. Or you may prefer an alternative explanation that they came across the Pacific from Polynesia. Whichever is correct, and perhaps both are, these people, the American Indian, have populated Mexico for at least 300 centuries. At first they were crude hunters but by 4,000 B.C. they were building elaborate pyramids. Over the centuries that followed, three great centers of civilization grew up: that of the Mayans in Guatemala and Yucatan; that of the Zapotecs and Mixtecs in Oaxaca; and that of the Toltecs in the Valley of Mexico, a mountain rimmed basin at the extreme apex of Mexico's Y-shaped mountain fork. Virtually the whole of Mexico is studded with the ruined pyramids, temples and cities of these ancient peoples.

Advanced sculpture, mural paintings and picture writing attest to their culture. A thousand years before Christ the Mayans perfected a calendar and had achieved an enlightened civilization. About 500 A.D. they migrated to Yucatan and built the great cities of Uxmal, Tulum and Chichen Itza which even today overwhelm one with their immensity, dignity and strength. Meanwhile in Oaxaca the Zapotecans built an empire around their equally impressive Mitla and Monte Alban, both of which remain to this day.

But the greatest empire flourished in the Valley of Mexico. Until the 11th century the Toltecs ruled the Valley from their cities of Tula and Tulancingo both now a chaos of fallen splendor. After them, successive tribes moved in. Finally, about 1325, an Aztec tribe became dominant. They built their capital, Tenochtitlan, on two islands in Lake Texcoco in almost exactly the location occupied by downtown Mexico City today. By the 16th century their emperor Montezuma II ruled a vast domain spanning central Mexico from the Gulf to the Pacific. Fast courier services linked both oceans with Tenochtitlan so effectively that Montezuma enjoyed fresh seafood delivered daily.

In April 1519, within hours of their arrival, news reached Tenochtitlan that a Spanish fleet had landed at Vera Cruz. With a force consisting of 400 men, 15 horses and 7 cannons, the Spanish adventurer Cortes landed in Mexico in an enterprise that changed world history. On November 8th, 1519, joined by 6,000 rebellious Tlaxcalan Indians, he entered Tenochtitlan, where Montezuma laid out the welcome mat. What followed, too long and involved to describe here, forms one of the most fantastic tales of history. Suffice it to say that by 1521 Cortes had captured Tenochtitlan and with it, all of Mexico. From 1521 until 1821 Mexico, or New Spain as it was called, was ruled by a succession of five Spanish governors, two audiencias and 62 viceroys, practically all of whom selfishly exploited the country and the Indians for their own personal gain and that of the Spanish crown.

Systematically, and aided by the church, the Spaniards set about destroying every vestige of pagan Indian culture. Wherever an Indian temple stood, it was razed and a Catholic church built on the ruins. In Cholula, site of 400 Aztec temples, the Spaniards determinedly razed every single one and in their place built several hundred magnificent churches. Tenochtitlan was utterly destroyed and colonial Mexico City built in its place. Like the Romans, their ancestors, the Spaniards built on a massive scale, a simple matter in view of the wealth of Indian slave labor available. Wherever a native town stood it was torn down and a Spanish town built instead. For their cities, the Spaniards were ultra careful. Sites were chosen only after the most studious consideration of climate, health and soil fertility. Today, these charming Old World cities occupy the most beautiful and strategic locations and few boast anything but an ideal climate. Nowhere else on earth is there such a concentration of fascinating cities so perfect for retirement.

Until 1550, the Spaniards built in the heavy fortress-like Gothic style. Later, their buildings leaned towards the lighter, more ornamental *plateresque*. In 1680 the still more elaborate baroque became popular and this in turn gave way to the intricately carved and gilded *churrigueresque*. Every colonial city is replete with each style of architecture. Baroque facades and severe church towers loom over colonial homes with grand staircases and over palaces, patios, cloisters and arcaded plazas almost untouched since the day they were built.

Their churches were the Spaniards' most significant contribution. Designed with traditionally European baroque facades and austere towers and richly decorated inside with gilded cherubs, they nevertheless reveal ample evidence of the half heathen Indian craftsmen who interpreted the plans and carried out the work. Equally obvious are the Moorish style domes which dominate every Spanish ecclesiastical building. These tiled domes, their glazed faience visible for miles across emerald valleys, are the calendar picture symbol of Old Mexico. No other country anywhere has so many domes. Yet domes are not Spanish. Mexico's domes are as purely Moorish as the Moorish blood which flowed in Spanish veins after centuries of Moorish occupation.

Having arrived without wives, the Spaniards cohabited freely with Indian maidens. The offspring, half Spanish-Moroccan, half Indian, in turn cohabited with other Indian maids. Gradually a new race appeared, the *mestizo*. By the end of the colonial era, the *mestizos* numbered some 2,600,000 as opposed to approximately 500,000 inhabitants of pure Spanish lineage and some 3,500,000 pure Indians. Since then, through intermarriage, the *mestizo* proportion has increased to some 85% of Mexico's entire population. The Mexicans are, therefore, not only partly Indian and Spanish but also partly Moorish and partly Semite, Goth, Celt, Vandal and Roman—all races which at some time or other left their blood in Spain. The language of Mexico today is fundamentally that of the Roman legions who held Spain for 700 years.

Long before the Spaniards arrived, the great mass of Mexico's Indian population had been ruled by despotic Indian chiefs to

11

whom such refinements as slavery and human sacrifice were everyday phenomena. To most, domination by the Spaniards was no worse, and sometimes better, than domination by leaders of their own. For the average Indian, the Spaniards proved but a substitute master; the Catholic church became an apt substitute for pagan gods and pyramids; and Christian themes and music were artfully substituted for the pagan themes of pre-conquest songs and dances. In remote areas, even today, pagan idols are worshipped side by side with the Christian and the popular fiesta dances depicting the Christian triumph over the Moors are identical with pre-conquest pagan dances, the characters being changed to satisfy the church.

Less content were Mexico's half million Creole or Mexican born Spaniards who found themselves restricted to mercantile and minor administrative roles while, according to colonial law, all key positions still had to be filled by Spaniards born in Spain. This dissatisfaction reached its climax in 1810 when at Dolores Hidalgo in the Bajio country a Creole priest, Miguel Hidalgo y Costillo, issued a declaration of independence accompanied by his "Grito de Dolores" or independence cry. On the anniversary of this day, September 15th, the same declaration and cry are repeated by the President in Mexico City and by the leading citizen in every town throughout the republic.

Starting out with a small Indian band, Hidalgo and his successors finally forced the Spaniards out and in 1821 Mexico became independent. Out of the chaos that followed rose the complex general and politician, Santa Anna under whose military oligarchy Mexico was ruled, on and off, until 1855. Santa Anna a) abrogated the rights granted to American settlers in Texas, b) defeated the Americans in the well known battles of the Alamo and Goliad, c) lost his entire army in twenty minutes to General Sam Houston, at San Jacinto, in 1836, upon which he agreed to recognize the independence of Texas, and d) later disavowed the independence of Texas as being agreed to under duress.

While our own part in this affair does not bear too close scrutiny, that of Santa Anna proved a series of disastrous blunders. In 1846 the United States invaded Mexico and in 1847 the American flag was hoisted on the National Palace of Mexico City. The following year both Mexico and the United States signed the Treaty of Guadelupe Hidalgo, which, for compensation amounting to $15,000,000, gave us all Mexican territories north of the Rio Grande including Texas, New Mexico, part of Arizona and present day California.

More years of strife followed for Mexico, a period known as the War of the Reform, aimed against the power of the church. The secular party led by Benito Juarez, a Zapotecan Indian, won. And in 1861 Juarez triumphantly entered Mexico City, confiscated all church property and suspended for two years all payments on Mexico's foreign debts.

This angered the European powers. In 1862, for the third time, foreign troops invaded Mexican soil. A combined British, French and Spanish force landed at Vera Cruz. Alarmed, Juarez signed an agreement recognizing Mexico's foreign debts. British and Spanish forces withdrew. But the French forces of Napoleon III pressed on with reinforcements. With the American Civil War looking black for the Union, Napoleon now saw a trifold opportunity: to create an American empire; to seize Mexico's mineral wealth; and to aid the Confederates in overthrowing the Union. The following year French troops occupied Mexico City and in 1864, Napoleon's representatives, the Austrian archduke Maximilian and his wife Carlotta, became the rulers of Mexico.

By now the Civil War was over, Juarez was a refugee in Texas and the U.S. became thoroughly alarmed at Napoleon's invasion. At American insistence, the French withdrew. Maximilian was shot at Queretaro and Juarez again became president. Until Juarez' death during his third term as president in 1872, Mexico prospered quietly under his secularist state.

Four years later Juarez' successor was deposed in a revolution led by Porfirio Diaz. From 1876 until 1910 Diaz held Mexico in a dictatorial vise. During these 34 years Diaz initiated more material progress than did the Spaniards in four centuries. Foreign investments were welcomed, railways built, compulsory free education inaugurated and the Valley of Mexico drained. For 34 years Mexico enjoyed peace and prosperity—but at a price which reduced the populace to serfdom.

Americans who complain of bureaucracy when buying real estate in Mexico have only Diaz to blame. Here's why. Since Aztec times, Mexico's lands had been owned and farmed on a communal basis. When the *conquistadores* arrived, they received vast land grants or *encomiendas* from the Spanish crown. But outside their *encomiendas* (later called *haciendas*) the Spaniards continued to give free communal land to villages. These lands, called *ejidos,* belonged to the villages and were communally worked by village farmers. Under Diaz, the *ejido* lands were broken up and distributed to individuals. Since most parcels were too small to yield a living, their owners were forced to sell. Thus the *ejido* parcels were picked up en masse by *hacienda* owners. Within a few short years, the *haciendas* numbered over 8,000 and covered most of Mexico. During the Diaz regime, the entire wealth of Mexico belonged to a mere 70,000 individuals, of whom at least half were foreigners.

With their lands gone, the rural populace was forced to work for the *hacienda* owners. Each *hacienda* was self sufficient and run like a feudal estate. The workers, constantly in debt to the *hacienda* store, received slave labor wages and lived under the most appalling conditions. The United States abolished slavery, which had never affected most people, in 1865. In Mexico, *the majority lived under serfdom until just over fifty years ago.*

A revolution led by Francisco I. Madero (who was, incidentally, substantially hindered by powerful American business interests) finally overthrew Diaz in 1910. The *haciendas* were burned, the people freed. Chaos, turbulence and bloodshed followed. Not until 1917 was order restored and a new constitution phrased. This constitution, issued on February 5th (the same day as the previous one in 1857) is of more than passing interest. For it is the constitution under which Mexico lives today.

Briefly, the constitution broke up the haciendas and restored all *ejido* lands. It forbids the church to own lands or to operate schools. It gives the ownership of all mineral, oil and subsoil rights to the nation of Mexico. It expressly forbids non-Mexicans from owning land and developing oil wells or mines. Foreigners, it states, may be granted these rights by concession only if they agree not to ask protection from their own governments and to abide as Mexicans before the law.

In addition, the constitution specifies an eight hour working day (7 hours for night work) with one day free per week. Regardless of sex, equal pay must be made for equal work. Unions, collective bargaining and legal strikes are permitted. Industry shutdowns are allowed only when excess output would lower prices below the profit level. Not fewer than 90% of the employees in any industry must be Mexican. Then there are provisions for accident and sickness compensation and for minimum wages.

Embodying as it does the entire spirit of the revolution, this creed has been closely followed by each succeeding president to the present day. Notwithstanding that each new president brings with him a fresh political climate and policy, all to date have unswervingly followed the constitution's aims. A series of eleven presidents in the three years prior to 1920 prevented much actual progress. But commencing with the term of General Alvaro Obregon in 1920, the reconstruction of Mexico really began. Land continued to be distributed at an unfailingly steady pace.

In 1934, General Lazaro Cardenas accelerated land distribution. Under his Six Year Plan for Reconstruction, large land holdings were expropriated en masse and broken into *ejido* parcels. Land as an investment became distinctly unpopular. For the first time in history Mexican investors began placing their money in industry instead. Thus began Mexican industry's leapfrogging progress.

To encourage foreign investment, the Diaz regime had passed a law granting ownership of mineral rights to those who held the land above. As a result, American and foreign interests had acquired huge oil fields in Mexico. Under a law passed in 1924 the oil was declared Mexican property. But the companies continued to operate under concessions. Poor working conditions, however, led to growing discontent. In 1937, the workers' union called a strike. And the government's mediation board ordered the companies to increase both wages and compensation. This the companies flatly refused to do. Instead, they launched a publicity campaign against the Mexican government. On March 18th in the following year, the companies having failed to comply, President Cardenas expropriated their lands. The oil fields were nationalized and by now, so were the railroads and various other industries.

Came 1939 and a flood of European refugees, many with industrial skills and capital. This gave Mexican industry another jab in the arm. The following year President Camacho with his Good Neighbor policy smoothed the way for fresh American investments which could benefit Mexico without surrendering national rights or exploiting the workers. War year shortages caused Mexico to manufacture many items she had formerly imported. New industries received a five year exemption from taxes and Mexico's economy entered into an all out boom which hasn't slowed since.

Meanwhile, land distribution continued until today 90% of Mexico's agricultural lands are once more functioning on the *ejido* system. Some of this land is operated by large collective farms. Much has reverted again to communal village property and is operated collectively by the villagers, who, as a group, are entitled to credit from the Ejido Bank. The rest is owned and operated by individuals. As in Diaz' time, the first parcels proved too small for individual operation. But today the average irrigated parcel being distributed consists of at least 25 acres or, if of dry land, as much as 200. Due to this foresight coupled with vast irrigation projects, Mexico's agricultural output has increased 50% in recent years.

What, you may ask, is the significance of the *ejido* to your residence in Mexico? First, the information is useful in helping to understand how village agriculture functions. As this was written, there were *ejido* lands at both Ajijic and Chapala, two of Mexico's most popular retirement villages. Secondly, the entire *ejido* system has, in the past 30 years, changed rural Mexico from a nation of serfs to a nation of upright, proud and independent people. Third, and among its shortcomings, *ejido* inefficiency is responsible for the often inferior quality of Mexican meat and poultry and the unhealthful practice—now dying out—of using human excrement for vegetable fertilizer.

Over the past 20 years Mexico has moved in a single direction—upwards. In May 1942 the republic declared war on the Axis, made a valuable contribution in supplies and material, and sent a small air squadron into action overseas. Social insurance has been effective since 1942 providing benefits for occupational accidents and disease, general illness, maternity, disability and old age. After his election in 1946, President Miguel Aleman embarked upon an enormous public works project. And his successor in 1952, President Ruiz Cortines, carried on the free spending tradition. New highways and railroads sprouted in all directions, irrigation and hydro-electric projects were begun and private investment encouraged. With the Good Neighbor policy firmly established on both sides of the Rio Grande, U.S. capital flowed into Mexico to avoid our high taxation.

Mexico boomed! But not without sacrifice. Since 1933, the peso had already been devalued four times—from two per dollar down to 8.65 per dollar. President Cortines' immense public works projects plunged Mexico into a $96 million deficit abroad and in 1954 the peso was once more devalued (to the present 12.50 per dollar). By 1958, Cortines' budget was $66 million in the red. Yet Mexico's gains had been tremendous. During his term, Cortines established Mexico's role as the leading nation in Latin America, diversified the country's economy and built up a worldwide system of exchange agreements, foreign investments and export trade. In contrast to most other Latin American countries, Mexico is no longer a boom-or-bust, one-industry nation. In both politics and economics it ranks as one of the most stable countries in the western hemisphere today.

In 1958, President Lopez Mateos rode to victory on the Revolutionary Institutional Party ticket—the same party which had been in power since 1929 (the official party in power is the only effective political party). Opposing him was Luis Alvarez on the ticket of the Party of the National Action. A third candidate, who failed to rally sufficient membership to make the ballot, was nominated by the Communist party. Symbolic of Mexico's politics over the past two generations has been the swing from militarists to strictly civilian administrators. For the first time in Mexico's history, Mateos' administration was strongly sprinkled with the nation's younger intellectuals. Almost immediately, Mateos balanced the budget, strengthened the currency and set out to eliminate graft, corruption and inefficiency in socialized industries (i.e., 400 plants including a steel mill and tractor factory, the railways and the gigantic Pemex oil monopoly).

Including weak and company unions, most Mexican industries now are unionized. Thanks to all this, Mexico's industrial production entered the 1960s with a history making annual growth record of 8%—an achievement equalled only by such twentieth century colossi as West Germany and Japan. Mexico City has risen to tenth place among world capitals and is the fourth largest metropolis in the western hemisphere. Today, Mexico is outstripping, percentagewise, the economic and population growth of the United States, a feat reflected in the pride which every Mexican feels for his nation.

THE NEW MEXICO. The peace, prosperity and progress achieved since the 1930s are transforming all of Mexico. From a nation which in 1910 could boast only two classes—the very rich and the very poor—is emerging a new strata of society, a middle class. This new middle class is buying consumer goods—TV sets, appliances and even cars—catapulting demand for manufactured goods to constantly new highs. Since 1930 the population has doubled and is now expanding at the explosive rate of 3½% annually, a pace which, if maintained, will mean a population of 55,000,000 by 1980. From one end of Mexico to the other, rapid progress and the growth of industry are raising national income.

What is the driving power behind all this? Getting the "feel" of something in Mexico is called getting "the wave." Most Americans fail to get the "wave." Thus a little inside knowledge is helpful. The driving power behind Mexico today is the spirit of the revolution of 1910. Haphazard as the face of Mexico appears, the spirit of the revolution as embodied in the constitution guides and inspires all progress and politics within the republic. Starting with the land reform, the entire progress of Mexico since 1920 has followed these principles almost to the letter. The army has been curbed and the money spent instead on health and education.

What has been achieved? For centuries, infant mortality claimed one out of every three poorer class Mexican babies. Other

Useful Publications About Mexico

A large selection of inexpensive English language books on Mexico is available by mail from Sanborn's Insurance Service, McAllen, Texas.

A wide selection of other useful and nominally priced booklets is available from the Pan American Union, Washington 6, D.C. Among these are the two volumes entitled *A Statement of the Laws of Mexico;* and also *A Tourist's Guide to Holidays and Festivals in Mexico; a copy of the Constitution of the United Mexican States, 1917.* Other good books are sold by mail by Minutiae Mexicana, Ave Alvaro Obregon 286, Mexico 7, D.F.

diseases took an incredible toll. In recent years, however, enormous strides have been made. Public health and welfare centers have been set up almost everywhere and such tropical scourges as smallpox, typhus, cholera, yellow fever and plague practically eliminated. Each year, every dwelling in Mexico is sprayed to combat malaria (accounting for the number painted on every house). Miracle drugs have eliminated most of the hazards of childbirth and as industry raises living standards, longevity is on the increase everywhere. Today, the chief causes of death are waterbourne diseases, intestinal parasites, gastro-enteritis and colitis; pneumonia and TB; heart diseases; diseases due to promiscuity; leprosy, accidents and homicide.

Crime in general? The rate is about the same as in the U.S. Risk of robbery is greatest in the largest cities. Yet to our knowledge no American has ever been robbed who was not frankly inviting trouble. We ourselves have never lost a penny. We would suggest, however, that your car, including the hood, should always remain locked. And in cities, it has been customary from colonial days to employ a *cuidador* or watchman to keep an eye on your home or apartment while you are out. Prostitution still flourishes in cities and, we are told, despite their being registered and given a weekly penicillin shot, these girls are invariably infected.

In 1910, 63% of Mexico's population could neither read nor write. Schooling gradually reduced this proportion, but some years ago the problem still remained so acute that writer Torres Bodet inaugurated the "Each One Teach One" movement. Practically every literate Mexican taught another to read and write and the government chipped in by publishing a large library of low cost, simple books. Results were so sensational it was not surprising to find Torres heading education in the Mateos administration. As this was written, only 28% of Mexico's population remained illiterate.

Even so, educational standards are abysmally low. As late as 1960, 81% of rural school children were dropping out by the third grade and of every 1,000 only 22 reached high school. Under Torres' able leadership a new drive for education began. Prefabricated schoolhouses were shipped out by the thousands and as this was written, 72% of all children aged 6-14 were attending school. Notwithstanding low teacher pay and lack of modern aids, standards seem high. Time after time, mothers of American children enrolled in Mexico's public schools have told us that at the same age, Mexican children are more advanced than in the United States. Among the best are Catholic schools, once banned but now permitted to operate again as private schools or *colegios*.

Where does Mexico really stand today? Of the total population, one half are still engaged in agriculture (compared to 18% in the U.S.) and fully one third of Mexico's population still exists at a subsistence level. In small towns and villages the average wage seldom exceeds $1.50 per day while women are fortunate to make $5 per week. Even in cities $100 a month represents a good income and an aggressive city salesman is well satisfied to take home $150. Though tremendous progress is being made in every field of endeavour, the fact remains that overall, Mexico still lags behind the United States by some 75 years.

THE UNITED STATES OF MEXICO *is organized* as a republic with a federal type of government, similar to that of the United States. Executive power is vested in the president who is elected by popular vote. Nowadays, all men and women over 21 may vote and failure to comply carries such civil penalties as denial of a passport. The president serves a six year term and cannot be re-elected. Besides his role as chief executive, the president is also an important originator of legislation. Although the states are free and sovereign and each has a dual hierarchy of internal government, the federal government is the dominating political force to a far greater extent than in the United States.

Federal power is split into tripartite division: executive judicial and legislative. Legislative power is vested in a bi-cameral General Congress consisting of a Senate and a Chamber of Deputies. There are two senators from each of the states and the federal district—sixty senators in all—each chosen by direct popular election for a six year term. One deputy is elected to represent every 170,000 inhabitants for a three year term (deputies recently numbered 162). Congress meets annually on September 1st and adjourns the following December 31st. During the recess, a Permanent Committee of 14 senators and 15 representatives carries on their work. At lower levels, the legislative branch includes numerous commissions, boards and agencies created to aid Mexico's growing economy.

Judicial power is vested in a Supreme

For Further Reading . . .

Here are some good books on Mexico available in most larger American public libraries: *History of Mexico*, Henry Parker; *Mexico Today*, John A. Crow; *Timeless Mexico*, Hudson Strode; *The Winds that Swept Mexico*, Anita Brenner; *Mexico and its Heritage*, Hudson Strod; *Mexico Reborn*, Verna Millan; *My House is Yours*, Elisa Larrolde; *The Days of Ofelia*, Diamant; *Tempest Over Mexico*, Rosa A. King; *Viva Mexico*, Charles Flandreau; *Little Mexico*, William A. Spratling; *House in the Sun, Village in the Sun*, Dane Chandos; *The Mexican Nation*, Hubert Priestley; *Mexico—a Land of Volcanoes*, J. H. Sharman; *Many Mexicos*, Leslie Simpson; *The Conquest of Mexico*, Prescott; *Mexico South*, Miguel Covarrubias; *A Treasury of Mexican Folkways*, Frances Toor; *My Heart Lies South*, Elizabeth Borton de Trevino; *Mexico* by William Johnson; and Frank Tannenbaum's *Mexico: the struggle for Peace and Bread*.

Court and in circuit and district courts which are duplicated by the states. Not generally known and of vital importance if you plan to live in Mexico is that *Mexican law operates under the Napoleonic legal code*. Which means to say that a person is guilty until proven innocent. This system, the very antithesis of ours, is largely based on old style civil law systems prevailing in continental Europe. In reality, it is lightly applied to American offenders. If you do have the misfortune to be arrested, you can usually count on being released within a few hours. The stories of Americans being held in Mexican jails for months without trial are factually true . . . but the stories fail to add that most of these prisoners were actually caught perpetrating crimes and that the majority also physically resisted arrest. While a Mexican jail is no place to linger in if one can help it, by and large you will find justice meted out in Mexico as fairly as in the United States.

Below the state level, all towns and villages are administered by a municipal council (*ayuntamiento*) elected by the populace. City police are uniformed like ours and aided by a highly intelligent mobile highway force. Small towns and villages are policed by *rurales*, easily recognized by their khaki uniforms, beige pants, black ties and ten gallon Texas style hats. Upon request, soldiers may be called in to assist the

16

police or to maintain order in small un-policed communities. In this role the soldiers are called *federales*.

Since 1947 women have held the right to be elected to municipal office and since 1953 have enjoyed full national sufferage.

THE STATES OF MEXICO. The Constitution of 1917 provided for a Federal Republic of 29 states, two territories and a Federal District. Since you will live in one of these regions, here is a brief review of the outstanding features of each. Given in brackets after the name of each state is the postal abbreviation followed by the area in square miles, the state population (latest estimate) and the state capital. The location of each state is shown in Figure 2.

AGUASCALIENTES (Ags.): 2,530, sq m; pop 215,000; Aguascalientes.

A small state in the Mesa Central with an average elevation of 6,000', Aguascalientes is famed for its numerous mineral springs and fertile soil on which are raised grapes and an enormous variety of fruits. Aguascalientes, the pleasant capital, manufactures cotton, pottery and leather and is surrounded by vineyards, orchards and *ranchos* raising fighting bulls.

BAJA CALIFORNIA (B.C.) This 1,015-mile peninsula, averaging 40-200 miles in width, is an unspoiled region rich in desert and mountain beauty. Below the central sawtoothed mountain range, gulfs, bays and beaches line both coasts. Almost rainless in parts, the climate is pleasantly tropical throughout the year. With its vast mineral resources and unsurpassed sports fishing, this region has great potential as a future western Florida. The 28th parallel of latitude divides the peninsula into the North and South Districts.

North District: 27,980 sq m; pop 578,-000; Mexicali. This state is fast becoming prosperous. The region around Mexicali, an extension of California's rich Imperial Valley, raises vast crops of cotton. And the two resorts of Rosarito and Ensenada, within easy reach of Southern California, carry the highest price tags in Mexico. Numberless bays and coves line both shores.

South District: 28,308 sg m; pop 71,000; La Paz. Dipping into the tropics, this isolated territory is rimmed by white beaches and almost entirely unknown. With the exception of La Paz and a few decaying villages and hidden *ranchos*, the whole area has remained stagnant since the first white man

arrived in 1533. Roads are few and passable only to jeeps while iguanas and giant cactus dominate the landscape. Outside La Paz, the native population seem personally clean and honest, shy, content and indifferent to money. Some of them, fair in pigment, may be the offspring of pirates whose activities gave rise to the numerous tales of buried treasure.

CAMPECHE (Camp.): 19,902 sq m; pop 160,000; Campeche.

A low lying and sparsely populated tropical state. The pinktoned capital of Campeche is a musty tropical port built over subterranean Mayan catacombs. Ciudad del Carmen, the second city, an Old World island fishing port, is being transformed by a shrimp boom. Both export plywood, veneer, copra and henequin.

CHIAPAS (Chis.): 29,070 sq. m; pop 1,171,-000; Tuxtla Gutierrez.

Seldom visited Chiapas is a varied, colorful and highly interesting state of rugged mountains covered with primeval pine forests, deep jungle clad valleys and spectacular landscapes of immeasurable distances. Home of ancient civilizations, it is the site of three wel known archeological zones; beautiful Palenque, remote Yaxchilan and even more inaccessible Bonampak. Prior to 1920 access was limited to burro trains and only in 1950 was the highway completed from Mexico City. As a result, Chiapas' rich Indian life is almost unchanged. In the mountain city of Las Casas—an overlooked colonial gem— the variety of Indian tribes is revealed by the babel of tongues and abundant vivid costumes. Collectively termed the Chamulas, the Indians stem from the Mayans. Chief tribes are the true Chamulas from whose be-ribboned hats and tunics one may deduce village, occupation and marital status; the handsome Zinacantanes and their cousins, the Tzotzels and Tenejapans; and the primitive Lacandones who inhabit the rain forest near Bonampak. Among their distinctive apparel are the Chamulas' high heel guards, facsimiles of those on Mayan sculptures; the bare midriff worn by both men and women from San Bartolome de Los Llanos; and all over Chiapas, the women's hair braided with long colored ribbons. Suffice it to say Chiapas deserves far more attention than it receives. Tuxtla Gutierrez, the capital, is a modern, bustling city at a hot, dry 1,700'; San Cristobal Las Casas, the other city, lies at a high, cool 7,500'.

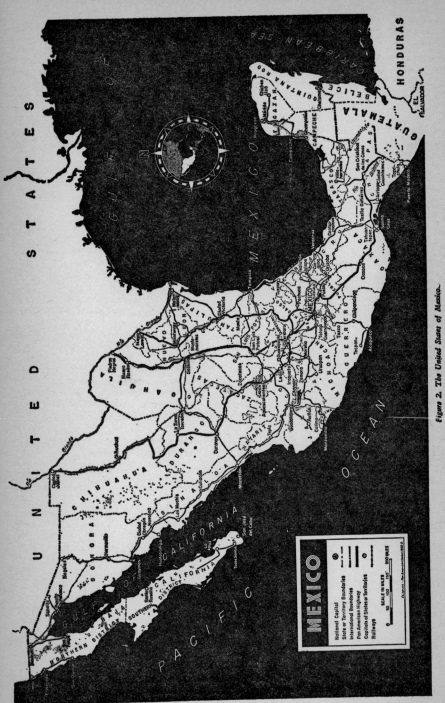

Figure 2. The United States of Mexico.

CHIHUAHUA (Chih.): 95,945 sq m; pop 1,109,000; Chihuahua.

The largest Mexican state and one of the richest, Chihuahua occupies a plateau averaging 4,000' in elevation and rising to 8,000'. Among the immense *barrancas* that slash its plains are those of the Urique River, some 8,000' deep, 50 miles in length and more spectacular than Grand Canyon. Vast underground water resources tapped by artesian wells aid the state's mining, cotton and cattle economy. Living in the biggest state with the tallest people, Chihuahuans are apt to be the Texans of Mexico (but are easily dissuaded when reminded of their diminutive Chihuahua dogs). Part old, part new Chihuahua is a bustling business town while Parral, the second city, still bears the bullet scars of earlier revolutions. As the state is predominantly a parched desert carpeted by spiny cactus, trees here are limited to pine forests in the rugged western Sierras. Inhabiting the subtropical *barranca* floors are fast disappearing Tarahuma Indians, some of the world's fleetest runners, who are distinguished by their turbans, long hair and crude violins.

COAHUILA (Coah.): 58,750 sq m; pop 915,000; Saltillo.

Mexico's third largest state ranges from hot tropical lowlands to beautiful fertile valleys and high, cool mountain country. Cotton is primarily responsible for the prosperity of the amazingly new, clean and modern city of Torreon while Saltillo, the serene, cool mountain resort capital, thrives on the state's overall economy of mining and cattle, wheat and sugar production.

COLIMA (Col.): 2,010 sq m; pop 154,000; Colima.

One of the smallest states, Colima borders the Pacific and owes its prosperity to the lusty tropical seaport of Manzanillo, nearest port to Guadalajara. Colima, the capital, is a languid colonial town in a luxuriant valley under the shadow of a still active volcano.

DISTRITO FEDERAL (D.F.): 580 sq m; pop 5,000,000 plus; Mexico City.

Located in the southwest part of the Valley of Mexico on the site of former Lake Texcoco now drained by the Desague Canal, Mexico City is a booming, fast paced, ultra modern world capital. Utterly un-Mexican, it is yet the central heart of the republic, as Paris is of France. It has no rivals, no competing Chicago or San Francisco. Here is the unified center of Mexico's government, finance, industry and transportation. At a cool 7,347', this oldest metropolis in North America is today slowly sinking (as much as 50 centimeters annually) into the mire of Lake Texcoco. Nevertheless, surrealist skyscrapers are rising left and right while on the outskirts is an ever expanding ring of plush suburbs and satellite cities studded with *multifamiliares.* Administering the Federal District is a governor general appointed by the president and who, in federal affairs, ranks in status next to the chief executive.

DURANGO (Dgo.): 48,250 sq. m; pop 800,000; Durango.

An extensive state on the mountainous Sierra slopes consisting of semi-arid lava plains slashed by deep *barrancas.* Among Durango's vast mineral resources is an entire mountain of iron. Cotton, wheat, sugar and cattle bring prosperity to Durango, the pleasant capital city dominated by its enormous cathedral. Largely still wild, Durango state is home to numerous bears and wolves.

GUANAJUATO (Gto.): 11,945 sq m; pop 1,700,000; Guanajuanto.

A mountainous state on the Mesa Central with broad, fertile valleys rich in fruits and flowers and an array of mineral springs. One of Mexico's most attractive states, Guanajuato has huge mineral resources and raises corn, wheat and tobacco. Leon is a neat and prosperous leather manufacturing town while Guanajuato, the capital, is one of the most flavorful and atmospheric colonial cities in Mexico.

GUERRERO (Gro.): 25,720 sq m; pop 1,124,000; Chilpancingo.

A rugged and mountainous Pacific Coast state cut by the Rio Balsas and countless smaller streams. From the Sierras and Mesa del Sur, vast tropical hardwood forests reach down to the Pacific Coast, a beach resort region boasting famed Acapulco and the hideaway Eden of Zihuatanejo. Inland lies the fantastic Old World town of Taxco, whose silver mines have produced immeasurable wealth. The capital city is of minor interest.

HIDALGO (Hgo.): 8,155 sq m; pop 927,000; Pachuca.

A small mountainous, highly mineralized and untouristed state, site of Real del Monte, the world's richest silver mine. On the high plateau are: Tula, once capital of the Toltec empire; the hilly colonial mining capital of Pachuca; and nearby, the picturesque mining village of Real del Monte. Rich forests of mahogany and ebony thrive on the state's eastern slope. Throughout Hidalgo, one finds relics of Otomi folk art and these Indians, living today much as in pre-conquest times, produce outstanding textiles. Within easy reach of Mexico City, southern Hidalgo is fast becoming the site of new manufacturing towns.

JALISCO (Jal.): 31,520 sq m; pop 2,100,-000; Guadalajara.

Romanticized in song and tradition, this rich and progressive state begins at an average elevation of 6,000' on the Mesa Central and plunges down through deep, unexplored *barrancas* to exotic jungles on the lush and fertile Pacific shore. Centrally located on the semi-arid plateau stands the modern yet distinctly Old World capital of Guadalajara, Mexico's second largest city; and nearby, on Lake Chapala, largest lake in Mexico, are clustered the retirement villages so popular with Americans. This is a land of sweeping panoramic views, golden sun-filled valleys and distant purple mountains, white villages with ancient church domes and towers, crumbling *haciendas* and working ranches, and *vaqueros* in broad brimmed hats on fiery Arab steeds. n the beach rimmed coast lie the two idylic resorts of Barra de Navidad and Puerto Vallarta. Extensive forests crowd the mountains; rich mines pour forth an abundance of silver, copper, iron and tin; fruits, tobacco, sugar and cotton flourish wherever irrigation waters flow; and modern plants produce leather, steel, sugar, textiles, pottery, and glass. As in Michoacan, the music loving Tarascan Indians dominate Jalisco's plateau; each village has its own song and the state is home of Mexico's wandering bands of *mariachi* troubadors.

MEXICO (Mex.): 13,380 sq m; pop 1,400,-000; Toluca.

A small state, the eastern half mountainous, the western half a plain. Within this state are three of Mexico's highest volcanoes, Popocatepetl, Ixtaccihuatl and Toluca peaks, which stand guard over two major valleys, those of Mexico and Toluca. From their snow clad slopes comes the Rio Lerma, which flows into Jalisco's Lake Chapala. Proximity of Mexico City and a state law granting industry ten years' freedom from taxation have brought hundreds of new factories, including many wheat mills and dairy processors, to Mexico state. Elsewhere, timeless villages and pre-conquest remains dot the countryside, which is inhabited in the north by the Otomi tribe and in the south by Aztec races.

MICHOACAN (Mich.): 23,476 sq m; pop 1,680,000; Morelia.

A rolling mountainous state of diverse scenery, beautiful Michoacan is a land of flat topped volcanoes, fertile semi-tropical valleys filled with orchids, tall forests and singing streams, waterfalls and canyons and a virgin untouched Pacific sea coast lined by magnificent white beaches. High spots of this picturesque state are: the pink hued colonial capital of Morelia splendidly situated in a green valley at 6,200'; Lake Patzcuaro with its butterfly net fishermen and charming lakeside colonial town of Patzcuaro; and the semi-tropical garden town of Uruapan. Here, too, are numerous spas including the famed resort of San Jose Purua. Essentially still famed for its handicrafts rather than for industries, the big new Tepalcatapec hydroelectric project should give an impressive boost to Michoacan's future economy. Ancient *yacatas* or pyramids tell story of the states' Tarascan Indians who still preserve their costume and culture in hundreds of timeless villages. Tall, proud, intelligent and volatile—polit but never servile—the Tarascans are an independent race of excellent weavers whose culture dominates west central Mexico. The women in their red or blue checked pleated wool skirts, blue *rebozos* and silver earrings are numerous in Patzcuaro on market day. Each village has its own band, composer, music and dances and here one may hear the purest of Mexican folk music. In the Uruapan area, many Tarascans possess features distinctly Chinese.

MORELOS (Mor.): 1,940 sq m; pop 390,-000; Cuernavaca.

A picturesque and artistic state of high, forested mountains and lush river valleys with numerous waterfalls. Here is a wealth of spas and resorts with good hotels and the towns abound with colonial monuments. Colonial Cuernavaca, today an international playground, contains Old World charm and modern sophistication and, once home of Cortes and Maximilian, now plays host to scores of wealthy Mexico City businessmen and American retirees.

NAYARIT (Nay.): 10,670 sq m; pop 377,-000; Tepic.

From the volcanic Sierra ranges, 17 deep

river valleys cut through this undeveloped state and enter the Pacific along Nayarit's 300 miles of practically virgin coast. Tropical villages dot the shore and the numerous coastal lagoons teem with wild fowl in season. Chief among the coastal towns is the Tahitian-like village of San Blas. Inland at 3,000', the colonial capital of Tepic reflects civic pride in its reputation as one of the cleanest and pleasantest small cities in Mexico. Two interesting Indian tribes inhabit the state: the Huicholes, a surprisingly clean and placid people who lead isolated lives in the Sierras, practice hypnotic dances and pagan worship and produce magnificent embroidery; and the Mongol-like Coras, also pagan worshippers, who bury their dead in caves and make excellent blankets, bags and ornaments.

NUEVO LEON (N.L.): 25,430 sq m; pop 977,000; Monterrey.

Center of a rich farming and dairying region, Monterrey—often called Mexico's Pittsburgh — is a modern, Americanized, commercial metropolis built at the meeting place of Coahuila's coal and Durango's iron ore. Here are big industries galore and golf courses, country clubs, Rotary luncheons, pure water and also crime and juvenile delinquency. Wealthy, ambitious and progressive, Monterrey frankly symbolizes the Mexico of Tomorrow (without the crime and juvenile delinquency).

OAXACA (Oax.): 36,800 sq m; pop 1,660,000; Oaxaca.

An undeveloped state of forested mountain ranges, luxuriant tropical valleys and a hot humid coast lined by surf pounded beaches. During the rainy season, its rivers overflow and minor earthquakes are almost a daily occurrence. Tapirs, pumas, jaguars and leopards roam the forest and crocodiles, alligators and boa constrictors are numerous. Equally rich in Indian remains and contemporary Indian life, Oaxaca is home of the kindly, highly intelligent Zapotecans whose ancestors built Mitla and Monte Alban, and the intensely colorful Tehuana matriarchy which inhabits the low isthmus region. Oaxaca, the Indian capital, rebuilt by the Spaniards in 1592, is a pleasant colonial town ideal for retirement while Tehuantepec and neighboring Juchitan, the Tehuana towns, are scenes of almost endless fiestas and wedding feasts.

PUEBLA (Pue.): 13,280 sq m; pop 1,990,000; Puebla.

Snow peaked mountains, rich valleys, forests and rivers form the setting for this historic state's wealth of archeological sites and colonial monuments. Here is Cholula, a city of tiled blue and yellow church domes; the resort spa of Tehuacan; and the sedate, very Spanish, colonial city of Puebla famed throughout Mexico for its Talavera tileware.

QUERETARO (Qro.): 4,485 sq m; pop 329,000; Queretaro.

Mountains to the north, fertile plains and valleys to the south, are what you'll find in this mineral rich state. A wide range of fruits and vegetables is protuced, opals and mercury are mined, and the state abounds in mineral springs. Flower filled plazas and neatly kept houses typify the pleasant colonial capital of Queretaro.

QUINTANA ROO (Q.R.): 19,860 sq m; pop 37,300; Chetumal.

Within the confines of this jungly territory on the Yucatan Peninsula are the beach rimmed resort islands of Cozumel and Isla Mujeres and the ancient Mayan city of Tulum, now in ruins. The mainland coast is lined by long, white and beautiful Caribbean beaches, stil largely inaccessible (roads are expected shortly). Chetumal, the ramshackle tropical seaport capital, is straight out of Maugham. Predominately inhabited by Mayan Indians, Quintana Roo is also home to a surprising proportion of Negroes from neighboring British Honduras.

SAN LUIS POTOSI (S.L.P.): 24,705 sq m; pop 1,052,000; San Luis Potosi.

In the center of Mexico and on the high plateau with the tall forested Sierra mountains to the east, S.L.P. is a semi arid mining state (gold, lead, silver, copper) and cattle raising region. Irrigation is needed to produce crops. The rather severe colonial capital is a busy railroad center and site for numerous smelters, tanneries, textile mills and other plants.

SINALOA (Sin.): 22,845 sq m;pop 797,000; Culiacan.

A long, skinny Pacific Coast state 50-150 miles in width and flanked by the Sierra Madre range which towers above a low and fertile coastal plain varying from 1-40 miles wide. Culiacan founded in 1531, is center of a thriving winter vegetable trade while farther south lies the shrimp port and winter beach resort of Mazatlan. Predominantly agricultural, the state raises an enormous range of products.

SONORA (Son.): 71,312 sq m; pop 689,-000; Hermosillo.

A large desert studded with giant cactus. Sonora's economy is being transformed by large new irrigation projects on the Yaqui and other rivers. The northern part adjoining Arizona—a desert region broken only by huge volcanic craters, basalt mesas and old Kino mission towns—resembles the Sahara. But farther south, both Ciudad Obregon and Navojoa are thriving centers of new agricultural booms. Interesting towns are the part colonial, part modern winter resort of Hermosillo; the sports fishing coastal resort of Guaymas; and the ancient mountain mining town of Alamos, nowadays a popular American retirement spot. Still inhabiting Tiburon Island and the adjoining mainland are the last of the fierce Seri Indians, a curious and primitive race who still paint their faces and live in crude rush huts. The small Mayo tribe still flourish around Navojoa, where they sell their beautiful blankets and rugs. And just south of Guaymas, if you are lucky, you may still occasionally witness the dances of the warlike Yaqui tribe.

TABASCO (Tab.): 9,895 sq m; pop 449,-000; Villahermosa.

Hot, damp, low, fertile and heavily forested, this little known Gulf Coast state is traversed by some of Mexico's largest rivers. Here are rain forests alive with brilliant tropical birds and also with pumas, tigres, ant eaters, tapirs and monkeys. Sizeable quantities of bananas, copra, cacao, rice and sugar are exported through Villahermosa, the state's distributing center and river port.

TAMAULIPAS (Tamps.): 31,100 sq m; pop 1,068,000; Victoria.

From the treeless plains and cotton fields along the Texas border, this big Gulf Coast state rolls south to irrigated valleys with exuberant tropical vegetation and wide deep rivers; and eastwards it climbs to the cold rugged peaks of the high Sierras. Rivers, marshes, lakes, lagoons and jungles lie back of the 270 miles of Gulf Coast, much of it lined by beaches and small, hard-to-reach resorts. Key cities are the fishing and oil port of Tampico; the oil refinery border town of Reynosa; progressive Nuevo Laredo op-posite Laredo, Texas; modern Matamoros opposite Brownsville; and sophisticated Victoria, the attractive capital of tall buildings, and beautiful parks. One of the most progressive border states, Tamaulipas is making great strides in business, cattle, industry, highways, schools and irrigation. Despite this surging activity, it offers much to the winter vacationer. Principal Indian tribe is the Huasteca who live in the south and overflow into bordering states. Characteristic of Tamaulipas is the heavily embroidered cuera leather jacket worn by charros and the fiery huapango songs and dances, Huastecan in origin.

TLAXCALA (Tlax.): 2,515 sq m; pop 285,-000; Tlaxcala.

The Rhode Island of Mexico—a tiny, relatively unknown state in the wooded mountains east of Mexico City. Home of the Tlaxcalans who aided Cortes, Tlaxcala abounds in colonial churches and monuments. Tlaxcala, the picturesque Indian capital, is famed for its magnificent, low cost tweeds in pre-conquest designs. Several small factories also make excellent Orlon blankets and textiles.

VERA CRUZ (Ver.): 28,085 sq m; pop 2,503,000; Jalapa.

The garden of Mexico, this beautiful state climbs from charming Gulf beach resorts to rugged Sierra peaks culminating in the symmetrical cone of Orizaba, highest in Mexico. Orchids grow wild in the exotic coastal jungles and the fertile valleys blaze with tropical flowers and vanilla plantations. In size and importance the mountain towns, Old World Jalapa and conservative, colonial Cordoba, are overshadowed by the gay and lighthearted old colonial port of Vera Cruz. Delightful resorts like Nautla and Tecolutla dot the northern coast while inland is the typical tropical town of Papantla with its Totonac Indian flying pole dancers. South of Vera Cruz city lies the peaceful peninsula port of Alvarado, starting point for mailboats proceeding up the Papaloapan River. Higher up this tropical river and overlapping into Oaxaca is the huge Papaloapan Dam Project, a Mexican TVA. Immediately south you find the strange, almost unreal Catemaco Lake, a tropical Shangri-La. And away down the coast, almost in Tabasco, is Coatzacoalcos or Puerto Mexico, a beach resort and sulphur port. In spite of the activity, the industrial and reclamation projects, oil installations and seaports, thatched villages are far more commonplace than industry. Back in the Papaloapan hinterland live some of Mexico's mist primitive Indians: the Papolucas whose women go naked above the waist; the Mazatecos who use a whistle code for long distance communication; the chronically debilitated Jarochos; and the Sierra dwelling Chochos who live by weaving palm straw hats.

YUCATAN (Yuc.): 15,045 sq m; pop 624,000; Merida.

Sea rimmed and isolated for centuries by impenetrable jungle, Yucatan's descendants of the ancient Mayans have retained much of their traditional customs and dress. Even today, Yucatecans—who also include a considerable proportion of pure Spanish people —remain aloof from the rest of Mexico. Friendly, good humored, hospitable, intelligent and clean, the Mayans live today in well built thatched houses much as they did when the Spaniards arrived. The men dress in tropical white and are fond of baseball; the women wear beautifully embroidered white *huipiles* and satin shoes and are remarkably good cooks . . . all in all a fine people whose passion for cleanliness has led to Yucatan's fondness for the Turkish Bath. These people are the direct descendants of the same Mayans who between 900 and 1,400 A.D. built the extensive and graceful cities of Uxmal, Kabah, and Chichen Itza, so admired today. But Yucatan has endless other attractions: pleasant Gulf beaches; several hundred varieties of tropical birds including the quetzal, parrots and macaws; and great hardwood jungles teeming with jaguar, ocelot, lynx, cougar, javelina, alligator, deer and wild fowl. Iguanas run wild everywhere and there are also harmless boa constrictors and rattlesnakes. Not generally known is the state's extensive labyrinth of underground rivers, caves and *cenotes* or wells, some containing blind fish. From these subterranean rivers, the cities obtain their water. Merida, the clean atractive and picturesque colonial capital, is studded with water pumping windmills.

ZACATECAS (Zac.): 28,455 sq m; pop 769,000; Zacatecas.

A state of rugged mountains and sandy plains on the high central plateau, Zacatecas lives from cattle and its fabulously rich mineral resources. There are two towns of importance: the dusty smelter city of Fresnillo and, at a high 8,200', the hilly cobblestoned mining capital of Zacatecas.

WHO ARE THE MEXICANS? By now, you know enough of the Mexican background to hazard a guess. Latest estimates give Mexico's population as 37,000,000 composed thus: of completely pure Spanish or European descent .17% of the *mestizo* race 85% of pure Indian race 14.83%. Of these, almost half the *mestizos* share with the Indians the primitive life of the *ejido* village or city slum. Many still cannot read or write, must still go shoeless and acquire necessities by barter. Corn is their staple food and since it is most easily produced on the Mesa Central, this is where most of them live. Of the pure Indian population, there are 56 different tribes, many still speaking variations of the 13 principal indigenous tongues.

These figures reveal a totally different Mexico from that which greets most tourists visiting Mexico City. There one sees only the capital's cosmopolitan concentration of scientists, intellectuals and executives—most of whom are of European extraction or are foreign nationals. The real Mexico enjoys a mixed racial inheritance, largely *mestizo*. From this group have come many of Mexico's outstanding leaders and statesmen. The Mexican today wears Indian *huaraches* and a *mestizo* straw hat and speaks the Andalusian of Spain. The highest compliment you can pay him is to call him *Puro Mexicano*.

Racial prejudice as such does not exist. But race very definitely is allied to social and economic position. Though you find occasional villages of poor whites, most Mexicans of pure Spanish ancestry—the descendants of the *conquistadores*—have managed to hold on to the bulk of their ancestral wealth and today, they enjoy the higher education and social prestige that goes with it. The educated *mestizos* and Indians are fusing into a small but rapidly growing middle class. And the great mass of the others — almost entirely Indian and *mestizo*—are forced to remain in backwardness and poverty. For proof of these racial-economic stratas, one has only to examine illustrations in Mexico's advertisements for consumer goods. Invariably pictured alongside the gleaming automobiles, TV sets and refrigerators are people of unmistakably European or strongly European-*mestizo* race. Unconsciously, the Mexican himself still associates the Indian with the lowest social and economic level. The *mestizo*, caught between top and bottom and frequently conscious that his ancestors were born out of wedlock, all too often suffers from a racial inferiority complex.

Living in Mexico brings you into contact with all three races and their respective social-economic backgrounds. For example, your maid may be pure Indian from an *ejido* village; your doctor a *mestizo,* able to enjoy comfortable middle class surroundings; and your lawyer a socially prominent and relatively wealthy Mexican-born European educated in the United States.

THE INDIAN TODAY is a disappearing race. In northern Mexico he is moving into towns and villages, mating with *mestizos* and forgetting his tribal customs and culture. In central Mexico the same thing is happening but with a stronger tendency to follow the traditional Indian way of life. Only in the Deep South—in Oaxaca and Chiapas—does Indian life continue unaffected by the 20th century.

Physically, the American Indian of Mexico possesses a short, square stocky build which is most noticeable in the women. The women are short legged and well developed. There are few flat-chested Indian girls. With their curvaceous build goes—when they are younger—a honey-toned skin, a flawless complexion, long dark hair reaching below the shoulders and lustrous, dark, sloe-shaped eyes. Generations of carrying water jars atop the head have produced an erect, regal carriage beside which the American woman appears to be slouching. These Indian beauties, all astonishingly alike, can be seen in their hundreds during village *serenatas.* From their union with Spaniards—a race also noted for the beauty of its women—has sprung the almost universal beauty of Mexico's *mestizo* girls. Notwithstanding their having lost in the process something of the Indian's queenly gait, the *mestizo* women are responsible for the high proportion of natural beauties in Mexico today. (Due, unfortunately, to an inadequate diet, many lose their looks and figure before age 30.)

Depending on his proximity to 20th century influence, the contemporary Indian wears anything from ready cut cotton clothes to the most elabortely embroidered and handloomed traditional attire. But on their feet almost all wear the Indian *huaraches,* soled in these times with old automobile tires. In fact, half the nation walks on its worn out auto treads. Too, depending on his background and environment, the Indian (and those *mestizos* alongside whom he may live) can range from those quite indifferent to personal hygiene to others who bathe twice or more each day. Generally speaking, the Indians of tropical coastal regions tend to be those with the cleanest personal habits.

Approximately one fourth of Mexico's population—both Indian and *mestizo*—lives in primitive rural villages lacking paved streets, running water or sewage. The typical village has dirt streets lined by low one story houses, either of adobe brick with tiled roofs or, in the tropics, of thatch or wattle construction with a thatched roof. The typical house consists of 1-3 small rooms, limewashed inside and decorated with a calendar, a shrine and several religious pictures. The floor is dirt, there is no ceiling and from the roof hangs a single, low wattage electric bulb. Furniture consists of a plain wooden table and a few wooden chairs, an ancient sewing machine, a sofa and a single bed for the parents. Children generally sleep on straw *petate* mats. There is no bath and the toilet consists of a primitive outhouse. Surrounding the house, or in back of it, is a dusty yard in which the more ambitious raise fruit. At night, the yard serves as a corral for the family's livestock and by day, as a poultry run. Cooking is done in an outdoor earth oven. Privacy is unknown. And wherever one walks, care is required to avoid animal droppings. Only in the most modern villages is water piped to individual houses, often by a network of pipes which lie on the ground. Elsewhere, the women must carry it as in ancient times from the communal well. Without a single modern appliance, the woman's lot is hard. She must spend long hours scrubbing clothes at the village pool or stream where, frequently working bare to the waist, she plunges into the cooling waters and thereby obtains the rudiments of a bath. Other long hours are spent grinding corn on ancient *metates.* Wheat, where available, is still threshed by horses' hooves as in archiac times. (It might be added, to allay your suspicions, that such rural villages bear no resemblance to the delightful colonial era resort villages in which Americans retire.)

From this bare existence, the Indian finds escape in two ways: through the tequila bottle; and at the weekly market. Few Americans casually traveling through Mexico appreciate the role of the market. It is the villagers' day off. The goods he brings to sell cost little or nothing to produce. Thus profit is secondary. Instead, the village market is a great social event. Outside Americanized northern Mexico every village has its *Día de Tianguis* or market day (city markets are open seven days a week). Craftsmen bring their products from miles around. And everyone swaps gossip as he barters. For the villagers, the arrival of an American in these markets is something to talk of for the rest of the week. They are sadly disappointed if you fail to bargain. They are delighted by the knowledgeable American who can bargain astutely and, however poor his Spanish, who can add some conversation. Such *simpatico* Americans find the markets a constantly engrossing pageant of Mexican life and since there is neither middleman nor any value set on time or labor, a source of wondrous bargains in magnificently executed arts and crafts.

Lacking refrigeration, the villagers also lack fresh milk and meat. In large villages and smaller towns a red flag outside the butchers' shops indicates that meat freshly killed that morning is available. Strangely, however, all the butchers seem to kill on the same day, leaving towns of as many as 15,000 people meatless several days of the week. Poultry, sold live, is always available of course. Otherwise, the small town dweller relies on canned foods to supplement his corn.

His bare life also accounts for the Indians' love of fiestas and weddings. Although less careful in protecting the chastity of girls than the upper class Spanish, comtemporary village courtship closely follows Spanish custom. Most couples meet during the weekly *serenata*, a picturesque custom in which all eligible young men promenade in an outer circle around the plaza while the girls walk in an inner circle facing the boys. Glances are exchanged and under the watchful eye of chaperoning *duenas*, couples pair off and stroll together. Even today, this custom is followed in such large cities as Guadalajara.

Down in Oaxaca's Tehuantepec Peninsula, the Tehuanas follow a still older pattern. In fishing villages, courtships may begin when a young man throws his fishnet over a girl. In towns, they meet in more conventional fashion and uniquely, since the Tehuanas are matriarchal, the young man sends a deputation of his friends to the girl's mother to ask for her hand. The mother may then expect the boy to live in her house and help in the family business (Tehuanas are great traders), thereby paying for the girl and at the same time learning more about her. In towns, this practice is dying out. Eventually however, after the boy and his friends have built a new home, a wedding feast is held. Halfway through, bride and groom leave to make love. A bloodstained handkerchief tossed from a window is a signal for more rejoicing (rarely is the girl other than a virgin; if not, the more conservative Tehuana families may still call off the wedding). Only at this stage does the church wedding take place. Then for a solid week afterwards, the couple go from home to home, from banquet to banquet, from dance to dance. Visitors are welcome at these celebrations which in ithmus towns like Juchitan, are constantly in progress.

While not typical of all of Mexico, the Tehauna practice is an important aid to understanding the role of marriage in Indian life. From then on, the wife's task is to produce children and to provide love and care. The weekly market apart, her social life is henceforth found in other weddings, in fiestas and in funerals . . . in short, in religion.

All Mexicans are Catholic at birth and most remain Catholic throughout their lives. Every village has its church and patron saint and its most influential citizen is invariably the priest, though the Catholic religion in Mexico today still bears strongly pagan overtones. The fireworks preceding every fiesta are, as in China, a symbol to drive away evil spirits. And since every village has its saint, these fiestas are numerous. With its fiestas and national days of celebration, Mexico has more holidays than any other country. Every fiesta is celebrated for the full 24 hours. Starting at dawn with a battery of rockets, the celebrations begin with band parades and church bells, followed by dances from pre-conquest times and climaxed by an evening *serenata* to band music and a brilliant late-evening display of whizzing fireworks built into a *castillo* or bamboo tower.

Fiesta calendars are distributed free by the National Tourist Office and for the knowledgeable American resident are an excellent guide to the country's finest folklore. For example, at Huejotzingo, Pue., one fiesta takes the form of a day-long play in which the entire town takes part. During Holy Week at Taxco and elsewhere one may see *penitentes* carrying bundles of thorns and wearing thorned crowns, following religious processions to church on their hands and knees. In mid-October a tremendous procession of costumed Indian dancers, mounted *charros,* and military and *mariachi* bands, all led by the Bishop of Guadalajara, return the miraculous *Virgen de Zapopan* to her church in one of Mexico's most spectacular displays of pageantry.

There are pagan overtones in other aspects of Mexican life. In the deep fastness of mountain valleys, *velorios* (witches) and *brujas* (sorcerers) still ply their trade. Even in quite large villages, the traditional wake accompanying a death is often led by a *bruja.* Within sight of Christian churches we have seen the pagan copal burned while, to the accompaniment of cabalistic signs and the flourishing of talismans, amulets, potions and similar aids, *brujas* have stuck pins in human effigies or consigned them to flames. The *brujas* are still consulted to bring rains, solve marital differences or to cure the sick. There are even printed textbooks on magic. The sacrifice of chickens or small animals is still far from unknown. And fear of the evil eye is still so universal that one must exercise care when photographing Indians *everywhere in Mexico.*

Small wonder that education has presented such problems. Entire Indian tribes have risen in opposition to schooling for their children. Only by adapting educational methods to Indian patterns of culture has the Mexican government been able to establish schools in backward Indian areas. Nowadays, mobile cultural missions tour Indian areas training the teachers in methods acceptable to the tribes. So successful has this system proved that the United Nations center for training rural teachers was set up at Patzcuaro and today serves as a model for teacher training throughout the Indianist Americas.

From these backgrounds, from the impassive stolidity of the Indian, from the utter reliance placed on religion, from the belief that whatever happens is inevitable, stems the Mexican's almost universally fatalistic attitude. "It is God's will" is the most common Mexican expression. Why worry about the future? ask the Mexicans. Thus ulcers, tension and high blood pressure are relatively rare.

This attitude, sometimes an obsession, possibly explains the indifference to planning ahead, the forgetfulness of Mexico's uneducated classes. Cookstoves run out of gas, carpenters out of nails, lighting plants out of oil because someone failed to think ahead. All too often, Americans conclude that the Indian (or lower class *mestizo*) lacks the ability to handle modern equipment. This is untrue. The same Indian skill which produces superb textiles, pottery and lacquerware is— with a little education—equally efficient with mechinical or electronic equipment. The *trained* Indian or *mestizo* mechanic ranks with the world's best. Masters of improvisation, they can tackle a repair job, without proper tools or spare parts, that would defy an American mechanic. Half the trucks of Mexico run on improvisation. The fault is not lack of mechanical skill. It is failure to think ahead and have the spares on hand.

Aware of these skills, Mexican industry is hiring the villagers in numbers. Hundreds daily are forsaking the primitive *edijo* village for life in the towns. There, for most, adjustment is difficult. Ambitious schemes to house these newcomers in modern *multifamiliares* (apartment houses) have proved a dismal failure. The transition is too abrupt. (Even in England, slum dwellers transferred to public "council houses" used the bath for storing coal.) Sociologists called in have advised the planners to leave newcomers in the slums until they become cognizant of the comforts and conveniences of modern living. Cruel perhaps. But in part, it accounts for the large slum sections which exist in Mexico's industrial centers today.

After several years, the more fortunate of these newcomers find a place in the *multifamiliares* of new satelite cities, Eventually, they then move into Mexico's new middle class.

How does all this affect you? In all likelihood your maid will come from a family which is at some point in the transition between *ejido* culture and the middle class. The girl you hire is not likely to be so primitive as the *sirvienta* hired by one of our friends in rural Oaxaca who, each morning, rolled up every mat in the house in the belief they were used as *petates.* But the background we've given should prove invaluable in helping to understand the way in which your maid thinks, believes and acts. It should materially assist in recognizing her innate weaknesses and in training her to become an efficient, capable and faithful employee in a minimum of time.

Further, and even more significant, this brief review points up the colossal future that awaits the Mexican economy once this vast segment of the population attains middle class prosperity. The steady emergence from *edijo* to city life is one of the most imporatant indicators of the enormous growth

26

potential that awaits those who invest in Mexico's common stocks today.

THE COLONIAL TRADITIONS of Spain are rigorously upheld in Mexico by a small but highly influential nucleus of pure European stock. Often fabulously wealthy, these direct descendants of the *conquistadores* are aristocratic, polished, educated, cultured and absolutely cognizant of the 20th century in everything but family life. This pattern of family life, most rigidly observed among themselves, has spread downwards into almost all strata of Mexican society.

The family is the soul of Mexican life. From cradle to grave most Mexicans remain within the family circle. Girls seldom leave home before marriage. And a few will marry if it means leaving their parents' home town. Children grow up within the bosom of the family; the old die with their families. There are few old folks' homes, youth camps or youth centers in Mexico. Every Sunday sees the Mexican countryside filed with picnicking families . . . the entire family unit from grandparents down to the latest newborn child. Once a week the family circle gathers for dinner at the home of the oldest member. For children, this means unending indulgence; seldom are they scolded, at worst they are mildly pinched. Despite all this, Mexican children are among the world's best behaved. Their manners are charming. And among those raised in families, even the poorest, *juvenile delinquency is virtually unknown.* A seldom broken tradition is that the last married girl remains at home to look after her parents.

Until marriage, girls are carefully chaperoned. Outside the wealthiest families, most today are trained for such white collar occupations as teachers or bookkeepers. But marriage means the end of work. From then on, the Mexican woman devotes herself exclusively to her husband and home. Large families are a national ambition, perpetuation of the family almost a fetish.

Particularly in northern Mexico, industrialization is modifying chaperonage. Girls of the new middle class are appearing on dates without chaperones. And at the Indian cultural level—which has always had its own moral standards—chaperonage is far less common. But by and large, and particularly in the provinces, chaperonage not only extends to unmarried girls but also to younger married women. One American girl who married into an aristocratic and wealthy

The Mexican Charro

The national figure of Mexico is the *charro,* an elegant gentleman cowboy attired in embroidered jacket, striped pants and wide hat and magnificently mounted on a thoroughbred steed with silver encrusted saddle. In real life, the *charro* is a business or professional man or rancher. On Sundays and holidays he carries on the best traditions of Mexico's mounted *caballeros* and their reputation as Latin Robin Hoods. Throughout Mexico, the stylized *charro* dress is a symbol of courage, valor and bold male gallantry which the *charro* displays each weekend at a rodeo or *charriada*. At these *charriadas,* gay and colorful events frequently accompanied by lively folk music and national dances, the public the welcomed. Besides seeing such dangerous sports as the *coleada* (bull tripping) you may also witness the *jarabe tapatio*, Mexico's nation dance performed in costume. For this spirited dance, popularly known to us as the Mexican hat dance, the men wear *charro* attire, the women a striking national costume called *China Poblana*. Consisting of a green cotton skirt with red yoke, white embroidered blouse and red-green-white striped *rebozo,* it is a modification of the Chinese costume originally brought to Puebla in the 17th century by a Chinese princess.

All *charros* are members of the Associación Nacional de Charros which has a branch in each large town. *Charro* dress is frequently worn by the groom at Mexican weddings.

Spanish family found herself entirely hedged in by relatives. Wherever she went, a female relative accompanied her. Finally she begged her husband to abandon these "feudal" traditions and move out of the huge family mansion into an apartment of their own. The man, though American educated simply could not bring himself to oppose the family traditions. The result: the American girl finally sneaked out, never returned, and the marriage broke up. (American girls seeking romance south of the Border might well pause first and consider whether they could ever resolve themselves to live with this outdated, half-oriental way of life.)

Chaperonage is the result of the Mexican male's double standards. For him, women are either good or bad. The bad are considered fair game and estimates say that one of every two married Mexican men has extra-marital affairs. But seldom if ever will he permit this to break up his marriage. (Incidentally, maids are frequently seduced by the youths of the family; one maid in three has an illegitimate child. Within the maid group one finds most of Mexico's lower class of unwed mothers. Prostitution is the only alternative to domestic service.)

All of this should sufficiently explain why younger American women should not, outside cities and resorts or the sophisticated American retirement colonies, go about unescorted. It also explains the rarity of invitations to higher class Mexican homes. An invitation to his home is the highest compliment a Mexican can give. He is inviting you into his most sacred precinct, the family circle.

Even the houses are built to shield the family from the outside world. The Mexican house faces inwards, all doors opening onto the central patio where the family gathers. No daughter can come and go without being seen by *mamacita* or an elderly aunt. The Mexican is indifferent to the exterior of his home which faces the street. For this reason, many unknowing Americans are disappointed by the chipped and faded exteriors of Mexican homes. Whereas if they looked inside, they would discover an orderly flower-filled patio surrounded by comfortable rooms.

Because servants are cheaper than appliances, even the wealthiest Mexican homes are short on gadgets. The kitchen—where, incidentally, one *never* eats—is a hive of industry. Both school and business hours are interrupted by a long afternoon siesta during which the family can unite. This makes both lunch and dinner late and accounts for the charming custom among older Spanish families of serving a *merienda* of chocolate or tea in the late afternoon.

Most Mexicans are married once . . . for keeps. First the young man proposes to his bride, then visits her parents to request her hand formally. Several days before the religious ceremony, the civil wedding takes place in the home of the bride. The religious wedding day begins with a two hour mass and religious ceremony followed by a *mole* banquet with the families and guests. To most upper class Mexicans a wedding without a religiuos ceremony is no wedding at all. The lower classes are less particular. Among the poor, common law marriages are commonplace.

Significant, if you intend to invest in Mexican stocks, is the Mexican's love of large families . . . admirable enough in itself but still more to be admired since it means a rapidly growing population. By the year 2000, this prolific trend should have produced 100,000,000 well educated Mexicans consuming ten times the industrial output of today. And with today's great strides in education, this is exactly what should transpire. With his impeccable manners, the Mexican child never interrupts the teacher with unruly behavior. Nor, thanks to the chaperonage tradition, does interest in the other sex distract the Mexican child from study. In almost all Mexican schools, the sexes are strictly divided.

THE NEW MIDDLE CLASS is almost entirely *mestizo*. Absorbed within his make up is the individuality of the *conquistadores* and their tight-knit family circle, the ability of the Roman and Moorish builders, and the stoicism and fatalism of the American Indian. Physically, the *mestizo* has a graceful body with the small hands of a craftsman; psychologically, he is a curious mixture of rugged individualist yet strongly responsive to communal demands; and religiously he is semi-polytheistic, placing saints and other religious figures on the same level with Christ or the Virgin Mary.

This complex personality far outnumbers other races and is the one with whom your contacts will be most numerous. Among these is likely to be your doctor, landlord, and repairman and also most tradesmen, shopkeepers, white collar workers, hotel staffs and so on. Installment buying is transforming this group into a solid middle class as surely as it paved the way for the universal prosperity of the United States.

Within the *mestizo* is the best of many races; he is hard working, friendly and easy to meet. He is also slightly puzzled. As we remarked earlier, his origin in violence and out of wedlock makes him feel inferior. So do the European faces in Mexico's advertisements. He reads Mexican history books idolizing Indian heroes. Yet he is ashamed of the backward Indian population. With Americans he feels inferior in stature, experience and education. His knowledge of the outside world is small. He is socially at ease, his formal manners are impeccable, yet he is far from sure of his role in life. He has no *mestizo* tradition behind him. How can he? His role as a vital part of his nation's history is relatively new.

The truth is that today the *mestizo* is still surging forward in a state of flux, seeking stability in a national identity. His short history has characterized the *mestizo* as a race capable of rapid bursts of energy followed by long periods of slumbering *siesta*. For example, throughout Mexico one can see homes, factories and highways built in these tremendous bursts of vigor only to be allowed to fall apart for lack of maintenance. His Indian ancestors did the same: built up civilization only to watch them crumble, instigated revolutions then watched the country go politically to pieces. Aware of these inherited shortcomings, enlightened *mestizos* are trying desperately to live them down.

You will find the *mestizo* gregarious and fond of loud, lively music; privacy is for his family with whom he enjoys a unity we have lost. For his supposed inferiority he compensates with an unflagging, never hypocritical courtesy which often bewilders Americans. To admire anything belonging to a Mexican is to have it presented to you on the spot. Naturally, you are not expected to accept. This special courtesy is carried so far that merchants sometimes offer you the products off their shelves. Again, if you accept, you are expected to pay. Outside tourist areas, Mexicans will frequently perform favors for which they ask no payment. Courtesy, however, demands that you should offer a present in return or, if they are poor, then a cash donation "for the children."

Because it is considered unkind to say "no," Mexicans will often answer your questions with untruthful pleasantries. Many an American tourist, told a certain highway is well paved, finds it filled with potholes. In their eagerness to please, many Mexicans will make promises they cannot possibly carry out. And since meals are considered a slow, leisurely ceremony, swift service would be the height of discourtesy.

With his Old World grace the *mestizo* is hospitable and sociable yet careful in his choice of friends. He won't greet you with an *abrazo*—a hug—on first meeting but once you do become his friend, you are his friend for life. From his Indian forebears the *mestizo* has inherited a deep respect for communal affairs. At the same time, he has inherited a wholesome slice of Spanish individuality. Repetitive work soon leaves him bored. He prefers challenging tasks which

provide an outlet for his artistic Indian skill. (Symbolic of this individualism are the Mexican consuls in the United States. No two ever give the same answers and from questioning, we are of the opinion that no two *immigrantes* have ever been admitted to Mexico under identical conditions!) Because Mexicans do not function well as groups, the country remains semi-organized. Uniformity is noticeably absent.

Hand in hand with his individuality goes a love of art and beauty. Every Mexican is an artist or a poet both at heart and in fact. From end to end, Mexico is one vast art gallery of paintings, murals, architecture, handicrafts and sculpture dating from earliest times to the present day. Here the intellectual is never spurned. Love of art is not considered effeminate. Nor does the Mexican lack fighting courage. He may not be the best material for a disciplined modern army, but in the name of patriotism he will not hesitate to face a hail of bullets or to jump to his death wrapped in the national flag.

Often illogical to the point of following heart rather than head, the Mexican is a born romanticist. He likes romantic places, prefers romantic older hotels to modern luxury places, and loves romantic music. The quip, "Latins are lousy lovers" is, so I am told, entirely without basis. Making the *mestizo* appear even more of an enigma are the flowery phrases of the Spanish language. It is best not to accept everything at face value.

Look deeper for an explanation of the *mestizo's* complex character and you'll find it exemplified in the cult of *machoism* or ostentatious manliness. Undoubtedly, says Mexican poet Octavio Paz, *machoism* grew out of the *mestizo's* traditional hatred for his Spanish father who, in turn, considered his Indian wife and *mestizo* children as racial inferiors. To compensate for this paternal hatred, the *mestizo* has set up a defense mechanism which glorifies his Indian mother while at the same time frenziedly cultivating the manliness and power associated with his European father. Thus practically every adult Mexican male practices *machoism* constantly and consistently in a hundred different ways.

Whenever he can bluff another motorist into giving way, a Mexican feels *macho*. And practically all male behaviour, from his elaborate language to his overwhelming hospitality and exaggerated courtesy, can be traced to that same inner conflict which constantly urges the Mexican male to prove his manliness and virility. The result: the Mexican is more of an enigma than you might suppose. In fact, the Mexicans themselves often find it difficult to understand other Mexicans. For to compensate for his inferiority complex, the Mexican all too often inhabits a fantasy world which he himself erects as a barrier against the reality of his sordid environment. Hence it is not always easy to break through his outer shell of formality and really get to know a Mexican.

That, in general, is the picture of the Mexican today. How do we appear to him? By consulting Mexicans educated in the States, we gleaned the following. At the back of most Mexicans' minds is a suspicion we are out to exploit them. The basis? The Mexican-American War of 1946-48 when we took by force or intrigue over one half of Mexico; the Diaz regime when Americans acquired almost one fourth of Mexico's soil and half her mineral wealth—until 1938 foreigners controlled practically all of Mexico's oil; the American government's efforts to suppress the 1910 revolution and to restore the Diaz regime; the poor treatment accorded *braceros* in Texas and the racially prejudiced treatment of Mexicans in Texas and other border states. Added to this is the fear that Americanization may eventually turn Mexico into another United States (as it already has done to northern Mexico).

Regardless of the fact that to Mexicans we appear large, ungainly creatures with masculine women, the Mexicans as a whole like and admire Americans. While the Mexicans themselves are far from perfect—for example, those perennially late or who never show up, those who cheat tourists or go all out to fleece them—neither are we perfect. A small segment of Americans is responsible for such bad feelings as do exist.

Item: tourist girls in slacks and shorts who enter village churches without head coverings or hats. Such villages are not enthusiastic about Americans settling there.

Item: the sprinkling of alcoholics, degenerates, oddballs, sour quarrelsome critics, the perennially dissatisfied and the social snobs who settle in Mexico's American retirement colonies and create a bad impression which the decent Americans must then live down.

Item: racially prejudiced American tourists and residents who consider the Mexican a second class citizen in his own country.

This is beginning to read too much like *The Ugly American.* So let's cut it short by saying that apart from our brusque, loudmouthed minority, we are well and truly welcomed. Our main shortcoming, say our Mexican friends, is that we tend to be spectators rather than to join in Mexican activities and have fun.

HOW TO LIVE SUCCESSFULLY IN MEXICO. If you've read this chapter so far, you probably know as much about Mexico and its people as the average American who has lived in Mexico for several years. You have learned that, far more than we are, the Mexican is a true product of the Americas yet he is not truly western nor is he Latin. You have learned how in background, temperament and psychological make up, he differs substantially from us.

Your entire success in Mexico will depend on how well you apply what you have learned. In terms of hard cash, we sincerely believe that through adapting yourself to the Mexican character, you can slash at least 10% from your daily expenses. With a basic knowledge of Spanish you can slash a further 5%-10%. Whatever you do in Mexico—whether you are retiring, fishing, touring or investing—your *simpatico* understanding of Mexico, its mores and folkways, will pay off with handsome dividends.

Through his gracious standards of formal courtesy, the Mexican attaches great importance to first impressions. So here, to help you avoid the most common *faux pas* is a rundown of helpful hints on customs and etiquette.

1. Always be yourself. Be natural. Never exaggerate politeness and never patronize. But leave the swift tempo of North America behind. Never try to hurry a Mexican and never appear to be in a hurry yourself. Slow down and live. Give yourself time to savor and to enjoy life as the Mexicans do.

2. Never shout, or talk in a loud voice above music. Strangely, Mexicans actually listen to what you say.

3. Avoid offending the Mexican's national pride. Mexico lies in North America and Mexicans are Americans too. Remember that you are a northamerican from the United States. (Never deprecate or criticize anything Mexican or compare it unfavorably with the United States. You can't change Mexico. The charm of Mexico lies in its difference,

in the Mexican's ability to industrialize his country without absorbing the machine age.)

4. Always shake hands upon meeting and especially upon leaving Mexicans. Grip lightly and formally and never pump vigorously up and down. Men should take the lead in shaking hands with women. Upon entering a roomful of people it does no harm to give a slight general bow. Afterwards, shake hands with everyone both upon arrival and upon leaving. Don't slap Mexicans on the back. Leave it up to them. Eventually, they may greet you with the *abrazo,* an embrace used by both sexes.

5. Do not praise the looks of a Mexican woman in the presence of her husband.

6. Carry plenty of small change, give a small tip for all services rendered but do not overtip. Along tourist routes never tip over 15% for normal service, 10% elsewhere and less for longer stays. We have seen Americans tip ten pesos for a 20 peso bill; in other cases Americans have given 50 pesos for a 35 peso bill and told the waiter to keep the change. This not only drives up prices but also offends Mexicans who cannot afford to tip at this scale. Too, waiters consider the action foolish and in poor taste. Never encourage the *mordida* or bribe.

7. Learn to think in pesos. Many tourists still ask for prices in "real" money, in dollars. Avoid brandishing your money. It is not only offensive but leads immediately to overcharging. Do not lay money in front of you on bars; Mexican bartenders trust you to pay the bill on leaving.

8. Wear formal city attire in larger cities. Regardless of how hot it becomes, never remove your jacket or tie. Outside resorts, men's shorts, and women's shorts, slacks and bare midriff costumes, are strictly taboo.

9. Before getting down to any kind of business, even when making a purchase in a small shop, exchange a few pleasantries first.

10. There are few teetotallers in Mexico but most Mexicans drink only with meals and seldom if ever exceed the light glow stage. There is no prestige in showing how much you can hold. So take it easy on drinks and bear in mind that at higher altitudes, lack of oxygen in the atmosphere lowers your resistance to alcohol.

11. Mexico is still a man's world and unaccompanied women should always exercise tact. In cities, where Mexican men have learned to allow for the American woman's emancipation, women may ordinarily go alone to the movies, theater and even to first class hotel cabarets. Otherwise, American women should not go out at night unescorted. It is permissible for unaccompanied American women to enter the cocktail lounges of better class hotels but bars and *cantinas* are still the exclusive province of men. You would also be well advised not to go out alone with a Mexican male. It is a popular custom for Mexican men to make complimentary remarks about good looking unaccompanied women as they pass in the street. Sex is *not* discussed in mixed company.

12. Ask permission before photographing people (or do it unseen). Do not offer to pay unless asked.

13. Gear your activities to coincide with the Mexican's daily schedule. Lunch and dine later and observe the *siesta.* (Personally, we dislike afternoon napping so use this period for correspondence or a country walk. But we never try to do business between 1 and 4 P.M.)

14. Learn some Spanish, especially the polite expressions.

15. Learn to call Mexicans by their correct names. Every male Mexican has two surnames: the first, that of his father's family; the second, that of his mother's. For example, Felip Manuel Saenz Arriola indicates that Saenz is the paternal family name and Arriola the mother's family name. To his friends, Felipe would be known as Felipe Saenz, not as Felipe Arriola. Assuming Felipe married Maria Sanchez Baeza, his wife would drop her mother's family name of Baeza and assume her husband's family name of Saenz, thus: Señora Maria Sanchez de Saenz, or less formally as simply Señora Saenz. Likewise, when the couple have a son, Juan Miguel, his full name would be Juan Higuel Saenz Sanchez. His friends would call him Juan Saenz. And he would be known more formally as Señor Juan Saenz Sanchez.

Make allowances for the Mexican temperament and observe these rules and you will find yourself well liked and perfectly at home. No one expects you to go completely Mexican. The ideal thing is to blend the best points of Mexican living with the best of our own. Do this and you too will discover the good life that awaits you South of the Border.

A FINAL WORD. Although Mexico remains a one party state and all presidents are chosen by the PRI to carry on the traditions of the revolution, each president nonetheless leaves on Mexico the stamp of his own personal projects.

During his 1934-40 tenure, Cardenas displayed strong leftist leanings, nationalized the oil industry and distributed *ejido* lands. Camacho's term, 1940-46, saw the birth of Mexico's industry. From 1946-52, Miguel Aleman pushed through a grand program of public works that changed the face of Mexico. During the six years between 1952-58, his successor, Adolfo Ruiz Cortines, did much to wipe out graft and he instituted Mexico's first attempts at economic planning. Between 1958-64, Lopez Mateos—veering neither to left nor right—offset nationalization of the electric power industry by creating more incentives for private investment.

Until 1970, Mexico is destined to follow the leadership of President Gustavo Diaz Ordaz, a tough anti communist whose avowed intentions are to strengthen ties with the United States and to remedy his country's problems of overcrowded housing and low farm production. At no other time have left leaning politics or expropriation seemed more remote.

Rest assured you will receive a gracious welcome wherever you go in Mexico and if you do hear criticism of the United States, more than likely it will be from Mexicans who are critical of America's tardiness in challenging communism elsewhere in Latin America.

Chapter II

Mexico's Treasure Trove of Sports
and Recreation

ALMOST ALL AUTHORITIES declare that ideal retirement involves adjusting to a slower pace of life and finding something new to do. Mexico admirably fulfills both objectives: first, because life in the republic is already geared to a slower, casual tempo and second, because by and large, the country offers a greater range of activities than does the United States.

In fact, the problem in Mexico is not finding something to do but choosing from the bewildering list available. Not only can you keep on with your present sports or hobbies—in a perennially warm climate and under stimulating new conditions and scenery—but you can choose from entirely new hobbies not available at home. Literally hundreds of retired Americans have become keen historians and archeologists, others collect pre-colonial artifacts or antique arts and furniture. Many an American housewife has become an avid painter, writer, rockhound or botanist. Birdwatchers find hundreds of new species to observe. Against Mexco's rich background of history and ancient civilizations, hundreds of American retirees have discovered unsuspected new talents; others have found a whole new life of recreations.

Within easy reach of a dozen popular retirement towns are the concerts, symphony, opera and ballet of Mexico City. Throughout the republic you'll find art galleries galore and endless subjects for painting and photography. You can play golf in the mountains or on tropical courses and you can keep your own riding stable for a fraction of the costs at home.

For the outdoor sportsman, Mexico can lay undisputed claim to the *world's finest ocean fishing.* Her 6,000 odd miles of coastal waters abound with gamefish of every variety and the Gulf of California forms *the richest fishing grounds on earth.* Here, sails and marlin run twice the size of those in Florida and a day's trolling which yields fewer than forty billfish is often considered way below par. From end to end the Gulf of Mexico is alive with giant tarpon and here, too, the smaller babies run well over five feet. Along both coasts you can battle with oversized bonefish in bays and coves that aren't even on the map. More than once we've hit into a fish that took a thousand feet of line at the first run then fought like an acrobatic two ton truck. Skindivers speak of Mexico's pellucid waters in whispers. And inland, there's fabulous fishing for really big brook and rainbow trout and bass in rivers and lakes where, as often as not, you'll find yourself the only angler for 100 miles around.

For hunters, Mexico is blessed with an abundance of wild life. Seasons, if they exist at all, are longer than at home and the limits far more generous. White tailed deer are common almost everywhere and you can bag coyote, fox, ocelot, mountain lion and jaguar without limit throughout the year. Hardly a hunter returns from Mexico without at least one fine tiger, bear or mountain lion skin. In winter, vast flocks of ducks and geese descend on both coasts and on inland lakes. Almost anywhere, from mid-November to mid-March, you can bag your daily limit of 15 in a couple of hours. Too, even few hunters are aware that you can hunt big game in Mexico under genuine safari conditions, penetrating deep into wild, unexplored jungle where you're just as likely to stumble on an undiscovered lost city as on a leopard, lynx or panther.

What does Mexico not have? Well, you won't find much in the way of the usual Stateside church circle routine nor can you enjoy your favorite TV program. Nonetheless, there *are* some surprisingly good TV programs showing Mexican boxing, wrestling and bullfights as well as other showing American films. Moreover, there *are* church groups and American societies and, if you enjoy social work, some really challenging pioneer projects. Many an American has his own pet project such as supplying eyeglasses to needy local children or educating a Mexican child. Then, too, some retired executives, professional and businessmen have found a niche as unpaid consultants to Mexican business firms (*unpaid* work is permissible, even for tourists). And after attaining *inmigrado* status, scores of retired Americans have launched profitable small hobby-businesses such as gift shops, restaurants, guest houses and posadas.

Of course, you don't have to live in Mexico to enjoy these recreations. Visitors enjoy them too. So to give you a better idea of what's available, here is a brief run down on each of Mexico's popular recreations and where you'll find them at their best. Naturally, if you're retiring, you'll want to locate as near as possible to your favorite leisure time pursuit.

FAMILIAR SPORTS AND PASTIMES. Almost every large city has frequent baseball, boxing, jai alai, polo and wrestling matches. Although gambling is illegal, pari-mutuel betting flourishes at jai alai games and at Mexico City's Hipodromo Las Americas racetrack, where, from October through July, you can always count on a good thrice weekly card. All larger and more modern Mexican cities have bowling alleys and in these same cities, golf is popular. Trips of half a day to two weeks are also favorite retirement pursuits and, naturally, being on the spot, you have at your fingertips the same choice of trips for which tourists must travel thousands of miles. Many Americans make a point of taking in every fiesta within a day's drive and during February, others spend an entire week enjoying the Mardi Gras carnivals held at leading coastal cities.

Riding is enjoyable throughout Mexico. You can rent riding horses almost everywhere. But most resident riders prefer to keep at least one riding horse of their own. Total cost for a good horse, saddle and all accoutrements of finest quality shouldn't exceed $100 while feed runs about 18¢-25¢ a day.

While culturally lagging behind similar sized cities in Europe, Mexico City is a focal point for some excellent ballet and music. Splendid concerts are given by the capital's two symphony orchestras and the ballet season—with performances by the "Mexican Ballet" and visiting foreign troupes—is al-ways outstanding. Summer is also the opera season. Most of these performances are duplicated during tours of the provinces. Then, too, in all large cities, first run English language movies are shown at modern theaters.

As an art lover, you can't afford to miss Mexico's great art galleries and museums. And even if you've never painted before, you can enroll as a beginner at art schools in Taxco, San Miguel Allende and similar places. All English language books and magazines are readily obtainable and in all larger cities, you'll find the well stocked Benjamin Franklin libraries of English language books.

Mexico is as photogenic as it is artistic. There are intriguing subjects everywhere. Color film is now obtainable and can be developed in Mexico City, and better photographic shops everywhere do excellent work in black and white.

Mexico is a gardener's dream world. Orchids grow wild and flowers spring up like magic. And with gardeners available for 90¢-$1.50 a day, all backbreaking work and lawnmowing is eliminated.

Mexico has almost 1,000 different varieties of birds, many unknown north of the border and still uncatalogued. You'll discover new varieties around any Mexican town. Shelling and beachcombing are equally rewarding. And around old mining centers such as Guanajuato, Queretaro, Taxco and Alamos, rock hunters can have themselves a field day.

Gamefish—Mexican Names

atun	tuna
bagre	catfish
baya	sea bass
cabrillo	rock bass
cherna, mero	jewfish
chilo-o-quijo	bonefish
corbina	sea trout
dorado	dolphin
garropa	grouper
guachinango	red snapper
jurel	jack
lobina	freshwater bass
palomita	moonfish
pampano	pompano
peto	wahoo
pez espada	marlin
pez gallo	roosterfish
pez puerco	triggerfish
pez vela	sailfish
picuda	barracuda
robalo	snook
roncador	striped bass
sabalo	tarpon
sierra	Spanish mackerel
tiburón	shark
toro	bullfish
totoaba	white sea bass
trucha	trout

NEW SPORTS AND PASTIMES AVAILABLE ONLY IN MEXICO. In most larger cities from October through March, world famed bullfighters perform every Sunday afternoon in the *plaza de toros*. Also on Sunday mornings, free *charreadas* or charro rodeos are staged. Top grade soccer matches are another low cost Sunday entertainment.

Learning Spanish is a popular pastime with all intelligent Americans and in larger towns, inexpensive classes are available at a variety of schools and institutes.

Even if ruins normally bore you, we guarantee that once you take up such engrossing studies as anthropology, archeology, and architecture, you'll find it the most fascinating pastime imaginable. For Mexico contains more archeological sites and more historic colonial cities than the rest of the western hemisphere put together. In the southern states, you can run a trench in almost any likely spot and dig up a treasury of artifacts and pottery hundreds of years old. Digging is still in progress at most archeological sites and new discoveries are constantly being made. Treasure is also constantly being found and untold millions are said to still be awaiting discovery in former pirate haunts and old mining centers. Under Mexican law, buried treasure or archeological discoveries must be split 50/50 with the owner of the property on which it is found. Items of historical or scientific value are purchased from finders at market prices by the Mexican government.

HUNTING. Because ammunition is exceptionally high priced and modern rifles out of reach of all but the wealthiest Mexicans, the republic teems with game of every variety. To hunt, you require a gun permit obtainable from your nearest Mexican consulate for approximately $16 and permitting you to import four different guns with 100 rounds of ammunition for each. In addition, you require a hunting license, good for six months' hunting in any one state and costing approximately $20. For further information and up-to-the-minute details, write the Mexican Government Tourist Department, 630 Fifth Ave., Rockefeller Center, New York 20. This effort and expense is well worth while for at less cost you can hunt big game under conditions as exciting as those in Africa.

Generally speaking, in northern Mexico you'll find antelope, bear (including grizzlies) and mountain sheep (protected in some years but quite plentiful in B.C., Chih., and Son.) Antelope are found in the northern deserts along with mule deer. For the big cats and bears which roam the high sierras in the north and the rain forests in the south (no bears here), you'll need dogs. And though you *can* hire hunting dogs in northern Mexico, we strongly advise you to bring your own. In most hunting areas, just off highways, you'll find ranches which specialize in hunting trips and which supply pack horses, guides and equipment at very reasonable cost. For that matter, almost any rancher whose cattle are plagued by jaguar will cooperate to the utmost in helping you to hunt. It pays to inquire where jaguar are troublesome. For jaguar frequently follow deer. Unless you've had previous experience with jaguar or wild boar, we'd advise your taking an experienced local hunter along—both animals are thoroughly dangerous when aroused. Even when hunting peccaries—the smaller pigs which trail wild boar in packs —it's comfortable to have a climbable tree handy.

Game are actually so plentiful in Mexico that hunting methods still follow those used decades ago in the United States. For example, you can hunt at night with a spotlight. And you can organize full scale game drives through canyons similar to the game drives of India or Africa. Boar are best hunted at night as are alligators. With such methods still in use, it's not surprising that most hunting is still completely uncommercialized and unorganized. Only near a handful of tourist resorts will you even find a duck blind. Elsewhere, you're *completely* on your own. You must be prepared to organize *everything* yourself and *to bring with you everything you'll need* from ammunition to dogs and decoys. The same principle applies to many other sports and pastimes including skindiving and even painting. *Bring in everything you'll need with you.*

SALT WATER FISHING in Mexico is undoubtedly the finest and most thrilling in the world. Big game fishing can be had out of *every* coastal port and every bay, cove, estuary and rivermouth fairly teems with fish. Mazatlan charter boat skippers think nothing of releasing 25 sailfish a day and for real thrills you can harpoon giant Pacific manta rays weighing a ton and measuring 20 feet across. Major fishing tournaments are held annually at Acapulco, Mazatlan, Manzanillo, Puerto Vallarta, Salina Cruz, Tampico, Tuxpan, Vera Cruz and Zihuatanejo, and the records of their catches exceed the angler's wildest dreams.

To get started, all you need is a Mexican fishing license obtainable at any fishing resort or from fish and game wardens. The license covers both fresh and salt water fishing for the whole of Mexico and non residents fees are ten pesos a month or 50 pesos a year. Owners of large boats must pay an additional 25 pesos for a 30 day permit and owners of small boats just four pesos.

Outside the larger resorts, sports fishing facilities scarcely exist and as with hunting, we advise your bringing in *all* needed equipment with you. Reasonable amounts are admitted duty free. Small boats and outboards are generally also admitted free of duty. Most Mexican fishing clubs offer reciprocal facilities to visiting American fishermen. For information on these clubs and on latest fishing regulations, write the Pemex Travel Club, Avenida Juarez 89, Mexico 1, D.F.

Game—Mexican Names

caiman	alligator
cordoniz	quail
faisan	pheasant
ganso	geese
guajalote	turkey
jabali	wild boar
leoncillo	mountain lion
lobo	wolf
mono	monkey
ocelete	ocelot
oso	bear
oso gris	grizzly bear
oso negro	black bear
oso pardo	brown bear
oso hormiguero	anteater
paloma	dove
pato	duck
perico	parrot
tigre	jaguar
venado	deer
venado burro	mule deer
yuguarondi	wildcat
zorro	fox

At leading fishing centers like La Paz or Mazatlan, charter boat rates range from $40-$65 per day including soft drinks, ice, bait and tackle. At Acapulco, they range up to $80 and closely approximate Florida levels. At most places, however, four fishermen sharing a 21' Chriscraft can enjoy a full day's fishing for $10 apiece. Worth knowing, too, is that at Mazatlan among other places, rates drop by as much as 40% from June 15 through October 16. Smaller boats and outboard skiffs run $15-$20 a day, guide included (whereas on the Florida Keys you'd pay $50). Few places yet have head boats but these are available at Guaymas for roughly $6.50 per head per half day; party boats, to date, are available only out of Ensenada. At smaller ports, launches can usually be chartered for $25-$35 a day and in the most remote places you may have to be satisfied with a local sailboat or *canua* at $15-$20 a day with crew. In these places, bargaining pays. For a total outlay of $12 a day, guide included, we have chartered outboard powered craft from remote Pacific Coast villages and enjoyed superb fishing for dolphin, roosterfish, Spanish mackerel and other gamey fighters.

What will you find and where? For the entire length of the Gulf of Mexico, tarpon is king. The world's record tarpon of 247

36

Fishing Tackle—Mexican Names

anzuelo	hook
cana	rod
carneda	bait
carrete	reel
chaleco	harness
cinto	belt
cuchara	spoon
empate	leader
gancho	gaff
hueso	bone jig
lisa	mullet
macana	club (weapon)
pez	fish (live)
pez volador	flying fish
piola	line
pluma	feather jig

pounds was taken at Tampico and fish up to 185 pounds are commonplace. For eight months of the year you'll find excellent tarpon fishing in river mouths and estuaries or by trolling in the Gulf. Only during the four winter months may your fishing be interrupted by blustery northers and in between, fishing still is good. Tuna, marlin and swordfish can be taken well offshore and sails are commonly caught off Quintana Roo. Among smaller species red snapper, yellow tail jacks and croaker are common everywhere and close in, among the surf, run shoals of pompano and Spanish mackerel. Sharks are plentiful everywhere, especially in river mouths.

The best fishing spots are these: *Camp:* Isla Aguada, Ciudad del Carmen. *Q.R.:* Cozumel Island, Isla Mujeres. *Tamps:* Tampico, Laguna Madre, La Pesca. *Ver.:* Alvarado, Coatzacoalcos, Nautla, Tecolutla, Tuxpan.

Mexico's Pacific Coast fishing is consistently good throughout winter and spring to the end of May, when brief interruptions may appear in the form of fierce *chubasco* squalls from the south. Among the more than 600 species of fish are three exceptionally tough fighters: the spotted rock bass averaging 10-25 pounds, roosterfish averaging 10-35 pounds and yellowtails averaging 10-15 pounds. Other sporty medium sized fish are rock bass running 10-15 pounds, white sea bass up to 150 pounds, Spanish mackerel 5-8 pounds, bullfish 15-25 pounds and red snapper 5-15 pounds. Hundred pound jewfish are everyday catches and in season, coastal waters swarm with tuna weighing up to 600 pounds.

Lagoons and rivermouths are the places to catch albacore, mojarra, pompano and yellow tail jacks. Close inshore or in the surf are the barracuda, bonito, roosterfish, tuna and Spanish mackerel. And farther, but not much farther, out are dolphin (30-100 pounds), marlin and swordfish (normally running up to 250 pounds) and sails, shark, manta rays, devil fish, giant turtles and just about every other tropical fish you can name.

Top place in Pacific Coast fishing grounds goes, of course, to the Gulf of California—a vast fish trap 750 miles long and 75-150 miles wide embracing 80,000 square miles of water equal in area to our three largest Great Lakes. Calm and surf free, this piscatorial horn of plenty is home to literally billions of game fish. Sails and striped marlin, the principal quarries, are most plentiful at the mouth of the Gulf between La Paz and Mazatlan, and the best seasons for these blue and purple giants are April to June and August to November. Smaller game are equally plentiful and you can fly cast in the surf for snapper or corbina; plug cast for bonefish, ladyfish, corbina and bonito; and spin and troll for sierra, jacks and pompano. Whatever you do, results are likely to be phenomenal. From October till April you can cruise the coast or central islands in boats as small as 16' and you'll find pleasant camping on thousands of miles of virgin beach.

The best fishing spots are these: B.C.: Ensenada, La Paz and neighboring resorts, Loreto. *Col.:* Manzanillo. *Gro.:* Acapulco, Zihuatanejo. *Jal.:* Barra de Navidad, Puerto Vallarta. *Nay.:* San Blas and nearby villages. *Oax.:* Puerto Angel, Salina Cruz. *Sin.:* Mazatlan, Topolobampo Bay. *Son.:* Guaymas, Puerto Penasco.

Freshwater fishing is at its best in the cool mountain rivers flowing down from the Sierras into both Atlantic and Pacific. Over 100 trout streams roar down through the western Sierras into the Pacific and from May 1 until October 15, big fighting brook and rainbow trout rise freely to the fly. On the Gulf of Mexico slope, summer floods interfere with fishing and the months of October through May are best. On both slopes, bass mingle with trout and lower down, where the streams enter the tropics, big catfish abound. High in the Sierras are streams which have still to be fished and in southern Mexico the big Gripalva, Candelaria and

Mexican Hobby Terms

amplicación	enlargement
barca	boat
boxeo	boxing
caballo	horse
caceria	the hunt
camara	camera
cartucho	cartridge
caza	hunting
cazador	hunter
cazar	to hunt
cine	movie theatre
culebra	snake
espuela	spur
estribo	stirrup
exposición	exposure
filtra	filter
fotografia	photograph
fusil	gun
lente	lens
mar	sea
mosquitero	mosquito net
negativo	negative
obturador	shutter
pajaro	bird
pelicula	film
pescar	to fish
playa	beach
rollo	roll of film
silla de montar	saddle
teatro	theatre
tripie	tripod

Usumacinta Rivers are almost virgin fishing grounds. Only in central Mexico near cities are you likely to run across waters restricted to fishing clubs. Elsewhere you can fish freely and it goes without saying that in the lower reaches of rivers, you will find both fresh and salt water species. Caution: there are some seasons on freshwater fish; check with the Pemex Travel Club.

Good freshwater fishing is available near these towns or in these areas: *Ags.:* Aguascalientes and surroundings. *Chis.:* Tuxtla Gutierrez. *Chih.:* Camargo, Lake Toronto and Sierra streams. *Coah.:* Don Martin Dam. *Gro.:* Rio Balsas, Acapulco. *Gto.:* Yuriria. *Hgo.:* San Miguel Regla. *Jal.:* Rio Tapalpa, El Estribo Dam. *Mex.:* Lerma, Tlalpan, San Angel, Amecameca, Valle de Bravo, Villa Victoria. *Mich.:* in Lakes Zirahuen, Zacapu, Tizapanito and around Uruapan, Villa Jimenez and behind the dams of Las Rosas, Santa Catarina and Puruato. *Pue.:* Rio Frio and dams of Valsequillo and Necaxa. *Qro.:* San Juan del Rio. *S. L. P.:* Panuco and Montezuma Rivers. *Tab.:* all tropical rivers. *Tamps.:* Roma, Hacienda Santa Engracia and the Tamesi and Panuco Rivers. *Ver.:* Jalapa, Orizaba, Fortin and also in the Papaloapan, Nautla, Cazones and Tecolutla Rivers.

Good Books on Mexico's Hobbies

ART, ARCHITECTURE. The New Architecture in Mexico, Esther Born; *Diego Rivera,* Bertram D. Wolfe; *Story of Architecture in Mexico,* Trent E. Sanford; *Idols Behind Altars,* Anita Brenner; *Modern Mexican Painters* and *Orozco, Man of Fire,* MacKinley Helm; *Mexican Architecture,* A. B. Ayers; *Modern Mexican Artists,* C. Merida and F. Toor.

ARCHEOLOGY, HISTORY. Mexican Archeology, T. A. Joyce; *Ancient Civilizations of Mexico,* H. J. Spinden; *History of the Maya,* Gann and Thompson; *Ancient Life in Mexico and Central America,* E. L. Hewett; *Digging in Yucatan,* A. A. Morris; *Aztecs in Mexico,* G. Vaillant; *Conquest of Mexico and Peru,* W. H. Prescott. Also write for archeological pamphlet and map, and booklet *Archeology in Mexico Today,* free from Pemex Travel Club, Juarez 89, Mexico City 1.

FISHING - HUNTING - GARDENING. Fishing in Mexico, free from Pemex Travel Club, Juarez 89, Mexico 1, D.F. *Hunter's Guide to Mexico,* $1.60 from Minntiae Mexicana, Ave Alvaro Obregon 286, Mexico 7, D.F.

Chapter III

NO PASSPORT, VISA, SHOTS
OR RED TAPE

THERE ARE THREE WAYS by which you can qualify to live in Mexico: as a tourist; as a visitor *(visitante)*; or as an immigrant *(inmigrante)*. Most newcomers to Mexico take up residence under tourist status.

And for very good reasons. Without payment, you can, at any border station, obtain in a few minutes a Mexican tourist card which allows you to remain in Mexico for 180 days or half a year. By returning to the border twice annually and renewing this card, you can therefore qualify to live permanently in Mexico without any red tape whatsoever. No passports or visas nor expensive inoculations or shots are required. You can enter or leave Mexico at any choice of border towns (it is *not* necessary to return via the same border point by which you entered). Once inside Mexico you can enroll at any school for a six-month period, engage in any kind of legitimate *unpaid* activity, hunt or fish or take part in sports or scientific activities and undergo any kind of medical treatment. You can take with you, *entirely free of duty,* your car, trailer, boat, portable typewriter and radio, TV, items of portable furniture and household linens as well as a substantial assortment of *used* personal possessions. A couple can take in two cars and double the quota of everything else.

You can rent a house or lease real estate *anywhere* in Mexico. You can invest in most Mexican securities. And you can, by making a private contract with a lawyer or bank, or through an easily arranged trust, *buy and own real estate anywhere in Mexico.* For an additional $10 a year you can go freely back and forth across the border whenever you like. You do *not* have to show possession of any minimum amount of money nor must you possess any minimum fixed income to qualify. Free lance artists and writers are permitted to work. And you can stay away from Mexico as long as you like and re-enter whenever you like.

As a tourist the only things you *cannot* do in Mexico are to accept paid work, engage in business, own real estate in your own name or remain longer than 180 days in the country at one time. Canadians holding a Canadian Government passport are also entitled to use the Mexican tourist card and to enjoy all the facilities just mentioned. Along with your tourist card goes a free car permit which, at press time, allowed you to import your car or trailer, etc., for the same 180-day period covered by your tourist card.

Far from being a drawback, the twice annual trip to the border means a pleasant change for tourist card holders. Via new highways or by public transportation, many retirees are able to make the round trip in two days. Car-less couples ride with car-driving friends and share expenses. Almost everyone uses this opportunity to load up on American made supplies, to enjoy salads and milk shakes, to shop and buy ready made clothes and shoes, and perhaps to visit relatives and friends north of the border. Your car, trailer and any other items listed on your car permit must go back to the border with you each time. But items not listed on your car permit can be left at home in Mexico.

To make it clearer, we repeat: you can retire in Mexico tomorrow without a passport, without any minimum income or capital and without any red tape or special documents other than some official proof of identification and car ownership. You do not need to visit a Mexican consul. You can obtain your tourist card at the border in a matter of minutes. You can live anywhere in Mexico, undertake any legal unpaid activity, rent real estate anywhere and through an agent, own real estate anywhere in Mexico including the coastal and frontier areas forbidden to inmigrantes. There is no charge. And the sole requirement is that you return to the border twice annually with your car.

Whatever your eventual plans, we suggest that you seriously consider entering Mexico in the first place on a tourist card. Should you later change your mind about living in Mexico, you will have lost nothing. For the regular tourist card is free. If, however, after having sampled life in Mexico as a tourist card holder, you decide to switch to *visitante* or *inmigrante* status, you can do so just as easily as if you had done so from the outset. So here's our advice: plan to spend your first six months in Mexico on a tourist card. During this time, you can then decide to: a) remain indefinitely under tourist car status; b) switch to *visitante* status; or c) change to *inmigrante* status.

Introduced in 1962 as part of a plan to liberalize the requirements for permanent residence, the *Visitante-Rentista* permit was frankly designed to allow American retirees to sample life in Mexico as permanent residents for a two year trial period. Provided you have a reliable income of $160 a month for one or $240 for two persons, you can obtain a *visitante* permit from your nearest Mexican consulate (or better, through a lawyer after you arrive in Mexico). With it, you can remain in Mexico for two years without having to return to the border and you can import your car and personal possessions, excluding household furniture and appliances, duty free but you cannot legally own real estate in your own name.

You may also, if you wish, enter Mexico from the start as an *inmigrante*. Entering as an *inmigrante* is a more serious undertaking than *visitante* and involves rather time consuming and cumbersome requirements. Not only do you need a U.S. passport but you must spend about $500 in fees, go to considerable trouble obtaining various documents and papers and you must wait 8-12 weeks or longer to receive your *inmigrante* visa. To qualify, you must either have a sizeable minimum fixed income or else deposit many thousands of dollars in Mexican securities or banks. Among the advantages are these: you avoid the twice annual border trip of the tourist card holder; you are permitted to buy and own real estate in your own name; and after completing five years' residence, you achieve full permanent residence status *(inmigrado)* which permits you to engage in business or to seek employment in Mexico. Even then, however, you may not purchase real estate in your own name within 66 miles of Mexico's land frontiers nor within 33 miles of the seacoast. And in view of the microscopic level of Mexican wages, the right to seek employment is of doubtful value.

In contrast to the freedom of the tourist card holder to do almost anything provided he returns to the border twice annually, an *inmigrante* must observe certain rules. As the law stood at press time, during your first two years you could not remain out of Mexico more than 90 days each year nor more than a total of 18 months during the first five years. Nor, until you have completed your first five years' residence in Mexico are you permitted, with one exception, to engage in business or to seek employment. You may bring in your entire household goods, appliances, furniture and car free of duty (an advantage which, car and appliances apart, is of doubtful value in view of freight rates and the cheapness of furniture which, as a tourist card holder, you can buy in Mexico in any case). But through having officially become a resident of Mexico, you are no longer entitled to the still liberal

40

United States Customs exemptions granted tourist card holders each time they return to the border.

Note that in no case—as a tourist card holder, *visitante, inmigrante* (or *inmigrado*)—do you lose your American citizenship. All these situations are concerned solely with your right to live in Mexico. You do not have to become a Mexican citizen. Nor are you required to return to the United States at any fixed interval to maintain your citizenship. Tourist card holders are officially considered residents of the United States, are granted the full U.S. Customs exemption allowing them to import $100 worth of duty free merchandise into the United States monthly and are permitted to vote in elections at home.

Of course, if you intend to engage in business or employment, you must enter Mexico as an *inmigrante*. But if you intend living off your present income, you can safely take your time about seeking *visitante* or *inmigrante* status. As a tourist card holder you are perfectly free to invest in most Mexican securities and to obtain a higher yield than *inmigrantes* can. In fact, you can invest in Mexico without ever visiting Mexico at all.

Nevertheless, a complete understanding of Mexico's immigration rulings will reveal some very interesting situations through which you may be able to realize substantial benefits. So let's examine the pros and cons of each in detail. (It must be understood that this information, though current at press time, is subject to change. For details of recent amendments, write the Mexican Embassy, Washington, D.C., or the American Embassy, Mexico City.)

Americans and other foreigners may enter Mexico as a) non-immigrants or as b) temporary immigrants.

Non-immigrants

BORDER ZONE. You may visit any border town or adjacent border areas with your car for a period of up to 72 hours without a tourist card, car permit or vaccination certificate. In B.C., this zone extends 9 miles south of Ensenada and to San Felipe. You may import a car as far as Ensenada for up to ten days without a car permit.

TOURIST CARDS are required by all foreigners aged over 15 entering Mexico for recreation. There are two types, both permitting you to remain in Mexico for 180 days. The single entry type now costs nothing and can be swiftly obtained from any Mexican Consulate or Mexican Tourist Bureau, through airlines or at any border point. To obtain one you must submit proof of nationality such as birth certificate, Armed Forces discharge, baptismal certifciate, voters registration card or a witnessed affidavit of place of birth. The multiple entry type permits unlimited border crossings, also free, requires completion of Form FM14 plus three 2"x2" front view photos, takes up to several hours to process and is best obtained in advance from a Mexican consulate. Children under age 15 traveling with parents are entered on the parents' tourist card and must accompany parents when entering or leaving Mexico. Children under 15 not traveling with parents require a duplicate notarized statement of permission from both parents and their tourist card must be issued by a Mexican consul. All tourist cards must be used within 90 days of issue. At border offices, you may be expected to tip 3 pesos; *pay it,* or you may be held up. Carry your tourist card at all times, failure to produce it may involve a 200 pesos fine. Extensions beyond 180 days are granted only in cases of serious illness and a doctor's certificate is necessary. If the tourist card is lost or stolen, apply immediately for a new tourist card to the nearest immigration office or to the Jefe del Departmente de Inmigración, Secretaria de Gobernación in Mexico City (see American consul before going) and the renewal fee is 30 pesos. If applying by mail, write in Spanish, giving details. If you are living in Southeast Mexico, you can renew your tourist card by crossing into British Honduras and obtaining a new one there instead of returning to the U.S. border. Presumably the same thing can be done by entering Guatemala—but check!

Along with your tourist card you may obtain a free automobile permit good for a full 180 days. At the same time the driver's tourist card will be stamped "Con Automovil." Since the driver cannot leave Mexico without the car, it makes sense to have this stamp placed on the card of the person in your party least likely to be called home in an emergency. There are no restrictions on house trailers which, with boats and boat trailers, will be entered on your car permit and subject to the same conditions as your car. For your permit, you will require your driver's license, car title and *annual registration,* and proof of ownership of trailer or boat, etc., in the form of a bill of sale. If driving a borrowed car, trailer, etc., bring a notarized statement from the owner authorizing you to use it in Mexico. If your car title shows a lien, bring a notarized authorization from the lien holder. At all Texas border stations, Sanborn's insurance agencies will swiftly notarize these documents for you.

Should your license plates expire while in Mexico, you can mail home for a new set. Allow one month for delivery or else have them sent to the border. New driver's licenses can be obtained more rapidly. If you wish to leave your car in Mexico while you visit another country you can do so by leaving it in custody of the Mexico City Airport Customs. Storage is free for ten days, nominally priced thereafter. Alternatively you can deposit a bond of roughly 10,000 pesos which Mexico City bonding companies will post for a fee of approximately 160 pesos (get details from U.S. Consulate). It is also possible, if you want to go to the trouble, to import a car into Mexico without a car permit by depositing a bond equal to the car's duty plus 10%, refundable on leaving. If your car is wrecked or stolen, get in touch immediately with the Protection Department of the nearest U.S. Consulate. (U.S. Consulates exist at all large border towns and at Guadalajara, Guaymas, Mazatlan, Merida, Mexico City, Monterrey, San Luis Potosi, Tampico and Vera Cruz.) Cars *cannot* be sold in Mexico.

To bring a pet into Mexico you must first obtain a certificate of good health signed by a licensed veterinary and visaed by a Mexican consul (fee $4). And your pet must also have a valid rabies certificate (standard injection is good for six months, nervous tissue type 12 months, chicken embryo type 36 months). These same documents are required to take the pet back into the United States. If they expire while in Mexico, they can be renewed very cheaply by a Mexican vet. Worth knowing is that you can, if you wish, transact business on a tourist card simply by appointing a Mexican agent such as a banker, lawyer or broker to conduct it for you.

VISTANTE-RENTISTA permits are issued to non-immigrants who enter Mexico for a period of two years to sample retirement living. The permit is theoretically available through your nearest Mexican consulate but is best obtained through a lawyer after entering Mexico on a tourist card. The primary requirements are a valid U.S. passport and proof of a minimum fixed income of 2,000 pesos ($160) per month for one person plus an additional 1,000 pesos ($80) for your spouse and for each child over age 15. The original permit is good only for six months but it can be renewed 3 times to cover a full two-year period without your having to return to the border. As a *Visitante-Rentista,* you are free to import your car and personal possessions (but not your furniture or appliances) for the period of your stay as a *visitante.* Furthermore, you are not legally entitled to buy and own real estate in your own name and any real estate purchases would have to be handled in the same manner as for ordinary tourist card holders. Upon expiry of your permit's two year validity, you are free to tranfer to *inmigrante* status (note that the financial requirements are higher and also that your two year's residence as *visitante* do not count towards the five years' residence as *inmigrante* which you require to qualify as *inmigrado.*) Alternately, when your *visitante* permit expires, you could return to tourist card status or, perhaps, renew your *visitante* permit. You can enter Mexico on a tourist card and change to *visitante* after arrival and unless you are perfectly certain you will like living in Mexico, this the course we suggest. Naturally, if you have already sampled Mexican life and are sure you will like it, there is nothing against taking out a *visitante* permit from the start. It's important not to confuse *Visitante-Rentista* permits with ordinary *Visitante* permits issued to traveling salesmen, theatrical people, etc., for remunerative work in Mexico of a special or temporary nature. You should also note that to qualify for *Visitante-Rentista* permits, you must be aged 55 or over and your income must be derived from sources outside Mexico. Fee for the permit is $5. A similar category of permit for applicants under age 55 is available; it is called *No-Inmigrante Rentista* and qualifications are identical.

STUDENT VISAS are issued to nonimmigrant students who enter Mexico for periods in excess of six months to enroll in day classes at an approved official or privately incorporated educational institution. The visa is issued for one year and may be renewed afterwards. To qualify, you must show proof that you will be enrolled at an acceptable Mexican school and that you possess the financial ability to complete your studies. Enrollment in Mexican schools is simple to arrange by mail. Although regular courses in Mexican schools and universities are conducted in Spanish, others such as those at San Miguel Allende are in English and you can, in fact, take only a single class such as Spanish which can cost as little as $10 a month. Since there is no age limit, this visa is a most useful document for anyone who wishes to remain in Mexico on a year to year basis without having to qualify for *inmigrante* requirements.

Immediately you enroll at a Mexican school, you will be sent a letter in triplicate stating that you have applied to enroll there (a small deposit of about $10 towards tuition will suffice). You then appear at the nearest Mexican consulate with this letter and the following documents: character and bank references in duplicate (if under 21 you must present sworn letter of consent from parents or guardian); proof of at least $100 monthly income over and above tuition fee for one year period; a valid passport; six front and six profile 2″ x 2″ photos with a white background; and certificates of good health and vaccination against smallpox (If studying under the GI Bill, the Certificate of Eligibility must be submitted in lieu of bank references, as well as a letter in duplicate from the V.A. stating the monthly subsistence to be received.) Authentication of the good health certificate costs $4 but the visa itself is free. After arriving and registering at the school, you must notify the authorities of your enrollment date and register at the Alien Registration Office. Students may not change schools without previous authorization and are not permitted to work or engage in lucrative activity or to own real estate in their own name. To renew your visa for the second year, you should have been enrolled at least nine months of the year, shown an attendance record of 80% and passed the annual examinations, if any. *You should note, however, that the simplest way to enter Mexico for study purposes is as a tourist. Every 180 days you then return to the border and re-enter on a new tourist card.*

Temporary Immigrants

An *inmigrante* is one who enters Mexico to establish residence and to acquire the status of permanent resident (*inmigrado*) which takes a minimum of five years legal residence. Until he attains *inmigrado* status, an *inmigrante* may not seek employment in Mexico nor, outside the exceptions given below, engage in business. There are seven categories of *inmigrantes* as follows:

1. *Rentista.* A person who lives off his pension, investments, bank accounts etc. To qualify, you require a fixed stable income of not less than 3,000 pesos ($240) a month plus a further 1,000 pesos ($80) monthly for each dependent aged over 15. This income can come from any reliable source, not necessarily in Mexico. Alternatively, you may deposit a sum of approximately, you may deposit a sum of approximately $14,400 for yourself and $4,800 for each adult dependent in a designated Mexican bank. Slight adjustments can sometimes be made if your income does not quite meet these specifications.

To be acceptable, your income must be derived from annuities, a U.S. Government or corporate pension, social security; investment companies, trust funds or a bank in either the U.S. or Mexico; or from a deposit in Nacional Financiera. Alternatively, you may use a letter of credit. Rental income from real estate in the U.S. is also acceptable. It is best to avoid a deposit in Nacional Financiera as no interest is paid to inmigrants. For more information, send for the booklet *This Is the Moment to Become Inmigrante Rentista,* free from Departmento Autonomo de Turismo, 1302 Connecticut Ave., N.W., Washington, D.C.

2. *Investor.* A person who invests his capital in some *stable* branch of Mexican agriculture, industry or export trade other

than through holding common stock. When applying, you must indicate the specific company etc., in which you intend to invest and where you intend to reside. You are also required to deposit in the Banco de Mexico a sum equivalent to 10% of your investment. If your investment is to be within the Federal District or nearby states it must total a minimum of 600,000 pesos, if elsewhere a minimum of 200,000 (if in virgin lands or in a badly needed new industry, a smaller investment may qualify). The investment must be made within 30 days of entering Mexico upon which half your deposit is refunded; the other half is returned at the end of five years when you attain *inmigrado* status. As an *investor inmigrante* you are permitted to work in connection with the business you invest in but not for anyone else.

3. *Invercionista.* A person who invests his capital in Mexico Government bonds, securities or a national credit institution as directed by Mexico's Ministry of the Interior. To qualify you must deposit $800 with *Gobernacion,* refunded if the agreed-on investment is made within 60 days of entering Mexico. The investment required must yield at least as much as the sums given above for the *Rentista* category. If required, *Gobernacion* will authorize you to make changes in your investments provided they continue to yield the required minimum amount.

4. *Profesionista.* A person who enters Mexico to practice a profession. Permission is so rarely granted you may as well forget it.

5. *Cargos de Confianza.* A person who enters Mexico to assume a position of management or responsibility in a Mexican institution or enterprise. Such opportunities are rarely available and must be sponsored by the Mexican employer. We have, however, known of cases in which Americans have been employed in such positions by Mexican friends who each year stated to *Gobernacion* that the Americans' services were indispensable.

6. *Tecnicos.* Persons who enter Mexico to render technical or specialist services that cannot be rendered by a Mexican. Again, rarely available other than under conditions described in #5. (However, you *might* arrange to work through an American firm that employs non-Mexicans: for a list, see *American Firms, Subsidiaries and Affiliates in Mexico,* $2 from the Department of Commerce, Washington 25, D.C.)

7. *Familiar.* A person entering Mexico to be supported by a spouse or relative within the third degree, who may be a Mexican citizen or an *inmigrante* or *inmigrado.* Male relatives over 18 are not normally admitted. Your application must be made in Mexico by your relative.

All information to the contrary, the only *effective* way to obtain a visa is through a reputable Mexican immigration lawyer in Mexico City. American Consuls can supply names and addresses. For the lawyer to get started, you will need a U.S. passport, certificates of good health and good conduct, various photos and other documents. The process usually takes from 8-12 weeks but can take six months. Your costs, including a special fee to the Ministry of Foreign Relations to allow you to own property, will run roughly $480. Within six months of receiving your visa, you must enter Mexico and within a further 30 days file with the Registry of Foreigners to whom thereafter you must report all changes of address. Your dependents within the third degree and minor children are entitled to the same status but children pay $103 entry tax.

During the ensuing 5 years your status will remain that of a probationary immigrant (*inmigrante*) during which you may not absent yourself from Mexico for more than 90 days during the first two years nor more than 180 days during the entire 5 year period. Annually, you must satisfy *Gobernacion* that you are complying with your *inmigrante* requirements and pay a fee of 50 pesos (plus 450 pesos for your lawyer to handle it). If during this time you fail to comply you must inform *Gobernacion* within 15 days and leave Mexico within 30 days.

After legally completing your 5-year residence as an *inmigrante,* and complying with all conditions, you apply within 90 days to *Gobernacion* who, for a further fee of 200 pesos, will declare you an *inmigrado* or permanent immigrant. As such you can come and go freely across the border, pay no further taxes (but must still maintain your U.S. passport) and you are free to engage in almost any kind of work or business. You may, however, still lose *inmigrado* status by remaining out of Mexico for two consecutive years or for over 5 years in any ten year period.

Granting of an *inmigrante* visa (or *visitante* permit) allows you to import your *used* furniture and appliances duty free.

All the larger American van lines can handle the move and store your furniture at the border while you're getting settled in Mexico. Your automobile goes in duty free and for as long as you remain an *inmigrante* (or *visitante*), so do any replacement cars you buy in the States. Also as an *inmigrante* (or *visitante*), all your income from sources outside Mexico is free of Mexican income tax.

Should you enter Mexico on a tourist card or *visitante* permit, you can switch to *inmigrante* status for an additional fee of $150-$300. If you reside in Mexico as an *inmigrante* for ten years yet fail to comply with *inmigrante* requirements, you are nonetheless entitled to *inmigrado* status. Likewise, after 20 years residence as an *inmigrante*, you pay no further taxes. Incidentally, if and when you retain an immigration lawyer in Mexico, never deal with one who demands over half his fee in advance.

As a foreign resident in Mexico you enjoy substantially the same civil liberties as do Mexican citizens. However, to own real estate you must agree not to invoke the aid of your own government and you cannot participate in Mexican politics. You must obey and respect the laws and institutions of Mexico and submit to the decisions of Mexican courts. By and large, federal rather than state laws apply to foreigners. You are exempt from Mexican military service but as an *inmigrante* you may be called upon to assist in emergency police work. Provided you follow these principles and comply with all immigration requirements, your domicile in Mexico can be regarded as safely permanent. Sources close to Mexico state that expropriation risks seem exceptionally remote. The only Americans we have seen expelled have been degenerates: incurable alcoholics, marijuana smokers or other objectionable types.

Now that you know the pros and cons of both tourist card and *inmigrante* status, here's a plan frequently followed by married couples. One spouse takes out *inmigrante* papers thereby qualifying to own real estate in his own name while the other remains a tourist card holder. Thus they get the best of both worlds.

TO BECOME a naturalized Mexican citizen involves renouncing your American citizenship and the chances that any American would want to do this seem so remote we shall not bother to give details. Nevertheless, there are two circumstances in which an American may acquire dual American and Mexican citizenships.

For example, a foreign woman who marries a Mexican and resides in Mexico is considered a Mexican by privileged naturalization. Unless she actually renounces her American citizenship, however, she continues to retain it.

Children born in Mexico of American (or Canadian) parents are also considered both Mexican and American (Canadian) citizens and hold dual nationality until age 21. They may then elect to be either a Mexican or an American (Canadian) citizen but can no longer be both.

As a native born Mexican citizen, such a child may seek employment, operate a business or own real estate. Parents can therefore assign to their Mexican born child any business or property rights they wish and operate the business etc., in the child's name as his legal guardian. If not *inmigrantes* already, the parents would, we think, have a strong case to qualify as *familiares*. If upon reaching age 21 the child elects American or Canadian citizenship, both child and parents would lose all rights unless in the meantime they had attained *inmigrado* status.

MEXICAN CUSTOMS. Upon entering Mexico as a tourist by car or bus, your baggage will be inspected at the border and seals placed on it which should not be broken until you are well inside the border zone. By rail, your baggage will probably be inspected in the train. By air, unless you have an unusual amount of luggage, in all probability you will need only to sign a statement that you are not carrying contraband.

Allowed in without payment of duty are from 100-160 pounds of personal effects, clothing and a reasonable amount of jewelry plus 2.2 pounds of tobacco, three bottles of liquor, a reasonable amount of camping and sports equipment, one phonograph, one portable radio and TV set, one movie and one still camera with 12 rolls of film for each, a portable typewriter, 50 books, scientific instruments and hobby tools, used toys, household linens, folding chairs, beds and tables, a reasonable amount of kitchen utensils and 12 artistic objects such as paintings. All this is allowed *each* tourist card holder regardless of age. Special permits are required for 35mm movie cameras, commercial cameras, tape recorders and sound equipment and firearms and ammunition. Boats, boat trailers and outboard motors are generally admitted free though in some cases you may be required to deposit a bond, refundable upon leaving. It's smart to have a notarized bill of sale for all larger items such as boats and to break seals on American tobacco, cigarettes and cigar boxes before entering. In preparation for writing this book, we personally brought in almost 1,000 pounds of personal effects, reference books, typewriters etc., by automobile. A small tip at the border helped smooth our way.

Whatever you take into Mexico, however, take it *with* you. Never have anything sent separately or by parcel post. If you receive it at all, you must pay duty almost equal to the value of the item itself. If you must send anything into Mexico unaccompanied, contact a customs broker through your nearest American consulate and have him handle the transaction. It's equally advisable never to send cash by the Mexican mails.

Strictly speaking it is forbidden to export colonial antiques and paintings and historic items like artifacts without a permit from the Direccion de Monumento y Museo in Mexico City.

To RETURN to the United States you require

Children in Mexico

Kids love Mexico! Many American parents enroll their children in the free Mexican public schools up to the eighth grade and find the standard of education more than adequate. Almost all younger children acquire fluent Spanish without instruction in under a year. In some heavily American-populated small towns such as the Lake Chapala villages, however, American enrollment at local schools has caused crowding. For the best education we'd choose a town where not too many Americans are living and which is not expanding to fast under the impetus of a mushrooming industrial population.

Teenagers can be a problem, though. While good private schools are established in most larger cities (with extremely low tuition fees and high scholastic standards) they lack the extra-curricular activities of American and Canadian high schools. And even in the largest American colonies, American teenagers find few opportunities for dating.

proof of citizenship such as that required to enter Mexico plus proof of vaccination, either in the shape of an International Certificate of Inoculation and Vaccination (free at U. S. Public Health Service offices and travel agencies) or in the form of a letter from a doctor. The vaccination should not be more than 3 years old. If necessary, you can be vaccinated in Mexico for less than in the United States. It is free at clinics. Or you can be vaccinated without charge by U. S. authorities at the border. (Occasionally, you may be asked to show proof of vaccination when entering Mexico so it's smart to be prepared by having your vaccination beforehand.)

As a returning United States resident (tourist card holder) you are entitled to import free of duty $100 worth of merchandise at retail value once every 30 days. These duty free exemptions are per person and subject to no age limit. Thus a family of five which makes two trips to the border annually may bring into the United States $1,000 worth of merchandise each year. In practice, there are no limits to the total amount of merchandise you may import providing you are prepared to pay duty on the balance in excess of your exemption; on most imports, duty is much lower than most people imagine, usually $8\frac{1}{2}\%$-15%. In addition, if you are willing to risk the Mexican mails, you are permitted to mail back each day one gift parcel not exceeding $10 in value to as many people as you like, including yourself. Such parcels should be marked "Gift Enclosed" with value shown.

How to bring back liquor: regardless of which state or Canadian province you are bound for, each person aged 21 or over is allowed one full quart except that Californians returning through a California gateway are allowed none. To import liquor through Texas, you must pay the small but annoying Texas State liquor tax. These exceptions are not available to *inmigrantes* or *inmigrados* who are not classified as residents of the United States.

For further details, we suggest your writing to the U. S. Treasury Department, Washington, D. C., for their free pamphlet *United States Customs Hints* (available, too, at all border points and most American Consulates).

Chapter IV

MEXICO'S FAT INVESTMENT PROFITS

MEXICO IS BOOMING! According to a recent U.N. report, Mexico has the world's second fastest growing population. The land of manana is fast moving into a world of tomorrow. Colossal agricultural and hydro-electric projects are paving the way for industry. Gleaming new factories are turning rural villages into prosperous modern towns. Modernistic new plants, office buildings, subdivisions and schools are transforming the Mexican landscape. Fleets of trucks ply the highways, tractors are replacing oxen and only six other countries can claim more air traffic.

From 16 million in 1930, Mexico's population grew to 33,000,000 in 1960 and is projected at 42,000,000 by 1970, 53,000,000 by 1980 and 100,000,000 by the year 2,000. But prosperity is racing ahead at *twice* the speed of population growth. National productivity, buying power and consumer spending are all increasing annually by over 6%. In 1964 alone, Mexico's gross national product increased 10% (versus 6½% for the U.S.). From end to end the republic is surging with new activity. Percentagewise, the Mexican boom ranks as one of the world's largest.

With a stable peso and government and the soundest economy in Latin America, Mexico has already become the financial center for the Latin American nations. Among foreign countries drawing private American investment, Mexico ranks third. Over 500 big American firms are doing business in Mexico. The peso is now ranked as a "hard" currency by the International Monteary Fund. And demonstrating further world confidence in Mexico are the huge recent investments made by the ultra conservative Vatican and by the Prudential Life Insurance Company.

The expropriation and nationalization of the 1930's is now just a memory. The Department of Commerce rates expropriation as "low among the hazards of Mexican investment."

Foreign money is pouring in. But not fast enough. The country needs new money badly and is willing to pay for it. In Mexico today, the *average* investment yields 9%. With safety comparable to similar investments in the United States you can place your money in a conservative Mexican bank and receive 7%-9% interest. AAA1 bonds pay 8%-10%. Mortgages secured by high grade property yield 10%-14%, others more. Stock dividends run 5%-10% and higher. Conservative mutual funds pay 5%-9%. And you can, if you wish, receive rates from 15%-18% on your money. Almost all dividends and interest are paid tax free and most fixed income securities pay interest monthly.

Though these may seem high returns, in Mexico they are considered quite normal. For generations, Mexicans have been accustomed to paying more for investment capital. The going rate for bank loans in Mexico is 12%. Mortgage borrowers have traditionally paid 18% interest. These high rates notwithstanding, Mexico's banks can show an excellent record. In many ways, the republic's banks and other investment institutions are more conservative than similar ones in the States. Over past decades, Mexico has had a far lower rate of bank failure than we have. All banks are strictly regulated by the National Banking Commission and by Banco de Mexico (Federal Reserve) and the Treasury Department.

Since most Mexican investments yield twice as much as ours, you can DOUBLE your investment income by investing in Mexico. Conversely, you can retire in Mexico *by investing only half the capital you would need to invest at home. And since living costs are less in Mexico, you can live as well on less income than in the United States. To live as well as you can in Mexico on the income from $25,000, you would have to invest $60,000 in the United States.*

As the oldest member of the dollar gold bloc, Mexico has never imposed restrictions on the free exchange of dollars and pesos. Money can be brought freely in and out and dividends received in dollars or in pesos. The official exchange rate is currently 12.50 pesos per dollar and banks deduct less than ¼% for making the exchange. The Mexican peso, currently worth 8¢ U. S., comes in bills of 1, 5, 10, 20, 50, 100, 500, 1,000 and 10,000 denominations. Each peso is worth 100 centavos, issued in the following denominations: copper coins, 1, 5, 10, 20 and 50 centavos; alloy coins 5, 10 and 25 centavos and 1 peso; and silver coins of 5 and 10 pesos (fast disappearing).

Because it may take a little time to establish a bank account in Mexico, you should bring sufficient funds in traveler's checks to cover immediate expenses for your first two months. Alternatively, of course, you can transfer funds to a Mexican bank before you arrive. Otherwise, transferring your funds to a Mexican bank will take from a minimum of ten days (at a Mexico City branch of the National City Bank of New York) to as long as a month at small town banks. Once your credit is established, however, Mexican banks will honor your checks on sight, even to the extent of a small overdraft. Don't under any circumstances, try to cash American personal checks or U. S. postal orders. If you need funds in a hurry you can have them wired to the Banco de Mexico through the largest American banks. Western Union will also wire funds to Mexico (payable in pesos). And with slightly more time, say up to two weeks, you can receive funds from the States in the form of an international money order. (Note: mutual funds and other institutions catering to American investors resident in the United States will accept Stateside personal checks but will not refund until the checks are cleared, usually requiring a minimum of 30 days.)

Once your money is in Mexico, you'll find a bewildering choice of high paying investments. Due to Mexico's need for foreign capital—plus the demand for investment information by retired Americans—many large banks now maintain English speaking investment counselors. Even so, Mexico offers no magic road to wealth for the uninformed. It's just as necessary to understand investment principles before investing in Mexico as before investing in the United States. Thus we recommend, as required prior reading, an excellent guide to investing for retirement entitled *Harian's Investing for a Sound 6% —and More,* available at $2.50 postpaid from Harian Publications, Greenlawn, New York.

Having grasped the principles of successful investing, you are ready to study the Mexican scene. Required background reading here is Chapter I of this book. You'll find that the very same characteristics, the identical customs described in this chapter extend into every field of Mexican business. Once oriented and prepared to invest in Mexico as a Mexican does, you are ready for the final step—familiarity with Mexican securities. To help you decide, you'll find below a short review of the principal types of Mexican securities together with their pros and cons. These facts are naturally offered for information only, are subject to change, and should not be misconstrued as a recommendation to invest in any Mexican institution or to buy or sell any Mexican security. In Mexico as elsewhere, there is no substitute for the old adage, "Before you Invest, Investigate."

For example, because Mexican banks etc., do not recognize the jurisdiction of foreign courts or executors in disposing of wills or estates, it is absolutely essential to include your beneficiary as a joint tenant when opening a bank account or buying other securities. If you do not wish your beneficiary to know, you may arrange for your attorney or executor to become a joint tenant with you. Under no circumstances, however, should you open a bank account or buy securities in your own name only if you hope to pass them on in event of your death.

As for income from American pension sources, social security payments may be received in Mexico by anyone who has been a U. S. citizen for more than ten years. Railroad and Armed Forces pensions may also be received in Mexico. For Civil Service pensions—some of which we know are being received in Mexico—you should check with the Civil Service Retirement Division in Washington. For state pensions, check with the state capital concerned. All commercial pension funds, mutual funds, bank interest and stock dividends etc., can be freely received in Mexico.

FIXED INCOME SECURITIES. Accounts in Mexican banks may be kept in either dollars or pesos. The yield on dollar accounts is always less than that on peso accounts. There are three types of private banks in Mexico, namely:

Deposit Banks: unlike their American counterpart, the commercial bank, Mexico's deposit banks may operate a nationwide chain of branches and several do. Like American commercial banks, no interest is paid on checking accounts and interest on savings accounts is low (i.e. 3½% for dollar accounts and 4½% for peso accounts) Proof of the ultra conservative attitude of Mexican banks in general is found in the withdrawal restrictions of deposit banks which limit withdrawals on sight to 30% of your account and require 30 days notice before you can withdraw the entire sum. Actually, the highest interest available on demand deposits is obtainable in the participation certificates issued by *Nacional Financiera,* which pay a yield of between 8½% and 9% (You may also hold gold on deposit in Mexican banks.)

Mortgage Banks: resemble Savings & Loan Associations in the States and issue attractive 100-peso ten year bonds paying 8% interest compounded monthly. These are considered one of Mexico's safest investments, the bonds seldom fluctuate in value and the banks are seldom oversubscribed. With an investment of $400 or more, most banks will hold your bonds in their Trust Department and automatically reinvest your interest.

Investment Banks: also called *financieras,* promote industry through the issuance of bonds called *bonos financieras.* They also accept savings in pesos on time deposit contracts (minimum one year limit) typically paying 8%-9%, interest from which can be compounded monthly. Owing to certain restrictions, these banks may become temporarily oversubscribed and unable to accept further deposits. Most *financieras* require a minimum deposit of $1,600-$8,000. In return you receive a promissory note and

return of your capital is not possible until the note matures. While not guaranteed by the government, *financiera* obligations are usually supported by the Bank of Mexico. The following Mexio City *financieras* usually welcome investments from Americans (mention does not imply our recommendation): Financiera Colon, Reforma 185; Intercontinental S.A., Paris 15; Corporacion Continental S. A., Reforma 107; Financeira Metropolitana, Juarez 42-B; Credito American de Mexico, Atenas 56; Financiera de Credito Mercantil, Reforma 45; Credito Mexicano, Isabel la Catolica 43.

Although Mexican banks are not insured, there hasn't been a loss since 1925. For more information, we recommend your writing for the interesting booklet *Mexico— Investing for Profit and Security* available free from Mr. William E. Hughes, Apartado 774, Monterrey, N. L., Mexico. Mr. Hughes, a popular and long established American banking agent in Monterrey, specializes in placing time deposits at high interest yields in conservative Mexican banks. There is no fee for this service. The average bank pays 8%-9% on peso accounts with interest often compounded monthly. Mr. Hughes' agency accepts personal or cashiers checks on American banks and you may open an account with as little as $1,000 for as short a time as 90 days. For deposits of $5,000 or more you can, normally, obtain yields one percentage point higher.

Such bank rates *compounded monthly* can provide astronomical yields. By compounding interest monthly over a ten year period at 7% your actual interest become 10% annually; at 8% it is actually 12.1% and at 9% actually 14.5. One man who invested $20,000 in a Mexican bank at 7% found 17 years later that his account totalled well over $65,000 and had outstripped all but the fastest growing mutual funds. In Mexican banks paying 8% interest compounded monthly, your money doubles in 8 years 9 months, trebles in 13 years 10 months, and quadruples in 17 years 5 months. A $1,000 deposit left untouched for 30 years at 8% becomes $10,900.

Operating a similar agency in Mexico City is the well known American run firm Industrias e Inversiones Alba S.A. de C.V., Reforma 336, Mexico 6, D.F., which is registered with our Securities and Exchange Commission. Like Mr. Hughes, Alba will also place your funds in well secured, short term loans to Mexican Investment Banks which pay from 8%-9% net on peso accounts and 5%-7% on dollar accounts. At press time, Alba preferred deposits of $8,000 or more for a minimum period of six months. On these very sound bank time contracts, interest is paid at frequent intervals with all Mexican income tax prepaid and the services of Alba are entirely free. At times, when the banks in Monterrey may be temporarily oversubscribed, you can often obtain higher interest rates in Mexico City and vice versa.

Note: it must be understood that all interest rates mentioned here are subject to fluctuation and that Investment Banks can become fully subscribed. Should this happen, agencies such as Mr. Hughes will recommend temporary placement of your funds in the Trust Department of Mortgage Banks which they represent.)

THE PESO'S past history of inflation—it lost about 9% annually from 1940 through 1960—made fixed income investments in dollars more attractive to investors outside Mexico. Now that the peso seems sound again, however, many investors in Mexico prefer to invest directly in pesos and receive the higher yields. Among other attractive fixed income securities are these:

Government Savings Bonds: double in value if held to full maturity over a ten year period and are available in denominations of 12.50 pesos up. In addition, four times annually a drawing is held and one of every 4,000 bonds receives a bonus equal to ten times the bond's purchase price. Because a bond can be purchased for $1, many investors buy an entire series of 4,000 bonds, thereby guaranteeing a premium of 1,000 pesos annually which adds a further yield of 1%.

Because they are issued by Nacional Financiera, the Mexican Government's Industrial Development Bank, and are guaranteed by a select portfolio of industrial stocks and bonds, we feel that the popular *Titulos Financieros* bonds might well be included in the classification of government bonds. Depending upon the issue, these bonds pay a minimum of 8% and are currently paying around 9% with coupons maturing quarterly. An interesting point is that you can reinvest the coupons immediately in additional *Titulos* so that your interest is compounded at a rate that over a ten year period

provides an average annual yield of 13.48%. Considering their safety, the *Titulos* compare very favorably to bank time contracts made in pesos. The *Titulos* can be purchased in pesos only for denominations of 100 up to 100,000 pesos and interest is also naturally paid in pesos. Anyone interested in providing a fixed income in pesos might well take a close look at these *Titulos.*

Corporate and other bonds average 1,000 pesos in face value, mature in 5-20 years (average 10) and yield 8%-10% interest payable semi-annually. Among such bonds are: 1. *Cedulos hipotecarias,* bonds secured by city real estate totalling twice the bonds' value and backed in addition by the borrower's note; they come in denomniations of 500 pesos up and yield 8% payable monthly (which can be compounded to yield a tax free 12.1% to maturity). 2. *Bonos hipotecarias,* similar to the above but secured by mortgage loans. 3. *Titulos financieras,* already discussed. 4. *Corporate bonds:* to discourage inflation fears, some Mexican bonds include a growth bonus. For example, Pemex 1958 issue sold to yield 7.6% will actually yield an interest which rises in step with the cost of living. The 8% bonds of Cerveceria Moctezuma pay, in addition, a preferred accumulative dividend of 4%, bringing the overall yield to 12%. Many other types of high grade government, real estate and industrial bonds yield 8%-11% at par and as much as 15% if bought at a discount.

Because sinking funds are not used by Mexican corporations, bonds are amortized by annual drawings, starting 2-5 years after issue and continuing until by maturity, all bonds have been paid off. Drawings are by lot and bonds so drawn are paid for at par. Not infrequently, good bonds can be bought at a disount and a capital gain realized when they are drawn. Commission on selling bonds is one half per cent.

Information on many good Mexican bonds can be obtained from brokers and also from such Mexico City banks as Banco de Comercio, Venustiano Carranza 44; Banco de Comercio, Depto Internacional, Gante 20; Sociedad Mexicano de Credito Industrial, Depto de Valores, 4th floor, Venustiano Carranza 54; and Nacional Financiera, Plaza de La Republica 31; also from other banks mentioned in this chapter. Interest

Brokers and Custodians

Because all Mexican seurities are issued in "street name" or bearer form and are readily negotiable, they should never be trusted to the mails. Moreover, to collect each dividend or interest payment, a coupon must be clipped and physically presented for payment. Thus for safekeeping and collection of dividends or interest, a Mexican custodian is *absolutely essential*. Many banks and brokerage houses offer reliable custodial service for a fee of ¼%-½% of the market value of the securities annually. Most Americans use the custodial services of the following banks, all in Mexico City: First National City Bank, Isabel La Catolica 54; Banco de Comercio, Venustiano Carranza 44; Banco Nacional de Mexico, Isabel La Catolica 43; Banco Comercial Mexicano, Isabel La Catolica 43; Banco Mexicano, 5 de Mayo 35; and Banco de Londres y Mexico, Bolivar y 16 de Septiembre.

For best results, most investors prefer to use a Mexico City broker. The following Mexico City brokers welcome American clients: Credito Bursatil, Isabel La Catolica 39; Banco de Comercio, 5th floor, Venustiano Carranza 54; Sociedad Financiera de Industria y Descuento S.A., Madero 47; Carlos Trouyet S.A., Juarez 14; Casusas, Trigueros y Cia., S.A., Juarez 100; Corretajes e Inversiones Bursatiles S.A., Isabel La Catolica 43-801; Valores de Capital, S.A., Hamburgo 70-305. In Guadalajara, there are Garcia Sanchez S.A., Condominio Guadalajara; and Allen Lloyd, Aptdo 1470, who caters to many Americans.

---

after taxes averages 8.75% and can be paid to you monthly in pesos or dollars.

Mortgages: as in the States, mortgages yield more than bonds and in Mexico reliable real estate brokers have well secured mortgages for sale to yield 9%-15%, with others bringing in up to 18%. Through banks and real estate brokers, you'll have no trouble in arranging a sound, secure first mortgage on AAA1 city real estate to yield 10%-12%. A word of caution: under no circumstances invest in mortgages, either in Mexico or the United States, without carefully studying the book *Harian's Investing for a Sound 6%—or More* mentioned earlier.

Private Loans: can be made to well established industries through Mexican banks. For example, well secured loans to major Mexican industries and even to the subsidiaries of American firms, can be made to yield an almost riskless 7% in dollars and more in pesos. Short term peso loans to sugar mills, for example, return a tax free 11%. Every Mexican bank has a wide choice of opportunities to loan money at high rates of interest to major Mexican industries. Here again, we stress the desirability of having a competent bank or reputable financial advisory service handle the transaction. Never make a loan or a mortgage on your own. (If you do, though you may be getting 18%-24% interest, you are definitely placing your capital in the risk category.)

COMMON STOCKS. Had you invested $2,000 in General Motors in 1909, you'd have been worth about a million dollars by 1956. Why? Because you'd have invested in a young, growing industry in a young country just commencing its period of fastest growth. Growth means phenomenal gains in stock prices. America's greatest period of growth covered the 80 years from around 1890 up to now.

Wouldn't it be convenient if you could turn the clock back to 1890 and invest your money in stocks which are worth a hundred times as much today? It's too late to do that in the United States. But Mexico, as we said in Chapter I, lags behind the United States by some 75 years. Industrial development in Mexico is just about where we were 75 years ago. Invest in Mexican stocks today and the chances for seeing your money grow are equal to, or better than, the chance you missed in the United States at the turn of the century.

Actually, your chances in Mexico *are* better. Mexico will make up that 75 year lag in far less than 75 years. The inventions, the developments which made America big are here already. Chances are good that Mexico will duplicate our 75 years of progress in a bare 25 years. This means your stocks *could* grow in value three times as fast as did ours. With population increasing 3½% annually and consumer buying increasing by over 6% per year, Mexico's future growth appears unlimited.

If in 1946 you had invested about $9,000 in two or three leading Mexican stocks, by

1966 you'd have received some $33,000 in dividends plus a capital gain of about $33,000. Fiscal privileges designed to permit capital for plowing back, allow Mexican stocks to yield far higher dividends than ours. All dividends are paid "net," with income tax already paid. And Mexico has no capital gains tax. Nor is the Mexican stock market affected by foreign recessions.

Mexico's stock market is about where ours was a century ago—in the pioneer stage. Although 350 different issues are listed on the Mexico City Exchange, most are jealously held in tight family circles and only some 25 issues enjoy an active market. The reason? Most Mexican stocks are such good buys, they never reach the open market. Instead, they are sold privately or over the counter. Despite a 500% increase in trading in a recent year, supplies still are thin, the spread between bid and asked prices considerable. For this reason, Mexican stocks are unsuited for short term trading. But for the longer pull, for retirement planning, they're ideal.

For the investor with foresight, new frontiers abound in the infant Mexican economy. Unlike the United States, where growth prospects are offered only by the space age industries, in Mexico almost every industry offers a phenomenal growth outlook. But selction is still important. *What* you buy is far more important than *when* you buy. As elsewhere, you *must* buy good stocks.

There are 3 exchanges: in Mexico City, Monterrey and Guadalajara. The two latter have teletype communication with the main Bolsa de Volores de Mexico in Mexico City, where two leading U. S. firms—Bache & Co., and Merrill Lynch—maintain correspondents on the floor. Both Mexican and American stock prices are quoted on the boards and you can buy and sell American stocks as readily as you can in the United States. Commissions are lower than those we're accustomed to paying and there are no transfer taxes or other charges. Due to the scarcity of Mexican stocks and the wide price spread, we recommend your buying or selling through limit orders, good till cancelled and with the price always named.

As this was written the average blue chip Mexican stock was paying 7% with the most optimistic growth stocks yielding around 4% and those with more emphasis on income up to 10% and more. In lieu of dividends, new companies are permitted to pay 9% in-terest during their first 3 years of operation. Often, however, they are able to pay a dividend in addition.

Which issues should you buy? That depends, of course, on your investment aim and unless you've read *Harian's Investing for a Sound 6%—and More,* mentioned previously, you won't have a clue. Nor, once having decided on the type of stock you require, will you find the wealth of market data which exists in the States. One guide is *Prontuario de Analisis de Empresas y Valores,* available in all Banco de Mexico offices, which reports on all leading companies in English. The best guide we have seen to the Mexican market, however, and one we can personnally recommend, is the *Investor's Mexican Letter,* published by Mr. Carl Ross, an authority on all types of Mexican investments. The monthly newsletter plus special reports costs $10 for two months or $58 per year (slightly less in Mexico) and can be obtained from Industrias e Inversiones Alba S. A. de C. V., Reforma 336, Mexico City 6, D. F., or from Suite 1005, 79 Wall St., New York 5. Daily stock market prices are quoted in English in the Mexico City *News* or may be had free from the Bolsa de Valores de Mexico, Uruguay 68, Mexico 1, D.F. Other market letters include *Mexletter,* $30 a year from Mexican Business and Investment Service, Hamburgo 165, Mexico City; and *Inside Mexico,* $45 a year from Aptdo 5-433, Mexico 5, D.F. A good free letter can be had from Allen Lloyd, Aptdo 1470, Guadalajara, who specializes in serving Americans.

For a start, we recommend that you buy only issues listed on the Mexico City Exchange and that you buy only through exchanges, banks, stockbrokers, or investment counselors. Secondly, you would naturally want to invest in the growingest industries and these, we are informed are: automotive parts, chemicals and fertilizers, construction and building materials, electrical and electronics products, paper, plastics, shoes, beer, cigarettes and steel. Among stocks most widely traded in these and other industries, the following are highly regarded: Altos Hornos (steel); Banco Nacional; Celanese (plastics, chemicals); Fabric Auto-Mex (cars); A.P. Green (refractories); I.E.M. (electrical equipment); La Moderna (cigarettes); Fundidora de Monterrey (steel); Moctezuma (brewery); San Rafael Paper; TAMSA (steel); Telefonos (telephone utility); Union Carbide (plastics, electrodes). If you seek preferreds, Mexico has these too.

MUTUAL FUNDS, organized under the Mexican Law of Investment Companies passed in 1955, are newcomers to the country's investment scene. To qualify under the law, a fund must have a minimum paid up capital of 50 million pesos, not more than 25% of its funds may be placed in any one company (30% in government bank stocks) and no fund may hold more than 30% of the stock of any one enterprise. At least 80% of their capital must be in cash or securities and 10% of dividends must be retained in a reserve fund. Although lacking the diversity of American funds—Mexico simply does not have the choice of stocks—the funds are well regulated by the commission whose laws seem to very adequately protect the investor. Loading charges are limited to a maximum of 5%, management fees to ½%-1% annually of the fund's value and you are given discounts on periodic payments and reinvested dividends.

The big advantage of the mutual funds is that they are able to buy large blocks of stocks not available to individual investors. To date, there are four Mexican funds, each associated with one of the country's large financial groups and each heavily invested in industries associated with that group. Thus through voting along with the managements, they are encouraged to buy more stocks of these companies. All funds welcome American investors.

Here are brief details on the four funds. Write for their prospectus and literature (addresses subject to change:

FIRME, V. Carranza 54, Mexico City 1, D. F. This largest and oldest of the funds is a balanced type fund invested in some 24 industries. Steady growth in size and in net asset value has marked its performance, and management is considered capable. Dividend is about 8½% of market value and sales load 3%.

Sogerin, Isabel La Catolica 44, Mexico City 1, D. F. A fund promoted by the Banco Nacional with securities purchased free of commissions by their Credito Bursatil brokerage affiliate. Recent yield has been 9.3% of market value; sales load is only 1%.

Other Sources on Mexican Investments

Recommended for study are: *A Statement of the Laws of Mexico Affecting Business* (including supplements), by Julian Bernal Molina (Pan American Union, Washington, D. C.); *Handbook for the Foreign Investor* (available from John M. Ryan, Aptdo 2179, Mexico City 1, D. F.); *Investing in Mexico* at $1.25 and *Establishing a Business in Mexico* at 10¢ (available from Superintendent of Documents, U. S. Government Printing Office, Washington 25, D. C.). The U. S. Department of Commerce, Bureau of Foreign Commerce, Washington, D. C., also has publications on investing in Mexico.

Other sources include *Mexican Market* (stock report) from Intercontinental, S.A., Paris 15, Mexico City; *Monthly Stock Market Report,* from Promociones y Corretajes S.A., Uruguay 68, Mexico 1, D.F.; *Securities Information* from Credito Bursatil S.A., Isabel La Catolica 39, Mexico City; the *Mexican American Review* (business magazine) $6 annually from the American Chamber of Commerce of Mexico, Lucerna 78, Mexico City; the English language *Comercio Exterior* (Economic Review) available free each month from Banco Nacional de Comercial Exterior S.A., Venustiano Carranza 32, Mexico 1, D.F.; *Estudios Especiales* giving the price, yield etc., of all securities listed on the Mexican stock exchange, free from Bolsa de Valores de Mexico S.A., Uruguay 68, Mexico 1, D.F.; and *El Mercado de Valores,* free each week from Nacional Financiera, V. Carranza 25, Mexico 1, D.F., (tip: Nacional Financiera also issues other excellent free publications in English). City banks also have helpful public relations departments and American consulates in Mexico can recommend banks, lawyers and accountants if required. You may also be interested in seeing the *Boletin Financiero y Minero,* Mexico's Spanish language financial daily, published at V. Carranza 69, Mexico 1, D.F.

FIMSA (Fondo Industrial Mexicana, S. A.), Juarez 100, Mexico 1, D. F. A new growth type fund under capable management by Casusas Trigueros y Cia., FIMSA has demonstrated rapid growth in both size and net asset value. Despite a 5% buying charge, yield is 9% of par price, the portfolio is excellent, and the fund is aiding smaller growth industries.

Inversora Mexicana S.A., Carlos Trouyet, Juarez 14, Mexico City. A smaller aggressive fund with a recent yield of 4% and a sales charge of 3%.

DIVERSIFICATION IN MEXICO is equally as important as in the States. The actual ratio between fixed income investments and common stocks or mutual funds will, of course, depend upon your investment aim and philosophy. Here, however, is how one man divided his $25,000 capital to yield approximately $211 per month, a return of 10.2%. He could naturally have obtained a higher yield. But he preferred to keep two thirds of his capital in common stocks as a stake in Mexico's growth.

Defensive Investments $10,000

Bank time contract, $2,500	Return $	225
Mortgage, $5,000	"	700
Industrial loan, $2,500	"	250

Aggressive Investments $15,000

Stock A, $5,000	"	425
Stock B, $5,000	"	475
Mutual Fund, $5,000	"	450

Total Annual Return	$2,525

You can make any of the preceding investments in this chapter without having to comply with any immigration requirements whatsoever. In fact, you can invest in Mexico without ever having visited Mexico at all. You can also, of course, invest in Mexico and live off the dividends when retired in the United States.

TO START A BUSINESS in Mexico you must enter Mexico as an *investor inmigrante* or else have achieved *inmigrado* status (see Chapter III). Once your immigration problem has been disposed of, the rest is not half so difficult as many people imagine. For example, there is no foundation for the popular misconception that all business must be owned 51% by Mexicans. This requirement applies only to vital industries such as transportation and to the liquor industry, publishing, advertising, fishing, motion pictures and radio broadcasting.

Mexico abounds with opportunities for new small business. A few years ago, two foreign engineers started a part-time business with a capital of 20,000 pesos. Today, they own a plant worth $300,000. Mexico is crying out for American know how and

opportunities to provide needed services exist by the thousands.

But don't rush in blind. Investigate carefully. One American firm spent vast sums to introduce root beer to Mexico only to discover too late that Mexicans disliked the taste. Once you discover a hot opening, however, go immediately to a competent lawyer and have him handle *all* the details. If you're buying a going concern, hire an accountant in addition. Although as we have said, outside certain basic industries a business can be entirely foreign owned, the majority of new businesses being formed today are joint enterprises with Mexicans. To incorporate your business will cost about $400 and with a minimum capital of 25,000 pesos and five shareholders you can either set it up as a simple *Sociedad Anonima* (S.A.) or, more advantageously, as a *Sociedad Anonima de Capital Variable* (S.A. de C.V.) which, above a certain minimum, permits you to change the capitalization by simply holding a stockholders meeting. (By becoming a silent, shareholding partner in such enterprises, you *can* share in business ownership in Mexico without having to comply with immigration requirements. But don't take our word. Check with a lawyer. And make sure you have full legal title to your share in the business before you invest a penny. Don't invest on trust. For dishonest Mexican businessmen have taken in non-*inmigrado* Americans as partners and simply taken their money and given nothing in return.)

Costs in Mexico being what they are, you can generally start a business in Mexico for considerably less than in the States. And with labor and taxes taking a very moderate bite, profits frequently run high.

What businesses are needed most? Among smaller enterprises within reach of individuals, the following products and services are badly needed in almost all larger, more modern towns: first class beef production, cheese, credit cards, drive-ins, electronic controls for industry, equipment rental (including industrial), frozen foods, greeting cards, hamburger stands, small inexpensive hotels and guest houses at new resorts, ice cream, high grade leather, lumber (everything from toothpicks to railroad ties), pasteurized milk, motels on new highways, pest control services, pleasure boats, first class poultry and eggs, waste products processing, professional fund raising services, quality control, quality vegetables, real estate agencies, refrigerated truck and warehouses services, modern stores of all types, subdivision development, supermarkets, dairies, personal loan agencies and trailer parks.

TAXES IN MEXICO. Most U. S. Citizens living abroad must pay income tax to Uncle Sam. However, there are some important exceptions and since these are too technical to discuss here, we suggest your writing to the Director of International Operations, Internal Revenue Service, Washington, D. C., for a free copy of their *Tax Guide for U. S. Citizens Abroad*.

Taxes in Mexico are much less burdensome than in the U. S. Compared to the U. S. Government which collects one fourth of the national income in taxes, the Mexican government collects only slightly over 10%. Thus while Mexico is not entirely tax free, it certainly is a haven for tax weary Americans. Thus far, all Mexican investments are exempt from the United States Interest Equalization Tax and are expected to remain so.

Inmigrantes and *inmigrados,* who are classed as residents of Mexico, pay Mexican income tax only on investment income from Mexican sources. Because in Mexico your income from different types of sources is reported and taxed separately under three different schedules, you are far less likely to be thrown into a high tax bracket than in the U. S. For a complete explanation of these taxes and the payment schedules, send 10¢ to the Superintendent of Documents, Washington 25, D. C., for the U. S. Department of Commerce bulletin *Establishing a Business in Mexico*. Though no agreement exists between Mexico and the U. S. to prevent double taxation, both countries in practice give credit for taxes paid on sources of income abroad. Hence as a resident of Mexico, the worst you can expect is to pay your present scale of income tax, the best you can expect is to pay very much less. If you are living in Mexico, your U. S. income tax statement need not be filed until June 15. All U. S. Consulates in Mexico keep forms and most are visited annually by a representative of the Internal Revenue Department to assist Americans in fiiling their returns.

As a tourist card holder, or non-resident of Mexico, you must pay U. S. income tax on all income derived from the United States. Don't forget, however, that no income tax is charged on U. S. social security pensions and that in many cases, couples 65 or over may receive as much as $5,333 in tax exempt retirement income. Too, on pensions received from your former employer's non-refunded current operating fund, you may enjoy full or partial exemption from U. S. taxes. Since as a tourist card holder you may not actively invest in Mexican business or real estate, the only type of income which may be taxed in Mexico is that derived from Mexican stocks, bonds, mortgages and other securities. Here, the good news is that: 1) such income is taxed only once, not at both the corporate and individual levels as in the U. S.; 2) almost all companies paying interest or dividends do so on a tax free basis; *such income is therefore free of further taxes;* and 3) income on mortgage bank and National Savings Bonds is also exempt. In other words, you may, by shifting your investments to Mexico and by living in Mexico, enjoy complete exemption from income tax.

Should you invest in non-tax-exempt Mexican investments, you would pay approximately 10% on fixed income securities and 15% on common stocks. Although capital gains is treated as income, capital gains on securities transactions are tax free for the very simple reason that such transactions are never reported. However, income from real estate rentals, exempt from taxes until 1962, is now subject to taxation and in larger towns, all houses for rent must be registered (tip: when renting, make sure your home is registered or you could be fined). The only capital gains tax on real estate to date is limited to a 5%-20% bite on land and buildings in urban areas.

As for Mexican inheritance taxes, there are none. In 1962, Mexico eliminated all her very moderate inheritance and estate taxes. No death duties are now in force.

Property taxes in Mexico, frequently based on outdated assessments, are astonishingly low. The highest on record runs about 1% of assessed valuation; the average home is taxed from $5-$35 a year.

Chapter V

Mexican Real Estate – For Gracious Living or Investment Profits

IN 1934, A MEXICAN and an American teamed up and bought most of the beach front property at a village called Acapulco. Today, this land for which they paid 2.50 pesos per square meter is a bargain at a hundred times the price. Their original investment of $35,000 has grown into several hundred millions. The same story is being repeated all over Mexico. During these same years, land prices in Mexico City increased by 20 times. In every city, exploding population growth is overflowing city limits and forcing up fringe land values. Downtown property in Guadalajara which sold at 500 pesos a square meter in 1955 was worth 7,500 pesos by 1965. Satellite towns are springing up outside the largest cities. In one, a few miles from Mexico City and aptly called Satellite City, lot prices rose from 80 pesos a square meter in 1957 to 800 pesos in 1965. As Mexico's population mushrooms while land supplies remain stable, a steady price rise seems inevitable. Says Mr. Henry E. Albachten, the well known Chapala developer, "I am personally convinced that real estate investments in Mexico have only one way to go and that is up."

Fortunes have been and are being made in Mexican real estate. The length of the Pacific Coast, investors are buying up beach property that sold in 1950 for a few cents an acre yet by 1965 was worth a fairly standard $25. Moreover, since the average Mexican has yet to learn of such real estate gimmicks as syndicates, cooperatives, leverage and lease-backs, being an *informed* investor is almost akin to being the only man with sight in a land of the blind.

Yet it's essential to know what you're doing. The average American knows literally nothing about investing in real estate. For example, can you tell the exact value of any lot? Can you tell what any given acreage is worth? When is the best time to buy a lot and the best time to sell? How can you tell if land is overpriced? How can you spot which land will grow in value five times as fast as other land nearby?

If you can't answer these simple questions, you should certainly not consider investing in real estate, either in Mexico or the United States. Just as with stocks, before you can invest successfully, you simply *must* know the principles for successful real estate investment. Fortunately, this knowledge is readily available in a book entitled *How to Retire on Real Estate Profits*, a complete guide to making money in every type of real estate as well as to getting a good buy in your own home and lot. This book, a standard work in its field, can be obtained for $2 postpaid from Harian Publications, Greenlawn, New York.

Having studied this book and grasped the principles of success in real estate, you are ready to apply them to the Mexican scene. You will find very few differences. Like the United States, Mexico's growth follows the patterns of the automobile age. Land along newly planned highways, for example, invariably rises in value by 300% before construction is completed. Almost all income property is identical in character to that in the United States.

On the assumption that you already have read, or plan to read *How to Retire on Real Estate Profits*, we shall not repeat the tremendous amount of information given in this book. We shall not warn of the pitfalls common to real estate everywhere.

We shall assume that you know *what* to buy and *when* to buy and sell. We shall also assume that you are sufficiently sophisticated not to buy or rent any kind of property sight unseen and that you realize the value of expert local guidance. For general advice on any aspect of real estate investment in Mexico, we have received high praise about Worth Realty of Insurgentes Sur 132-410 in Mexico City, which firm is headed by a very knowledgeable Mexican and concentrates exclusively on sale and rental of residential and industrial properties.

HOW CAN YOU acquire property in Mexico? As we've already discussed in Chapter III, there are two ways: a) as a non-immigrant (tourist card holder, *Visitante-Rentista* or student) you are not permitted to own property in your own name and must arrange for it to be held by a Mexican through a private contract, trust or renewable lease; and b) as an *inmigrante* or *inmigrado*. However, under Article 27, Section F of the Constitution, neither *inmigrantes* nor *inmigrados* may purchase land within 33 miles of the ocean or 66 miles of land frontiers. In purchasing such lands through an agent, they are in the same position as the tourist card holder. So let's review the various methods.

As a tourist, your first step in acquiring property is to consult a reliable lawyer recommended by the nearest American consulate. Your lawyer will then propose one of the four following alternatives and if agreeable, will conclude all arrangements:

1. *By private contract* with a lawyer or individual who agrees, for a small annual fee, to hold the property in his name and to sell or lease it as you desire. As the entire success of this plan depends on your confidence in the individual concerned, it is restricted to persons in whom you can have trust. Under no circumstances ever buy a home in the name of your maid and wherever possible, select a male, as a woman may marry and her property become subject to the whims of her husband.

This arrangement can be made fairly watertight in two ways. First, by demanding an irrevocable power of attorney which permits only you to sell, lease or change the title. Secondly, by taking back a mortgage in excess if the property's value. Naturally, the mortgage exists only on paper. (Example: you buy a $7,500 home and take back a mortgage of $10,000 with the lien written into the title. Your property could then be neither sold nor used as collateral for a loan.)

2. *By a trust* arranged through a government certified bank. Upon your instructions, the bank will then lease or sell your property and recover the proceeds. The trust may be terminated only by the purchaser. If later, you acquire *inmigrante* status, you may have the property transferred to your name and the trust ended. Of course, you must still trust the bank but in our opinion this is the safest way to own property through an agent. Not all banks arrange trusts but one can usually be found.

3. *By a quit claim* issued to you by the developing company who builds your home and holds title to it. You can sell the quit claim and thereby transfer ownership of your property. But the company or other title holder cannot sell your property.

4. *By a renewable lease,* a method fast becoming popular in housing developments catering to Americans. Under this arrangement, the developer holds title to the property and issues to you a ten year lease with irrevocable right of renewal every ten years. You can sell the lease at any time. Or if you later acquire *inmigrante* status, terminate the lease and have title transferred to your own name. Under an old law permitting foreigners to deal in real estate outside frontier and coastal zones, foreign owned real estate firms may also set up such leasing arrangements licensed for 50 years. It's smart to sign only a lease that provides for a bank to see that the terms of the lease are carried out in case the landowner dies; and that also allows you to sell the lease to a third party.

As an *inmigrante* or *inmigrado,* you must obtain permission from the Ministry of Foreign Relations before you can own land, a technicality done automatically by lawyers processing *inmigrante* applications. To secure this permission you agree to waive right of appeal to your own embassy and to stand as a Mexican before the law. All this has been discussed in Chapter III, which you may want to read again after having read this chapter.

Mexican Real Estate Terms

alberca	pool
alcalde	mayor
apartamiento	apartment
arquitecto	architect
arrendar	to lease
arriendo	lease
ayuntamiento	city hall
bienes raices	real estate
calefacción central	central heat
campo	field
capataz	foreman
charca	pond
ciudad	city
contratista	contractor
contrato	contract
copia	carbon copy
cuadra	city block
drenaje	drainage
edificio	a building
extensión	tract of land
fracción	a plot
fraccionaria	subdivision sales office
fraccionamiento	subdivision
fuente	fountain
gobierno	government
honorarios	fee
jefe	chief
ley	law
limite	boundary
lote	a lot
marmol	marble
moderno	modern
patrón	employer
piso	story of building
plano	plan, map
propietario, casero	landlord
pueblo	town, village
rentar	to rent
se renta	for rent
se rentan apartmientos	furnished apartments
amueblados	for rent
suburbio	suburb
terreno	a lot parcel
se vende	for sale
vista	view

How can an American (or Canadian) citizen acquire frontier and coastal lands? Regardless of your immigration status, you may acquire such property by any of the four methods just quoted. However, because the law limits foreigners to ten year leases on these lands, a more popular way is to take out a lease for 9 years 11 months, covered by a note from the owner for the value of improvements you intend to put up (this is purely a precaution, you need never actually build). The existence of the note, though, prevents the owner from releasing or selling. Written into the lease also is an irrevocable renewal agreement by which your wife or other relative takes over as lessee after your 9 years 11 months are up. For a third terms, you can take back the lease yourself and so on *ad infinitum*. For bigger deals, however, you'll find it worthwhile to organize a Mexican corporation (see end of Chapter IV) which, in turn, administers a 100% Mexican company which buys and holds the property. Although this involves some expense and organization, actually it is an almost watertight way in which to hold *any* kind of property.

Expropriation risks? As a foreigner you run no more risk from expropriation than a Mexican. For both stand equally before the law. Under the Agrarian or Land Law you may hold the following maximum areas of land without fear of expropriation: 100 hectares of irrigated land; 200 hectares of dry land; 150 hectares of cotton land; 300 hectares of plantation land; and corresponding areas of land for other uses. For example, you are permitted sufficient grazing land to maintain 500 head of cattle. Over and above these maximums, the surplus *could* be expropriated. But you can still obtain a specific exemption against expropriation from the Agrarian Department. The only expropriation against Americans in recent years concerned the seizure of an enormous ranch in Sonora for which a fair price was paid in full.

As in the United States, land is rising steadily in value and offers an excellent hedge against inflation. Already, fringe land values have soared around such fast growing centers as Mexico City, Guadalajara, Puebla, Monterrey and Cuernavaca, but there are bargains aplenty elswhere. Due for tremendous future growth, for example, is the Chapala-Ajijic resort area bordering Lake Chapala. Already some 400 new homes are going up annually. But recently, fringe land between these resort villages was being traded at 12 pesos per square meter. Land surrounding Guadalajara selling at $1-5,000 per acre had already been milked by speculators. But farther out there were any number of good speculations for the longer pull at $100-$200 an acre. In fact, everywhere in Mexico, farmlands below the expropriation limit are an excellent investment. Prime irrigated or grazing land not too far from cities can still be found at $3-$3.50 per hectare and eventually some will sell for factory use or subdividing. Meanwhile it can return a good income through being leased to farmers.

By now, you're probably wondering just what is a hectare and why land is sold by the square meter. These two measurements are the principal standards by which land is sold in Mexico. The following table illustrates their conversion equivalents:

.305 meters	= 1 foot
.914 meters	= 1 yard
1 meter	= 1.094 yards, 3.3 feet or 39.37 inches
1 square meter	= 10.76 square feet or 1.196 square yards
.836 square meter	= 1 square yard
10,000 square meters	= 1 hectare
.405 hectare	= 1 acre
1 hectare	= 2.471 acres
259 hectares	= 1 square mile
100 hectares	= 1 square kilometer
1 square kilometer	= .386 square miles or 247.1 acres
1 kilometer	= .62 miles
1.609 kilometers	= 1 mile

For long term land speculation, the best opportunities probably exist on the Pacific Coast. Along the entire length of this coast north of Acapulco, new paved highways are snaking down through jungles to remote fishing villages with unsurpassable beaches. Soon afterwards, the inevitable smart resort hotel appears. For the tremendous population of the American Southwest, this subtropical coast is the nearest thing to Florida (and far superior). Already, travel magazines are calling it the Americas' Riviera. Stupendous growth seems unavoidable. Small resorts like Puerto Vallarta and Barra de Navidad are turning into smaller Acapulcos and Americans are building homes the length of the coast. All such coastal lands must be held by an agent and thousands of parcels already are. Be sure, however, that you hold clear title. Often enough, in these undeveloped areas, titles must be traced back several generations before they can be cleared. Some Americans, having failed to take this precaution, have found their titles questioned. Watch, too, for big differences in micro-

climates. One side of a cove may be 15° hotter than the opposite side and, perhaps, subject to invasions of *jejenes* (gnats).

Another ripe area being largely overlooked is, in our opinion, the coast of Tamaulipas and northern Vera Cruz. Costs here still are low yet inevitably this seems destined to become the winter playground for millions from our south central states. A third good area is the Caribbean coast of Quintana Roo, slated to be opened up in a few years by new paved roads. (Incidentally, just across the Mexican border in neighboring British Honduras are scores of good buys in ranches, citrus groves, retirement estates and islands, all available free of Mexico's land owning restrictions. For details, airmail Tropical Real Estate, Box 107, Belize, British Honduras.)

Elsewhere, land near growing cities—and all Mexican cities are growing fast—is rising rapidly in value. From the old colonial city center located in the plaza, all Mexican cities tend to grow outwards, obeying exactly the same growth patterns described for American cities in *How to Retire on Real Estate Profits*. Without having read this book, you'll simply be investing blind. But with its aid you can readily spot the main path of growth and you can buy land squarely across it. For instance, Mexico City is growing south out along Avenida Insurgentes and is spilling out in a southerly direction beyond the swank Pedregal suburb. Exactly as forecast in *How to Retire on Real Estate Profits,* the business district is also growing south along Avenida Insurgentes. This same pattern is being repeated in *every* Mexican city today and land directly in the path of growth is doubling in value each year.

As you'll have learned from reading Chapter I, most Mexican cities were founded several centuries ago. Center of the city is the main plaza, bordered as a rule by the *palacio municipal,* post and telegraph offices and the cathedral. From the plaza, narrow streets run rectangularly in all directions, dividing the city into blocks as in the United States. Close to the plaza are fine old colonial homes with immensely thick walls which ensure summer coolness. These homes are entered from the street by heavy double doors leading into a *zaguan* or passageway which in turn leads to a floral central patio into which all rooms open. All floors are beautifully tiled and frequently, the rooms have atmospheric, rough-hewn-beam ceilings, baroque fireplaces and such added features as *al fresco* dining porches and bars.

These old colonial homes can often be bought or rented and with a little refurbishing, make attractive modern residences brimming with atmosphere and character. In some cities, their magnificence rivals that of palaces. Some years ago, an American discovered a host of run down colonial houses in Alamos, Son. Some, indeed, were little better than rubble piles. Seeing the possibilities, the American, through an agent, took leases on the more promising houses and with crews of low paid peons, set about rebuilding them. Today, some of his acquisitions, reportedly picked up for as little as $400, have resold for a much as $30,000. Over 90 Americans have purchased refurbished palaces, bringing a fortune to the developer.

Could you do the same? We'd definitely say yes. Almost any attractive colonial village with a benign climate, easy access and a respectable hotel could be turned into a new American retirement colony. You could start by taking options on properties and by leasing homes which could be temporarily rented to their present occupants. Then with an inexpensive publicity campaign like that developed by Mr. Robert Thayer at Ajijic, you can attract dozens, perhaps hundreds, of Americans. This is exactly how the big retirement colonies grew on Lake Chapala and Americans who held leases and property there made tens of thousands out of newcomers.

To be a dealer in Mexican real estate or to invest in income producing property you should, strictly speaking, have attained *inimgrado* status. But hundreds of Americans are handling such investments through a trust or agent. For example, you can build and rent single family dwellings, a proposition which yields an average of only 7% net in American cities but which in Mexican retirement centers, brings in 10% or more. Office and apartment buildings, when built by the owner, yield a fairly stable 12% net. Warehouses do even better and all are in demand. A word of caution: as we mentioned in Chapter I, Mexican owners are prone to let their buildings run down. So be doubly sure, when purchasing an older building, that it is in good repair. For this reason, you are generally better off constructing a new building yourself.

NOT LONG AGO, two retired couples each began building a two bedroom home beside Lake Chapala. Upon completion, one couple found theirs had cost $4,500 while the other, almost identical in size and equipment, cost $7,500.

Why the difference? The couple who built the $4,500 home used a modern, functional Mexican design, planned for living beneath a brilliant sun. Designed to combine outdoor beauty with indoor comfort, half their rooms had open walls making them literally an extension of the garden patio. Floor-to-ceiling picture windows and huge brick fireplaces lent their home a lavish look. Rooms were lofty and spacious with tiled floors and open ceilings exposing rough hewn wooden beams they'd had their contractor pick up from a wrecker. Magnificently executed stone and plaster work, done by skilled artisans, gave character to their home. Throughout, they had made extensive use of concrete, Mexico's principal construction material.

By comparison, the $7,500 home resembled a box. Designed to the contemporary style popular in the northern United States by the couple themselves, it seemed curiously out of place in a land where you can live outdoors ten months of the year. Rooms were small and tasteless, the whole thing poorly executed by Mexican builders unused to the design and materials. Later, realizing their mistake, the couple sold it and hired a Mexican contractor to design and build them a more suitable home at a saving of $2,000.

This same error is committed almost daily by newly arrived Americans. Told they can build an attractive two bedroom home for $4,500, they immediately proceed to design one like the bungalow they recently vacated at Cape Cod. Then they wonder why it costs twice as much.

By using a contemporary modern Mexican design and placing the task in the hands of an experienced Mexican builder, you very definitely could, as this was written, build an attractive Mexican home for roughly half the price it would cost in the United States. Naturally, homes, like cars, come in different grades. You can spend up to $18,000 for a home that would cost $36,000 in Florida and in swank suburbs like Mexico City's Lomas or Colonia Polanco, land costs are so high that the cheapest homes start at $30,000.

By and large, however, you'll find the following construction costs a good average:

for deluxe construction $6 per square foot or $60-$66 per square meter; for first class construction $5 or $50-$55; and for ordinary construction $4 or $40-45 respectively. In Mexico City, Cuernavaca and Acapulco among other places, costs may run 10%-15% more; in small towns and in southern Mexico, they could run 10%-15% less. These costs are for modern construction equivalent to the latest methods in use in the United States and include all wiring, plumbing and fixtures. Assuming that the average two bedroom home covers 100 square meters, such a house of first class construction would run about $5,000. First class construction of this type nearly approaches deluxe construction in the States. Thus in most places you can build a modern two bedroom home with large living room, patio, up-to-date kitchen, two baths, fireplaces, tiled floors throughout and a garage for around $5,000. Using ordinary construction, the same thing could be duplicated for as little as $4,000.

Land costs are extra. Typically, you can pay from 300 pesos per square meter in the swankiest new subdivisions at fashionable resorts and in big cities to an average of 80 pesos up in the best residential section of the average city. Elsewhere, as on Lake Chapala, your lot will cost 25-50 pesos per square meter with all utilities at the line. By and large, you can figure from $750-$3,000 for the average retirement lot. And in country districts where you can build among captivating mountain and valley scenery, from 10-15 pesos without utilities.

Representative of the packaged modern homes available complete with lot and all utilities are those in one of several well laid out subdivisions near Chapala. Figure 3 illustrates a typical rambling studio home built of stone, brick and steel at a cost of just over $4 per square foot. Actual prices complete with landscaped lot for a three bedroom home averaged $7,750 while attractive two bedroom homes with two full baths and fireplaces were being built for under $6,500. Lots of 6,500 square feet were priced from $1,800 and the entire subdivision was tastefully laid out on paved, well lighted streets so that each house enjoyed a lake view. Pure, pressurized water was piped to each house and nearby was a modern resort motel and 9-hole golf course. Similar subdivisions are appearing in many popular residential towns such as Ajijic, Chapala, Cuernavaca, Guadalajara, Ixtapan, San Miguel de Allende, Tequisquiapan and Valle de Bravo.

The Chapala homes, while emphasizing many of the better features of Mexican design, were planned and built by an American to cater to American tastes. By going completely Mexican you can do even better. With the aid of the concrete shell technique so cheap and popular in Mexico, you can have a bold, dramatically contemporary design featuring mathematical curves and ultra modern contours that would cost a fortune to duplicate at home. A good Mexican architect will produce a home which is a counterplay of contrasts, an amalgam of modern profiles, the brightly glazed tiles and textured wood panelling of Old World colonial, and the naturalness associated with the weathered look of rough hewn beams, worn terra cotta and Indian stonework motifs. Few Americans possess the imagination which allows the free and brilliant interplay of colors and contrasts characteristic of homes designed by Mexicans. Entire walls of glass are commonplace, as are French doors opening onto balconies with sweeping desert views. For a few hundred dollars over and above normal first class construction costs, you can have a home like those which grace the covers of home and garden magazines.

And why not, when in such places as Lake Chapala, skilled workmen like bricklayers and carpenters make $2.25 a day, plumbers and electricians $2.75 and laborers $1.50? All homes are of masonry, either of red bricks costing $8 per 1,000 or of larger adobe bricks which cost $18 per 1,000. The elegant red roofing tiles cost $14 per 1,000, water pipes cost half as much as in the States, lumber and wiring a bare three-fourths of prices we're used to. Magnificent ceramic floor and wall tiles cost just 4¢-12¢ per square foot. All floors and baths are tiled. In living rooms, bedrooms and patios, brick fireplaces are taken for granted. There are no basements or central heating plants to run up costs. Baths are generally showers but tub baths are available. Most larger homes include one or two maids' rooms with separate shower and toilet and out back, concrete laundry equipment which serves in lieu of washing machines. For any home located above 4,000' we recommend your specifying a fireplace in every room (a portable electric heater will suffice in the bathroom). In rural construction, in place of ceilings, rush or bamboo mats are placed directly under roof tiles. A small amount of dust trickles through each day but this is no problem, since it is cleaned up daily by your maid. Do be sure your home is designed with ample closet and kitchen cupboard space, a failing in many otherwise well designed Mexican homes. Be sure to choose a site free from noise: avoid building on or near plazas, churches, movie theaters, busy roads or dusty highways.

Most cities have satisfactory water supplies and sewage. Municipal water comes mainly from wells and in this dry, sunny country supplies are occasionally rationed (accounting for the numerous empty swimming pools you see in spring). Since few cities have adequate water pressure, all homes come equipped with an electric pump and roof tank. In villages, water is drawn from wells, either by electric pumps or by hand labor and likewise stored in your roof tank to supply pressure. Do make sure water supplies are adequate before you build. Otherwise, you must pay $1.50 per 1,000 gallons to have it hauled. Most modern homes have electric water heaters but in older places, water is heated by a geyser into which you insert a package of wood chips (called *fuego rapido*) and you light it whenever you require a bath. All this is, of course, done in practice by your maid and costs per bath work out to 4¢.

Because the best and cheapest building method is to use reinforced concrete construction, building in Mexico takes longer than at home. If, however, you re-evaluate your sense of time, building a home in Mexico can be an amusing and fun-filled experience. All to often, Mexican builders interpret the plans to suit themselves. For example, we've seen fireplaces built on the outside of rooms, toilets that flushed with hot water, living room switches which turned on bedroom lights and even rooms built without doors. With a little watchful patience, though, you can spot these errors in time and if your attitude is *simpatico,* you'll end up with a lavish, spacious home at comparatively little cost. By comparison, the impatient American who insists on using fast steel construction to carry out an American style job will end up paying twice as much for a disappointing home.

BUYING AN OLDER HOME already built is often cheaper than building a new one.

You'll find homes for sale advertised in all newspapers, both in English and Spanish (frequently Spanish language papers list the better buys). And for a few thousand dollars you can purchase a modernized older style colonial home in which the patio serves as an outdoor living room and the whole arrangement gives you a delightful sense of privacy. Beamed ceilings and balconies are standard in these charming old homes which often possess indoor living rooms up to 60' long and fountains, pools and garden patios all for the proverbial song.

Real estate brokers operate in all larger towns. As at home, however, few possess complete listings and their commissions add to purchase price. Before buying, we strongly recommend your surveying every neighborhood. Prices vary widely in different neighborhoods and you may find exactly what you desire in a less costly area. At all events, be on guard against buying from those Americans who have built homes at low cost and who are constantly trying to unload them on to newcomers at a substantial mark up.

A sound and common practice is to buy (or lease) an old house for $750-$1,250 (or $10-$15 a month on a long term lease) and to modernize it with up-to-date bath and kitchen and new tile and paint for a further $700-$1,200. As the least expensive method of obtaining a home in Mexico, this plan has much to recommend it. You can easily build corner fireplaces into rooms which lack them and though water pipes and electric wiring must run on the surface, they detract little from the flavor of these older homes. Furnished in free flowing contemporary Mexican style, they can rapidly be transformed into attractive homes. In some places, you will even find old haciendas you can buy or lease and convert.

One important caution: Americans who lease such homes then later decide to leave, frequently offer the lease for sale. (Example: an unfurnished house leased for ten years at $15 a month costs $1,000 to renovate. After two years, the lessees decide to leave and offer the lease for sale at $2,400. Over the remaining 96 months life of the lease, this works out to $25 monthly for the lease and $15 for rent—a total of $40 a month. While this may still sound an attractive rent, one should bear in mind that the total outlay to the seller was $1,000 in return for which he receives $1,600 profit plus, proprotionately, $800 of his original outlay.

While such a practice can be recommended as a profitable hobby for amateur real estate dealers in Mexico, as a tenant you should take a long, hard look at the figures and have the lease inspected by a bi-lingual lawyer before deciding to take it on yourself.)

THE BEST TIME to rent a house is April to June or September to November or outside the school term in college towns. In larger towns, rentals are widely advertised in both English and Spanish language newspapers and are listed with real estate brokers, who, however, may levy a charge for showing and, naturally, will add their commission to the rent. In smaller towns, news of vacant rentals is generally passed by word of mouth. In any case, don't expect to find the ideal rental property ready and waiting. Allow 2-4 weeks to find what you want.

To yield a satisfactory return, a house should be rented at 1% of its cost per month. On the average, therefore, you can expect to pay $65 for a $6,500 home, $100 for a $10,000 home and so on. And since land and building costs are higher in cities, at resorts and near the U.S. border, higher rents apply in these places. Rents also vary with demand. In an American retirement colony in which 24 couples are seeking rentals when only 12 are available, rents naturally rise. And vice versa.

Equally obvious is that furniture wears out much more rapidly than buildings so that rents for furnished places are roughly double those for unfurnished rentals. For a temporary stay in Mexico, a furnished rental is your only choice. But for permanent or semi-permanent residence, buying your own furniture reduces your rent by 40%-50%. As mentioned elsewhere in this book, there is no immigration ruling to prevent you from buying furniture in Mexico.

In fact, whether you are buying or renting, there is little advantage in taking your own furniture to Mexico. Freight costs are high, duty is higher still and to import it duty free, you must qualify for *inmigrante* status. A far better plan is to sell your furniture in the States and to buy new furniture in Mexico. Handsomely designed contemporary modern furniture is made by inmates of penitentiaries where it can be picked up for a song. Alternatively, beautifully made, custom designed furniture can be had in Mexico at under one half of Stateside prices. Using new fabrics and furniture ap-

propriate to Mexican living, you can furnish your home exquisitely for $750-$2,000 (depending, of course, on size of home and quality of furniture). For example, 5 rooms and a kitchen can be delightfully furnished for $1,000-$1,500, much of it with elegant rosewood pieces. A few sample prices: leather captain's chairs $4; single bed and mattress $37, double $47; dressing table $17; very large dining room table with 8 matching rosewood chairs, custom made $110; davenport $55; lounging chairs $15; leather covered coffee table $10; bookshelves $9; large wool rugs $11; rosewood writing desk $40; gas range with tank and mixer $60-$180; 7 cubic foot refrigerator $400. Only electrical appliances cost more than in the United States and since labor is cheap, few are ever used. Frequently you can buy a houseful of furniture from departing Americans at slightly less than cost and, in turn you can sell yours to incoming Americans for almost what you paid. If you prefer cheaper pine furniture, you can furnish a two bedroom home for as little as $650. A tip: all electric wall and ceiling fixtures, garden furniture and plants are removed by each tenant. Strangely, Venetian blinds remain with the house.

For permanent residence, you'll find an unfurnished rental by far the better choice. As we have said, various factors affect rentals. No one can say exactly what rent you will be asked. But by and large, you'll find the following quotations fairly representative for the most modern, desirable properties. Older places run 15%-30% less, super deluxe places 10%-20% more. In really off-the-beaten-path locations, costs are lower still and sometimes you can find country mansions with huge gardens and swimming pools for $50-$75 a month. Again, in the plushest suburbs of the largest, most fashionable cities, you can pay a good deal more. Given first is the typical rental spread when furnished and in barckets, unfurnished. Places in which range and refrigerator are supplied run between the two. These are all year rents; short term tourist rentals usually run higher.

In Mexico City and large, fashionable resorts: 1 b.r. apt. $85-$100 ($35-$60); 2 b.r. apt. $125-$175 ($60-$90); 3 b.r. apts. $135-$200 ($65-$100); 2 b.r. home $135-$185 ($65-$90); 3 b.r. home $140-$190 ($70-$100); 4 b.r. home $150-$210 ($75-$105); 5 b.r. home $160-$250 ($80-$125).

Other large cities, resorts and large retirement colonies: 1 b.r. apt. $65 ($35); 2 b.r. apts. $75-$100 (34-$50); 3 b.r. apts. $85-$110 ($38-$55); 2 b.r. home $80-$100 ($35-$50); 3 b.r. home $90-$120 ($40-$55); 4 b.r. home $95-$130 ($42-$60); 5 b.r. home ($65 up).

Smaller towns, small retirement colonies and non-tourist areas: 1 b.r. apt. $25-$60 ($20-$30); 2 b.r. apt. $35-$65 ($25-$35); 3 b.r. apt. $40-$70 ($25-$40); 2 b.r. home $40-$70 ($25-$40); 3 b.r. home $45-$75 ($25-$45); 4 b.r. home $50-$80 ($30-$50).

Included in the furnished rates above are all linens, silverware and kitchen equipment. For unfurnished rentals, you can bring in your own linens free of duty. In most places, you'll find a fairly wide choice of rentals—say a dozen to choose from—but you could conceivably just be unlucky and find none at the moment. Whatever you do, avoid arriving in resorts just before or during the tourist season. It might be added, too, that rentals just outside or on the outskirts of towns are somewhat cheaper than those listed above. Good bus service is usually available.

To guard against rent rises, always sign a lease when renting for one year or more. Most leases are made for 2-3 years and to be legal, involve a 2% tax, customarily shared between tenant and landlord. Two months' rent is normally demanded in advance. Before signing, have your lease checked by a bi-lingual lawyer and make sure all utility bills have been paid by the previous tenants (who often will sell their utility and telephone contracts).

As tenant, you are normally responsible for repairs and maintenance, the landlord for furnishing an adequate water supply. It pays, however, to be watchful for gouging landlords who look upon American tenants as a heaven sent answer to their maintenance problems.

Outside the popular American retirement colonies, don't expect to nd a supply of vacant renovated older homes with modern plumbing. Instead, you'll be better off paying slightly more to rent a newly built home. Most new homes in Mexico can readily be rented. A common "for rent" sign is a white rag in the window or on a wall or fence. Also for rent, of course, are houses bearing the more conventional "Se Renta" sign.

Further information on how to buy real estate in Mexico can be obtained from the Foreign Department, Banco de Comercio, Gante 20, Mexico 1, D.F.; the Trust Department of the Banco Nacional de Mexico at Isabel La Catolica 4, Mexico 1, D.F.; or from the First City National Bank of New York, Isabel La Catolica 5, Mexico 1, D.F.

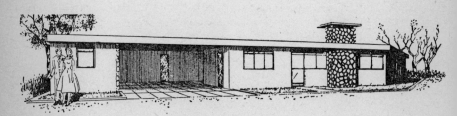

Figure 3. Typical Studio Home.

CHAPTER VI

HOW TO LIVE A CAVIAR LIFE
ON A SARDINE BUDGET

LOOKING FOR A HAVEN where you can enjoy tranquillity without pills for as little as $3.50 a day It seems incredible but there are still idyllic spots in Mexico where prices look like the 1930s and nobody worries.

In Mexico not long ago I sat in the patio of my $40-a-month lakeside villa sipping a 10¢ bottle of excellent beer and smoking a 7¢ pack of cigarettes while the local barber cut my hair for 32¢, tip included. As he worked, I read the mimeographed literature published for newcomers by the American Consulate in Mexico City. One paragraph in particular caught my eye: "Living costs in Mexico have increased greatly during the past few years and certain imported articles are and always have been more expensive than in the U.S., but most articles of prime necessity are less expensive and the resulting cost of living is lower."

Just as I'd completed this official acknowledgement of Mexico's soothing prices, my gardener—who was busily tending orchids for a wage of under 15¢ an hour—called out that someone was at the door. Then my 50¢-a-day maid ushered in a friend who poured himself a jigger of Bacardi from a gallon jug which retails at $4.50 and announced that he had just built a two-bedroom, two-bath home with twenty foot living room, patio and fireplace for less than $4,700.

If you're shopping for relaxation, you can find tension free Utopias in some of Mexico's almost perfect climates with prices guaranteed to make you purr. Americans haven't been slow to take advantage of these costs. Since the great American exodus to Mexico began in 1949, some 50,000 of our expatriates are estimated to be enjoying the good life south of the border.

Here's how one contented Chapala retiree aptly summed it up: "Make your money in the United States—the world's highest paid and most expensive country. When you've got enough, invest it in Mexico—where investments yield twice as much as ours. Then live in Mexico—and enjoy gracious low cost living in one of the world's most charming lands. Back in the States, I was planning to save $70,000 so that I could retire at 60. But the fast pace brought on a heart attack before I reached 45. At that time I had $25,000—one third of what I needed to retire. So I came to Mexico and invested it here. Now it brings in as much as $60,000 would on Wall Street. And I figure that with the lower cost of living I'm far better off. I have a three-bedroom home with two baths and two full-time servants. To duplicate that in the States, I would have needed at least $150,000 invested at 5%. Furthermore, I'm living in a climate superior to that of any place in the United States."

How have other couples fared? To find out, we briefly canvassed over 40 couples in the Chapala-Guadalajara area, a region in which living costs represent a good average for the entire Republic of Mexico. Among them all, we finally selected four who met our standards: a) each of the four was in a different income bracket; b) each had previously tried out retirement in the United States; c) each was living in Mexico on the same sized income they had retired on north of the border and each still had approximately the same amount of debt or financial burden; d) each was still following the same pattern of providing shelter, i.e. either renting with or without his own furniture or owning a home; e) each was living in approximately the same sized city, town or village to that in which he had previously been retired; and f) all had been in Mexico nine months or longer and in their present residence six months or more. We then interviewed each of the couples again to find out how they had fared. Here are reports of four couples, each in a different retirement income bracket:

COUPLE A, with a very low retirement income by Stateside standards, had found it progressively inadequate in the U.S. Forced to eke out a bare existence in a modest Ozark retirement cottage, they had had to subsist on a very moderate diet without much meat, had been unable to afford any drinks or social entertainment, were hard put to meet medical expenses, could not afford to operate a car and did not maintain any life insurance.

In Mexico, though still forced to live by austerity standards, their income nevertheless paid the rent of a rather rustic though quite cheerful small apartment in an old *colonia*. They enjoyed a tequila cocktail before dinner and often invited friends in for a drink. They ate meat once daily and also enjoyed a bountiful supply of fresh vegetables and tropical fruits. Though their income still did not cover a car, it did cover the services of a part-time daily maid who did all their shopping, cleaning and laundry. Each week they bussed to Guadalajara and took in a first run movie or sometimes a concert or ballet performance. The past winter they had also gone by bus for a two weeks' vacation at a Pacific beach resort village. Though they had to budget carefully, they found their income now covered doctor and dentist bills and the drugs they required cost half as much as at home. Since moving to Mexico, the couple had enjoyed better health. Mrs. A's arthritis had completely disappeared and they had made many new friends. Mr. A estimated that by and large, at their modest level of living, their money went a good 20% further than in the United States.

COUPLE B had previously lived in a low priced, one-bedroom home at an inexpensive Florida inland retirement town. Their rather small retirement income had covered all necessities but had left little over for enjoyment. Their car had been five years old and they were able to meet a nominal life insurance premium. Once each summer, they had spent a week at a nearby Florida beach resort when low off-season prices prevailed. They ate one meat meal daily and did a little modest entertaining at which Mrs. B had served beer. They could not afford domestic help. In short, by Florida standards, their mode of living had been rather austere.

In Mexico, they still didn't rate high on the totem pole. But they did live in a fairly modern two-bedroom suburban home and they kept a full-time cook-maid and a part-time gardener. They ate meat thrice daily, entertained quite frequently at home and Mr. B was once more able to follow his hobby of painting. They often went to the movies or live theater and were planning a month-long winter vacation at a Pacific Coast resort—this in spite of an operation Mrs. B had undergone several months previously in the best hospital in Guadalajara (for which the total tab ran under $250). In comparing living costs, Mr. B estimated that at their level, money went about 35% further than in the United States.

COUPLE C had moved to Mexico from a modern but inexpensive two-bedroom home in a popular Arizona retirement town. There, they had lived quietly but comfortably, had owned a three year old car, taken an annual vacation on the Oregon Coast, were able to eat quite satisfactorily, maintained a small but adequate life insurance premium, had a cleaning woman once a week, entertained at home about 4 times a month and gave modest sums to charity.

In Mexico, by comparison, they lived sumptuously in a 3-bedroom, two-bath home, kept two full-time maids and a part-time gardener, entertained extensively at home, kept two riding horses and belonged to the country club. In addition to an annual month long vacation at a Pacific Coast resort, Mr. C drove all over Central Mexico pursuing his hobby of photography. The Cs had filet mignon for dinner and kept a bottle of Scotch behind the Bacardi jug. Only recently they gave a dinner for 15 friends with an orchestra to play for dancing.

Mr. C met us at the door wearing a pair of custom made shoes and a hand monogrammed shirt. Their home, a Mexican designed house with a central patio, looked inward to a charming garden open to the sun and blue sky. We sipped cocktails on built-in masonry seats in a 3-sided dining room open to the patio. "Marvelously private," said Mr. C. "Back in Arizona we'd have been looking out on our neighbors' garbage cans. In the States we build on a 75-foot lot the same way we build on a country estate. The house occupies barely one third of the lot. But look at *this* house. Our walls extend right to the lot line, our house covers the entire lot. The garden—which is the patio—is inside the house and forms an outdoor living room. All our rooms look out on the garden-patio and the result is we have twice the floor space of the average American style home. Add on the patio and you'll see we have a home of roughly three-to-four times the living area of a similar American style house. The colonial Spaniards certainly knew how to live on a small city lot. And there's nothing cooler or more comfortable for a desert climate than a patio style home. This house is as big as the lot and for the same cost, you get 3-4 times as much living space as your money would buy in America."

Mrs. C joined us and explained how they'd had fun hunting up old colonial tiles, beams, balcony rails and columns from *demoliciones* (house wreckers). Their home would have done justice to the color pages of any home and garden magazine. Exuberant folk art covered the rough textured walls. "Once you know the folk arts and where to find them, you can furnish any home beautifully and without much expense," Mrs. C explained. "Here in Mexico the folk arts flourish as nowhere else on earth. All our American friends admire our home. But few take the trouble to go out to the villages and seek these wonderful bargains."

Rich, colorful handmade textiles had been adapted as wall, furniture and floor coverings. Handsome custom-made mahogany and rosewood furniture blended with other pieces woven in lovely and unusual palm designs. Color splashed primitive paintings gazed down from multi-hued stone walls on which a rich texture had been achieved through the old Aztec art of studding mortar joints with pebbles.

"As you've probably guessed, interior decorating is my hobby," went on Mrs. C. "But I simply borrowed the ideas from homes of Mexican friends. Mexico brims with new ideas. Compare the curves and changing

Christmas in Mexico

You won't see snow but Christmas in Mexico is nonetheless enjoyable. A few days before Christmas your Mexican friends will invite you to a *posada*, a re-enactment of Mary and Joseph's search for shelter. With other guests you arrive at the host's home carrying lanterns and sing Christmas songs outside the door. Like the biblical innkeeper, the host at first refuses admission but a little later you all troop in and the party begins. A popular feature of all Mexican family parties is the children's *piñata*, a large pot stuffed with candies and presents. Children, blindfolded, take turns to swing at the *piñata* with a broomstick while the host raises and lowers it from the ceiling on a rope. Once it is smashed, the children eagerly dive for the contents. Instead of a Christmas tree and Santa Claus, Mexican families construct a *Nacimiento* or Christmas scene and presents are distributed on January 6th, the Feast of the Three Wise Kings, when children lay out shoes instead of stockings.

---

planes of this handmade furniture with the severe straight lines of modern mass produced products. Look at the richness, vitality and integrity in these whimsical designs, all executed with the skill and sensitivity that only Indian artisans still possess. Yet all these beautiful custom made things cost less than half of what you'd pay in the States."

We dined beside the patio at an enormous refectory table set with Oaxaca weavings and buff-colored Tlaquepaque tableware. Starting out with oyster cocktail we passed on to delicious *caldo de pollo* broth followed by red snapper Veracruz style, charcoal broiled *filete* with guacamole salad and Manila mangoes and cheese for dessert—all capped with strong, black unblended Mexican coffee and the truly superb Kahlua liqueur. "Every item came from Guadalajara's Libertad Market and the meal cost under $1 per head," Mrs. C explained. "It's true that the steaks aren't quite up to American standards. But must you eat steak? Personally, I've found Mexico an epicurean delight. We have more charcoal braziers in the kitchen than gas burners. Our food bill runs 40% less than it did in Arizona, our liquor costs less than one third and we both smoke king sized filter cigarettes at 8¢ a pack."

Later, over a couple of long filler 7¢ Dorado cigars, Mr. C summed it up: "On our income, which was just average in Arizona, we're really able to enjoy some of the luxuries of Mexican living. To say we live like kings would be an overstatement. We really had to study Mexico before we could evaluate the folk arts and hunt them up, create and design our own furniture and enjoy the best of Mexico's food and drink. From comparison with our former Stateside budget, I'd say our money goes about 70% further in Mexico."

COUPLE D's earlier attempt at retirement had been spent in a typical middle income bracket three bedroom home in a typical middle class suburb at a North Carolina resort. There they had lived quite comfortably, owned a one year old car, had a part-time Negro maid, belonged to the local country club and had been able to afford one off-season trip to Europe. All in all, they had been able to enjoy a fairly satisfactory level of typical middle class American living and had even been able to save a small amount each month.

In Mexico, they enjoyed a luxurious penthouse scale of living. Their five bedroom, four bath home would have cost $40,000 in Tryon (though all they paid was $65 unfurnished) and this included some stables in which Mr. D, whose hobby was horses, kept a string of mounts. They had three full-time maids, a professional cook and a full-time gardener who helped Mr. D with the horses. Though they lacked the interior decorating ability of Couple C, their home was richly furnished in a harmonious blend of colonial plateresque, Renaissance, baroque and churrigueresque styles. There were antiques galore and embroidered linens, crystal and onyx everywhere. Since retiring to Mexico, the Ds had been able to afford a trip around South America and regularly took trips to every part of Mexico.

"Mexico really *is* a bargain," said Mrs. D. "Last week we hired a catering service to provide dinner for 35 guests and the bill was under $60. But you've *got* to know your way around. True, we're living regally but we didn't begin to approach our present cost of living until our third month in this house. For example, most tourists think Mexican clothes are expensive. But I'm wearing a Vogue design that a local seamstress duplicated for under $14 and Mr. D's English tweed suit was made in Guadalajara for much less than he paid for his last one on our trip to England. At our level of living, we estimate our money goes at least twice as far as it did in the States."

WHAT DO THESE REPORTS show? Obviously, you can no longer live in Mexico on $1 a day and you'd have a pretty thin time on $2. If your income is sufficient to live on in the States, however, then all other things being equal, you should find it more than adequate in Mexico.

Will you live better? Hark back to the conclusions of our four couples, all with different incomes. Couple A, forced to spend almost all their money on basic necessities, found it only went 20% further than at home. Couple B, spending about three-fourths on necessities, found it went 35% further. Couple C, spending about two-thirds on necessities, found their money went 70% further. And Couple D, spending an estimated half on necessities, found their income went at least twice as far.

In other words, on basic necessities such as food and shelter, you should not expect to save more than 20% (bread in Mexico is 21¢ a loaf, in the States 26¢). But with your necessities covered, the bargains come thick and fast. A $10,000 home costs only $5,000 in Mexico; a $20 jug of Bacardi just $4.50. And for $16 a month you can obtain a more willing, industrious maid than you could hire for $200 at home.

Conclusion: the real bargains in good living come *after* you have covered all your necessities. While you will save only 20% on needed essentials, what you have left over can go 2-3 times as far as at home. For example, assuming that a couple living in a certain home can cover all basic necessities for $200 a month, with $300 they should be able to duplicate the scale of good living enjoyed by Couple C and with $400 a good many of the features within reach of Couple D. In the States on the same scale, if $240 covered all your essentials then to duplicate the standards of Couple C *item by item* would cost at least $1,000 monthly and to live *exactly* like Couple D a good $1,600-$1,800 (remember that American maids are $200 a month, not $16).

Of course, it is not correct to say that you can retire in Mexico as well on $400 per month as in the States on $1,600. For instance, Couple D's, four servants and a gardner would, in the States, eat up $1,100 or more of their monthly budget. In labor saving America you would not require four servants. Nevertheless, this comparison does indicate the princely scale of living, the many Old World luxuries you can enjoy in Mexico which in the States are out of reach.

Obviously, then, figures alone give a misleading comparison. To arrive at any fair comparison of living costs involves also a consideration of space, time and relativity. Comparing life in Mexico and the States is like comparing life in a Southern country house of the 1850s with life in a contemporary suburban apartment. Despite some modern conveniences, *the domestic life of Mexico is still lived deeply in the 19th century, that of the United States in the 20th century.* In terms of modern compact space, electronic luxury and labor saving contemporary living, your dollar buys less in Mexico. In terms of living space, personal service and 19th century luxuries, your dollar will go very much further in Mexico.

SOUND ATTRACTIVE? So do somewhat similar reports in magazines and in mimeographed literature purporting to tell how you can retire in Mexico on a shoestring.

But consider this: all four couples whose budgets we have just analyzed had completed high school or had an equivalent education, one had graduated from a state university, another from an Ivy League college. Although none speaks Spanish fluently, *all* possess a working knowledge. All are reasonably intelligent, well informed people, cosmopolitan in outlook and cognizant of the arts, literature and current events. All sincerely love Mexico, are *simpatico* in outlook, draw daily inspiration from the Mexican scene and enjoy the spiritual values they found. *All are really outstanding examples of the way in which Americans can benefit from the attitudes and way of life of Mexico and merge it with the best of our own.*

Needless to say, other Americans have not been so successful. One has only to drop into a bar to find a typical group drowning their maladjustments in the low cost ambrosia of Mexican liquor. This is not the fault of Mexico. You'll find identically the same group drowning their problems at considerably higher cost in Florida bars. Actually, the percentage of failures in Florida runs almost as high.

Among the 40 odd couples we originally contacted, some were dejected because they had failed to retire successfully in Mexico.

As one disgruntled ex-plumber retorted, "Why live in Mexico when you can be happy?" Obviously, Mexico is not a paradise for everyone.

Mexico may be for you. Or you may find yourself completely out of your depth. How can you tell beforehand? Here is a short 14 point questionnaire which should give you a pretty good idea. Score 1 for each question you answer Yes. If you score 11 or more, you will undoubtedly enjoy Mexico. If your score is 7 or less, you'll probably be happier back in a Stateside suburbia.

1. Are you retired from the Armed Forces, a teacher or professor, or have you previously lived in or travelled in and liked foreign countries and their people?

2. Have you graduated from high school or do you possess an equivalent educational background?

3. Can you master elementary Spanish?

4. Do you deplore discrimination against racial minorities in the United States?

5. Do you enjoy the arts, opera, theater, photography and cultural activities in general?

6. Are you adaptable, patient, at least slightly sophisticated and cosmopolitan and something of an individualist? Do you possess a ready sense of humor?

7. Do you enjoy *doing* things rather than being entertained?

8. Do you prefer intelligent conversation to most TV programs? Can you find contentment through your own inner resources, keep busy with your hobbies, interests or sports?

9. Are you optimistic? Are you able to live successfully at home?

10. Do you prefer a more individualistic mode of life to the usual conformist type of American suburban living and church circle routines?

11. Can you live without American spectator sports and TV programs?

12. Although *you* will live hygienically in Mexico, you will unavoidably see some of Mexico's poverty, dirt and squalor. Are you sure this will not prove upsetting?

13. Do you value the luxury of servants, the charm of antiquity and the beauty of handmade art works in your home more than our super-efficient plumbing, push button appliances and mass produced furniture and household decorations?

14. If you travel abroad, do you prefer to make all your own plans and arrangements

(as opposed to buying a completely planned escorted tour or having a travel agent make all your arrangements in advance)? In other words, do you think you can face a few uncertainties, deal with problems on the spot abroad?

If you are an out and out conformist, if your entire horizon is based on American suburban living and church life, if you haven't a ready sense of humor and patience, if you can't live without the most super-efficient plumbing and sanitation, if your interests center around watching American sports and TV, if you don't think you could master elementary Spanish, if you can't stand the sight of poverty and dirt, then we recommend your taking a long, hard look at Mexico before deciding to retire there.

Are you at home in the company of worldly-wise people—generals, colonels, professors, writers, artists and retired executives? In Mexico you'll mingle with people like these—your income bracket isn't important. Your ability to mix and feel at home with them is. You needn't be a Ph.D. to retire successfully in Mexico. We know policemen and firemen in Mexico who thoroughly enjoy their retirement, who never got beyond the eighth grade and yet who are welcome at every social occasion. We also know retired admirals who are ostracized from every social activity and shunned by every decent American in Mexico. Mexico is no haven for misfits and the perennially dissatisfied. There are people who, having failed to live on $12,000 a year at home, also fail to make ends meet on the same income in Mexico.

Thus far, we trust we have made ourselves clear. If Mexico still sounds like the place you're seeking, then here's what you should know.

First, don't sell your home and rush off to Mexico to retire. Pay a visit first. You'll have an enjoyable vacation, probably for less than you'd spend in the States. Begin, if possible, by taking the tour of retirement towns described further on. Choose the area which appeals to you best. Then spend a little time there. If you have several weeks, rent an apartment and set up trial housekeeping. You won't achieve rock bottom costs at first but a month in any Mexican town will show you, as quickly, easily and painlessly as possible, how Americans *do* live successfully in Mexico, how problems *are* met and how you *can* live successfully

when you retire. You will meet other couples like the As, Bs, Cs and Ds and see how various people make out on different incomes. You will also meet those who fail to make out through their inability to adjust to Mexico and you can profit by their mistakes. Only then, when you are convinced you like Mexico, should you return home, sell your house and move down for good.

To reduce the cost of this experiment, think about renting out your own home while you're away. Use your regular vacation period, don't take off extra time. Or if you habitually spend the winter in Florida or Arizona, spend it in Mexico instead. At all costs, don't plunge headlong into Mexican living unless you can afford to go back if you find you don't like it.

Secondly, if you haven't been abroad before, plan to acclimatize yourself gradually to Mexico. Don't, for example, fly direct from a large American city to Guadalajara airport and take a taxi straight to a small inn at a village like Jocotepec. For most people, the transition is too abrupt. Instead, spend a few days in a tourist hotel in Guadalajara. Then move to a small resort hotel in a smaller town like Chapala. Finally, when you move into a village *posada* you'll find yourself fully conditioned and quite at home.

Do allow sufficient time for your preliminary inspection. People do fly down to con a Mexican town in three or four days. Not staying long enough to meet people and see inside their homes, nor to escape tourist prices, they return home with the misconception that Mexico is all slums and high prices. Others, in their rush to meet American residents, resort to striking up conversations in bars where, during the day at least, they meet only the discontented. It takes at least a week and preferably two weeks to thoroughly discover the charms of such retirement spots as San Miguel de Allende, Guadalajara or Ajijic. As at home, American residents don't come out and slap visiting tourists on the back. To meet fellow expatriates you must be seen around a while; you must at least give the impression that you are no casual, curious tourist. Be sure, too, before concluding that rentals are either scarce or overpriced that you have not arrived in the middle of the tourist season or a school term. Rental rates and availability during late fall may present a much more attractive picture than those encountered in crowded January.

If you do come straight to Mexico to retire, don't try to have everything cut and dried beforehand. Wait until you arrive, then capitalize on what you find. Be prepared to spend a few weeks hunting up the ideal rental. Avoid paying high prices just to get settled in quickly.

What is the ideal age for retiring in Mexico? Our investigations reveal that the most successful people are under 72. Unless you are very active, sharp and already conditioned to a foreign environment, we would not recommend retirement in Mexico after age 72 (though you'll enjoy a vacation or winter sojourn regardless of your age). And do be sure your funds are adequate. Time after time, American Societies have been forced to pass the hat to send home a retiree who couldn't make out.

Do distinguish between relaxation and idleness. Mexico, the land of 365 mananas, is ideal for loafing. Relax all you like. But do have some retirement activity in view (for suggestions see Chapter II). Idleness and cheap drinks are a combination which has ruined many otherwise well laid retirement plans. The more raffish American colonies all have their share of hopeless alcoholics (and none is anonymous). Choose an area where you can carry out your favorite sports and hobbies. In their November 1959 issue, the magazine *Mexico This Month* described how several American couples had built their retirement around such hobbies as lithography, photography, interior decorating and refurbishing old homes. Unlike those unsuccessful Americans who get away from it all with the aid of tequila, these Americans based their philosophy on the theme that time is something to be enjoyed, not killed. To the challenge of time, Mexico offers a magnificent chance to discover your self, your talents and an entire new life.

THE LURE OF MEXICAN LIFE means these things: practicing the art of loafing in a gracious environment of Old World charm and a whole new world of beautiful handicrafts; the luxury of servants at roughly 50¢ a day; and the opportunity to enjoy a full, rich and stimulating life of cultural activities or outdoor sports—all at somewhat lower cost than at home. The cheapest and quickest way to retire in Mexico is to enter on a tourist card, buy your own furniture and rent an unfurnished home.

What will you actually spend? Surprisingly enough, this wasn't easy to ascertain. For one thing, there are so many alluring things in Mexico that Americans buy many extra things they wouldn't buy at home. After covering necessities, luxuries are so cheap that most expatriates spend the rest of their money living it up. Some of the less successful couples don't keep track of what they spend and throw pesos around like trading stamps. Some couples get along very well on $200 a month, others fare no better on $400. But from our own experience and research, several facts stand out:

1. To live inexpensively in Mexico you *must* know the ropes and this takes a little time. Don't expect to achieve living costs as low as old timers until you've been in Mexico at least eight weeks.

2. Mexico today makes practically everything you'll need. Anything bearing the label "Hecho en Mexico" costs half as much as any similar item imported from the States and is frequently just as good. Any American made item in Mexico costs twice as much as in the States.

3. The chepaest thing in Mexico is labor. Capitalize on Mexico's low labor costs in every possible way.

A few examples: a full-time laundress costs less than a washing machine. On one occasion we went to a supermarket with an American woman who complained her food bill cost more than at home. Blithely, she went through the store picking out the same familiar American brand names she'd been used to in the States. When we pointed out similar Mexican made items alongside each, she simply said, "Oh, I can't read the labels." For an experiment, we duplicated her order in Mexican made goods and tipped the clerk to price it. Her bill was $30.65, ours $14.50. On another occasion, we bargained a garden urn down to $1.75. Then we sent in our maid who got it for $1.50.

So here are the rules for living inexpensively in Mexico. Never buy an American made product if a Mexican one is available. Supermarket price tags are often lower than those in corner groceries but prices in public markets are even less. So buy everything which is hygienically acceptable in the markets. Most Mexican storekeepers don't know that you are not a tourist and may charge higher prices. So let your maid do your shopping (which also saves your time and effort). Be prepared to bargain wherever it is practiced, which, regardless of written price tags, means almost everywhere outside supermarkets and department stores. Leave American imports for your twice annual border trips. Some things like ready made clothes and shoes and pipe tobacco are cheaper in the States. Load up on these when you visit the border and you'll save enough to pay for your trip (another good reasn for not taking out *inmigrante* papers).

Most of the people who complain that Mexico is more expensive than they thought are those who buy imported whiskey, cigarettes, foods, appliances and brand name goods. Certain items, however, do cost more in Mexico and these include: all American imports, ready made shoes and clothing, pipe tobacco, canned baby foods, electrical appliances, house cleaning powders and disinfectants, plastics and curtains and draperies. Tipping is also more frequently required though individual tips are far less. And sometimes costs are increased through breakages caused by careless servants. By contrast, Mexican products in which labor is a predominant cost are much, much cheaper: i. e., food, repairs, utilities, construction, furniture, decorations and medical bills. In fact, if during your preliminary visit you can postpone your annual medical check up, eye examination and new glasses, dental work, car repairs involving labor, tailored clothes and gifts, you can pay for your vacation by getting them all in Mexico.

TO LIVE THE GOOD LIFE in Mexico, you must know the ropes. This involves knowing sufficient Spanish to be able to shop and dicker about prices; to know Mexican values in pesos; to exercise the patience, time and understanding to bargain prices down; and to know *where* to shop, particularly the existence of factory, farm and wholesale outlets. Understandably, this is going to take at least eight weeks. Short term vacation renters cannot hope to match the lower costs of permanent residents. Imagine how much a Mexican would spend in an American town if he couldn't ask about prices or didn't know there were such things as laundromats, self-service stores, farmers markets, drive-ins, low rent shopping districts and surplus and wholesale outlets.

Without knowing the ropes, you can spend as much in Mexico as in the States. Many unsuccessful retirees still spend far more than they need, simply through not having acquired this know how. Some do

worse: bid up wages by offering more; and many fail to agree beforehand on the costs of repairs, taxi trips and other items for which no fixed price exists. If you expect to be popular, we suggest you do everything possible to help keep prices down.

Assuming you can follow out the foregoing procedures, how much will you need? Of course, spending habits are flexible and no two persons ever end up by spending exactly the same. But assuming you have no hidden debts, life insurance premiums or other burdens of any type at all, here's how your monthly budget might look:

Rent for three bedroom unfurnished house	$55
Food for two people and one maid	70
Utilities	9
Car operation and insurance	27
Maid's wages and household items	20
Medical, dental	12
Miscellaneous	10
Personal spending	40
Monthly prorated cost of tourist cards and border trips by car	7
Total	$250

This is the actual budget of a retired California couple living in Guadalajara under circumstances favorably resembling, but not quite equal to, those of Couple C. They own their own furniture which they purchased in Mexico. The budget does not include costs for purchasing a new car or for emergencies or sudden illnesses. They do not buy American made imports and they pay cash for everything.

Using this budget as a base, you can add or subtract to suit your own pattern. Costs might be 10% less in a village. In Mexico City or a very fashionable resort, they might run 25% more. Without a car you can shave off a flat $20. And you could, with care, shave a bit off other items. For each child in your family, you could add about 20% to the budget above, for each extra adult about 25%.

Which brings up the subject of bachelors. Don't assume that because two can live on $250 monthly one can live on half as much. Rent, maid and utilities run almost as high for one as for two. The minimum we'd recommend for a bachelor living alone is $150 and that doesn't cover a car. For this reason, we suggest that a bachelor should team up and share a household with another bachelor.

Such situations are very easily arranged as bachelors already in Mexico welcome others to share their costs. Another alternative is to live in a family style hotel or pension. You'll find many good ones supplying a pleasant room or even a bungalow complete with linens, meals and maid service for $4-$5 a day, others as low as $100 a month (or $180 for two). At still less cost, for around $75 a month, you can board under pleasant conditions with a good class Mexican family.

These same family style hotels—as well as apartment hotels which rent furnished apartments by the week—are excellent bases while seeking a permanent rental and establishing your household. Until you are settled and know the ropes, you will of course, spend more. So bring sufficient funds to see you through this ninety day period. Do have an emergency fund in case of sickness. American consulates are constantly plagued by Americans who have come down expecting to live on next to nothing and end up broke.

It's smart, incidentally, to avoid scrupulously any "Utopia" written up as a bargain paradise in a major magazine over the past 12 months. You can easily check by consulting the *Readers Guide to Periodical Literature* in your public library. For example, back in 1958 Life Magazine ran an eight page photo story on Ajijic and three weeks later the streets were packed with sleek American cars and station wagons. Within a few days every room was taken, every house occupied and the overflow had backed up to Guadalajara. There wasn't a rental left at any price. Costs soared, maids asked higher wages. A new subdivision appeared on the slopes behind the village and *inmigrados* began building apartment houses. There was no cheap living for the incoming hordes. Nine out of ten headed straight back home. A few wisely sought less publicized villages. Which all adds up to this one sage conclusion: never, never rush off to a Mexican "Utopia" because you've just read a glowing account of its low living costs in some magazine. Undoubtedly, costs were still low the day the magazine came out. There may have been a dozen low cost rentals. But the first dozen readers to arrive snapped those up. The readers who followed found no housing at all. Remember, bargain paradises are inexpensive because they *are* undiscovered, uncrowded and untouristed. A horde of magazine readers destroys the very Utopia they have come to seek. Gradually, over succeeding months, these publicized Edens return to normal. But it's simply asking for trouble to follow the advice in widely circulated national magazines.

HIGH LIVING IN MEXICO is yours for the shopping. These days, you'll find modern department stores and five and tens in the largest cities and in the capital, a host of specialty shops comparable to those on Fifth Avenue or in London or Paris. Here you can buy the products of modern Mexico as well as Swiss watches, foreign cameras, French perfumes and British woolens at less cost than at home. There is even a chain of national pawnshops headed by the big one on Mexico City's Zocalo. Apart from knowing that outside the capital, these shops invariably close for the 1-4 P.M. siesta, you can patronize these stores with the same ease with which you'd shop at home.

But shopping for Mexico's genuine folk arts requires special know how. In this world of beautiful things for modern living, nothing that outside the capital, these shops incan be custom made from a simple plan or drawing. To seek out the really distinctive designs and colors, you must leave the smart shops for Mexico's markets and her arts and crafts villages. Bargaining is the rule and if you're a skilled Yankee Trader, the bargains are fantastic. Because a good deal of poorly executed silverwork, gaudy rebozos and serapes, textiles and paintings are purposely made for tourists, it's wise—even as a tourist—to avoid shopping in strictly tourist shops or with a guide.

Likewise, though their products are good, resort and hotel shops grossly overcharge (yet most are susceptible to bargaining and will give discounts for quantities). Personally, we patronize non-tourist craft shops only for expensive items with which we are not too familiar. Everything else we buy in markets or in village workshops. If you're planning on furnishing in colonial or primitive Mexican styles, you can get loads of ideas by examining the interiors of old *posadas*, historic restaurants, hacienda hotels and museum houses. For other folk arts, your best orientation is to visit the National Museum of Native Arts and Crafts at Juarez 44 in Mexico City. The museum also sells art works albeit at somewhat higher prices than you'd pay in the villages. But a visit here *will* permit you to distinguish the genuine from the shoddy and to give you an idea of prices. Also well worth visiting are the regional folk art museums at Patzcuaro and Guadalajara and the better craft shops at folk art centers like Tlaquepaque, Uruapan and other weaving and pottery villages.

The best of these arts and crafts villages are centered in Mexico's four richest folk art regions. For example, within easy reach of the Mexico City-Toluca Highway are such outstanding craft villages as Tianguistenco, Tenancingo, Metepec, Oyoacac and Tenango where you can buy direct from working weavers, potters and embroiderers. For shopping expeditions elsewhere, we suggest three tours easily made from Mexico City by car or bus. They are: 1. to Toluca, Morelia, Tzintzuntzan, Patzcuaro, Uruapan, Guadalajara, Tlaquepaque, Tonola, Guanajuato and Queretaro; 2. to Puebla, Oaxaca and Chiapas—home of the purest Indian arts; and 3. to Puebla, Vera Cruz, Jalapa and Tlaxcala for outstanding textiles. Other good folk art centers are Tepic, Navojoa, Culiacan, Cuernavaca, Taxco, Iguala and Merida. The richest states are probably Michoacan, Mexico, Tlaxcala, Puebla, Guerrero, Oaxaca and Chipas—yet you'll find good buys everywhere but in the border states.

What are Mexico's best buys? Here is a list of the principal ones with some pointers for buying.

Antiques. In small shops in the provinces you'll find good buys in colonial antiques. Avoid buying them in Mexico City or in markets.

Baskets. Every market has hundreds of artistic baskets ranging from shopping bags to laundry hampers and also beautiful straw mats and hats. Prices are ridiculously low. Best markets are in Toluca, Mexico City, Oaxaca, Cuernavaca and Taxco.

Ceramics. Every region produces its own distinctive vases, lamps, dinner sets and handpainted tile. Carefully check quality of glaze before buying and look for discolored gray or white overfired pieces. Ceramics are best bought outside Mexico City in the following important centers: Tlaquepaque, Jal., specializes in beautifully made and painted primitive style ware which is, however, susceptible to chipping; in Oaxaca

City and nearby villages such as Coyotepec, Ocotlan and Atzompa, you'll find the heavily ornamented dark green or black volcanic pottery made by secret Zapotecan formulas; and in Puebla, home of the majolica Talavera ware originally brought from Spain, you'll find both durable hard baked ware resistant to chipping and the lighter baked ware similar to Tlaquepaque's, all in elaborate, sensitive designs. Other good places are: Guanajuato for hard baked ware and hand painted tiles; Iguala, Gro., for really ancient designs; Tzintzuntzan, Mich., for white glazed ware; Santa Fe de La Laguna, Mich., for black glazed earthen ware; Juchitan, Oax., for Tehuana Ixtaltepec pottery; and Las Casas for archaic types. Other good pottery centers are Toluca and Valle de Bravo.

Amazingly inexpensive everywhere are the brown decorated *ollas* and *cazuelas* used in kitchens. They should be cured by slow boiling before use. Delicate, paper-thin onyx tableware can also be found in Oaxaca and Puebla.

Copper, brass. Top spot for outstanding articles of hand hammered copper is Santa Clara del Cobre, Mich., also Mexico City and Taxco.

Furniture. We've already given you a pretty good idea of the wonderful buys available in custom made mahogany and rosewood items. Equally good is tropical palm furniture and such novelties as mosaic tables with wrought iron legs. Good knock down furniture is also available. Tamaulipas, Mexico City and Toluca offer a wide choice while bargains in modern pieces can be found at any penitentiary.

Glass. You'll find a fine assortment of vases, pitchers, glasses and just about everything else in free flowing or corkscrew forms and with hand etching that resembles Finland's. Avalos Brothers make the best and you'll find it in Mexico City or Guadalajara.

Gold. Like silver, gold is sold by weight without regard to styling and can be bought at savings up to 50% and more. Gold coins are available, so are diamonds. Most other Mexican gems, though attractive, possess little real value. Top bargain spots for gold filigree jewelry, etc., are Oaxaca and Las Casas.

Ironwork. Is of Spanish origin and comes in the form of delicately wrought candlesticks, wall sconces, candelabra and lamps. Best places are Guadalajara, Oaxaca, Puebla, Taxco and the villages of Acatlan and Izucar de Matamoros between Puebla and Oaxaca.

Lacquerware. This is best bought at Patzcuaro or Uruapan in Michoacan or, for items of aromatic *olinalau* wood such as clothes chests, at Olinala, Gro. Make sure the wood is well seasoned cedar and that the polychromed design is inland and not painted on. If the surface is smooth, it is genuine inlay; if bumpy, it's painted.

Leather. Calf products are not always up to par but good alligator bags and shoes are splendid buys. Good alligator is soft, flexible and light in weight with fairly evenly matched scales; cheaper stuff is hard and heavy. The best handbags are made by Lilly, Gout de Paris and Madeleine. Be sure your handtooled leatherwork *is* handtooled; best way to be sure is to buy it in a workshop where you can see it being made. You'll also find excellent suede coats, bags, gloves, etc. Mexico City is the place. Outside the capital, you can buy a comfortable pair of custom made sandals or *huaraches* for loafing for around $1.50 (you'll be asked more but *bargain!*). Splendidly made custom men's shoes run about $12 a pair, often less. Cuernavaca specializes in resort footwear. If buying elsewhere, smell the leather for a bad odor indicating improper curing. Another big bargain are leather captains chairs and matching round leather coffee tables available in the Guadalajara area; the chairs run about $4 apiece. Luggage, frequently priced at half U. S. levels, is also a top buy.

Paintings. Mexico is a haven for art collectors and at the outdoor Sunday art shows you can pick up those colorful Mexican primitives for surprisingly little.

Perfumes. Buy French perfumes only from the finest recommended stores as surreptitious dilution is a definite risk. Even then it's safest to stick to brands which are not bottled in Mexico. Guerlain is one.

Silver. Mexico is the home of silver styling, ranging from elaborate 4-piece sterling silver coffee services from around $90 to trinkets available for a few cents. Be sure to buy only sterling silver hallmarked

Souvenir Shopping

anillo	ring
arete, pendiente	earring
aretes	earring
billetera	billfold
cartera	wallet
ceramica	pottery
collar	necklace
cuero	leather
gangas	bargains
gemelo	cufflinks
muestra	sample
oro	gold
plata	silver
pitillera	cigarette case
polvera	compact
porcelana	porcelain
pulsera	bracelet
regalo	gift
venta	a sale

with an eagle containing a check number or with an "oM" sign or the name of the silversmith. Any silver not so marked is second grade and will involve an export tax of 4%-7½% if taken out of Mexico. A certificate goes with purchases of all silver items (which you'll need at the Customs). Silverware is made in Taxco and sold there and in Mexico City. In Taxco, silver is priced by the workmanship involved. In Mexico City, it is sold by weight regardless of workmanship. So here's how to get the best buy. For heavy pieces which do not involve a great deal of artistry, prices are lowest in Taxco. For lighter pieces involving a great deal of workmanship, prices are lower in Mexico City. Mexico's top silver artists are the Castillos, Spratling, Antonio Pineda, Martinez and Salvador. Don't forget to ask for the 10% discount customary on quantity purchases.

Textiles, apparel. Cotton is the only apparel available in Mexico at prices comparable to American ready mades. Plan to bring all ready mades with you or pick them up during border trips. Tailors and seamstresses everywhere are able to copy anything for a few dollars and this art reaches its height in Mexico City's small dressmaker shops which turn out remarkable facsimiles of the latest Italian and French fashions at substantially lower prices (they also have originals at prices lower than on Fifth Avenue). Men's tailors do equally good work. A tailored suit can be had for $50; for $80 you'll get a splendid suit of the finest British tweeds or woolens. Hand-painted or hand screened manta (muslin) sportswear, though not cheap, is a good buy in Mexico City, Cuernavaca and Acapulco. Outside resorts, a woman's hand embroidered blouse can be had for $2, a tailored hand-loomed monogrammed shirt for less than $4.

But the real bargains are Mexico's beautiful handloomed tweeds and the exquisitely designed and handmade shirts, shorts, dresses, suits and table mats made from them. For instance, three meters of 60"-wide hand-loomed Tlaxcala tweed cost only $18-$24 and a tailor will make it into a woman's suit for $15 more. You'll find the best hand-loomed textiles in Oaxaca, Toluca, Michoacan, Chiapas, Puebla, Mexico and Nayarit with prices as low as $2 a meter.

Serapes, used for covering furniture and as rugs or blankets, cost $5-$15. Plan to buy them in small town markets where typical designs are still found. Make sure the weave is close; test the dye with a dampened white handkerchief to ensure it doesn't rub off and lay the *serape* on the floor to make sure the corners lie flat. (Rugs should be checked the same way; the best handloomed rugs are those designed by Preaxor or Borisov.) The best *serapes* in our opinion, come from Teotitlan del Valle, Teposcalula and Oaxaca, all in the state of Oaxaca. Other good *serape* centers are Cholula, Tlaxcala, Aguascalientes, Puebla, Saltillo, Guadalajara, Santiago Tianguistengo and Texcoco, Mex., and in Michoacan at Patzcuaro, Santa Clara, Jiquilpan and many smaller villages.

Equally attractive are *rebozos,* spreads and blouses—usually sold together. The finest *rebozos* come from Yalalag, Oax., but are scarce. Other excellent ones, rich in pre-Columbus designs, are found in Oaxaca and nearby Mitla and Teotitlan and also in Tuxtla Gutierrez, Las Casas and Comitan. Other excellent *rebozos* abound in the villages of Tlaxcala—such as Santa Ana Chilautempan (Sunday market) and Chiconcuac—and also in Saltillo and the villages of Michoacan. The best *rebozos* are made on *otate* or belt looms. To wear one, center it across the stomach, cross over the back and bring the ends over your shoulders.

Tin. Gracefully punched, fluted and curved tinwork comes in the shape of candle-sticks, wall masks, trays, baskets and even cabinets and is best bought in Oaxaca, Mexico City, Taxco or Tlaquepaque.

Tortoiseshell. Attractive tortoiseshell items are made in Yucatan and along the coasts. Rare coral and pearls are also available.

Tip: if taking a load of loot back to the States, it's smart to have receipts for everything.

EATING AND DRINKING. Food and drink are abundant and inexpensive and like other half truths, the belief that Mexican food is hot and spicy has little foundation. You can let your maid shop for fruits and vegetables in the public markets where they're often astoundingly cheap. For other items, you'll want to know that modern delicatessens and reliable butcher shops are appearing in almost all retirement areas. Fresh pasteurized milk is delivered daily in all larger towns. You can choose among dozens of varieties of the delicious French style Mexican bread or the spongy pre-cut and wrapped American types. And you'll find a wide choice of canned goods. Most cities of any size now boast at least one supermarket complete with English speaking uniformed clerks and with well stocked shelves containing, alongside the inexpensive Mexican brands, prohibitively priced American imports. What most Americans fail to understand is that such American imports as U. S. packed turkey and meats are flown in specially for Mexican millionaires. Look instead for the "Hecho en Mexico" label and stick to domestic brands.

Most maids catch on quickly to American cooking. But you'll certainly enjoy some of the more popular Mexican foods. Soups are out of this world. Personally, we also enjoy *tortillas,* either toasted with chicken or beans or else wrapped around meat or chicken as *tacos* or *enchiladas. Tomales,* of course you've tried. Just as tasty are *quesadillas,* fried turnovers; *arroz Mexicana,* Spanish rice with beans; *guacamole* salad of avocado and onion; red snapper sauteed in the Vera Cruz style; the brown *frijoles,* fried or re-fried; whitefish, available at lakeside towns; *cabrito al horno,* barbecued goat kid; *bar-bacoa* or barbecued lamb; *carnitas,* deep fried pork; and the king of Mexican banquet dishes, *mole de guacalote,* turkey with mole sauce. Also good are the numerous rice and egg dishes. You'll find Mexican cooking highly nutritious and if you ask, chile and other sauces can be omitted entirely.

If you prefer, of course, you can live entirely on Stateside menus. Mexico has all the raw materials and here is a rundown on what you'll find.

Beverages: Coca Cola, Pepsi Cola, Squirt —name your soft drink and Mexico has it, along with the famous Tehuacan mineral waters—all safe and about half the price you'd pay at home.

Canned goods: if you can't resist American canned goods, at least stick to those made in Mexico by U. S. subsidiaries. Far cheaper and of good quality are Mexican canned goods which duplicate just about every U. S. line including new items in the shape of canned mangos, peppers, chiles and sauces. Only canned baby foods are really expensive. The best Mexican canned goods are made by Clemente Jaques y Cia., S. A.

Cigarettes: are a bargain. As against smoking imported American cigarettes at 40¢ a pack, you can choose from Mexican king sized filter tips such as Del Prado, Records, Filtrons (strong), Raleigh and Lords (mild) which run from 8¢-24¢ a pack or regular cigarettes from about 6¢ a pack. After smoking Mexican cigarettes for a few months, most expatriates prefer them to American brands. Personally, we enjoy the strong La Perla cigars at 25 for 36¢ but the aristocrats are Regente Medianos, Dorados, Aromaticos and Coronas which would cost 25¢-35¢ in the States but in Mexico are only 7¢-16¢.

Coffee: the strong, black, unblended Mexican coffee with its slightly burned flavor is reasonably priced. Most Americans, however, seem to prefer Nescafe, which costs about the same as at home. Drug stores sell healthful, inexpensive herb teas.

Dairy products: cost about half Stateside prices. Pasteurized milk is now widely available as are pasteurized butter, cream and ice cream. Mexico also makes a variety of excellent cheeses of which the hard, well cured types are safe to seat. Superior to American quality are yogurt (cheaper) and cottage cheese (more expensive).

Fruits: are much cheaper. Tropical fruits are superb and what is not generally known

is that delicious fruit salads can be made from the thick-skinned fruits without any health risk at all. Among the many varieties are: avocados; *caimitos;* the delicious *chirimoyas; guanabanas* with their mouth watering nectar; guava, a type of citrus; the sweet flavored *mamey;* flawless ripe mangos; the best papayas on earth, beneficial for the stomach; an dthe *zapote* of which you eat the sweet, juicy pulp with sugar and lime. In addition, there are the more familiar melons, watermelons and cantaloupes and several varieties of nuts. Strawberries are quite good but apples, pears and peaches are not up to temperate climate standards.

Liquor: is a best buy. Tequila, most popular of the drinks made from maguey, is a versatile substitute for gin or light rum in cocktails, sours, etc., and comes in the sharp, white "clear" or aged, yellow "anejo" types; best brands are Jose Cuervo, Pechuga, Almendrado, Sauza, Herradura and Providencia. Rum is also excellent and the best brands are the three types of Bacardi—the young, light *Carta Blanca,* the more mature, golden *Carta Oro,* and the dark, aged *anejo*—and also Bonampak and the dark, dry and rather sweet Ron Batey. Gilbey's Gin is also bottled in Mexico. Available at supermarkets among other places are Mexico's sherry (Tres Coronas is very good) and her surprisingly good domestic wines. Among these, we can recommend: red wines, Santo Tomas, St. Emilion, Santa Maria, Marques de San Pablo, San Marcos, Rancho Viejo and Noblejo; white wines, Marques de San Pablo Blanco, San Marcos, and Verdizo Blanco; and rosés, Santa Maria, Posada Riviera and San Lorenzo. Among aguardientes—the Mexican aquavit— we'd recommend Madero XXXXX, Palma, Marques de Aguayo, Dorado and Habanero. Brandies are excellent and the brands to look for are San Marcos Gran Reserva, Milenario, Cordon Real, Evaristo I, Presidente and Reserva. Of equal quality are the fruit liqueurs made in Tenancingo and the really fine coffee liqueurs, Kahlua and Kayamagui. Mexican beer is the equal of the finest Dutch and Danish beer and among brands we enjoy are the light Bohemia, Carta Blanca, Corona and Yucatan beers and the dark XX, Negra Modelo and Leon.

No worthwhile wisky is made in Mexico and imported brands are within reach only of those living at the penthouse level. Prices of other distilled beverages: Gilbey's gin is

Mexican Liquid Measure

.473 liters	1 pint
.946 liters	1 quart
1 liter	.26 gallons or 1.06 quarts
2 liters	.52 gallons
3 liters	.78 gallons
3.785 liters	1 gallon
4 liters	1.06 gallons
5 liters	1.3 gallons
7.54 liters	2 gallons
10 liters	2.6 gallons
11.31 liters	3 gallons
15.08 liters	4 gallons
18.85 liters	5 gallons
37.70 liters	10 gallons

For rough conversion, consider 1 liter equal to 1 quart; 4 liters are roughly 1 gallon; 15 liters are almost exactly 4 gallons, 18 liters almost exactly 5 gallons.

Mexican Weights

1 gram	.035 oz.
28.35 grams	1 oz.
453 grams	1 lb.
1,000 grams	1 kilo
1 kilo	2.2 lbs.
1,000 kilos	1 metric ton
1 metric ton	2,204 lbs.
.907 metric tons	1 U.S. or net ton

To quickly convert kilos to pounds, double it and add 10%. Example: 10 kilos equals 20 pounds plus two pounds or 22 pounds. For approximately ¼ lb. ask for 100 grams; for ½ lb. a quarter kilo; for 1 lb. a half kilo.

$2.10, vermouth $1, brandies around $1.45, liqueurs $1.10-$2 and tequila 95¢-$1.50 per fifth. Bacardi sells in gallon jugs at around $4.50. Beer by the case costs $2.50 per 25 bottles or 10¢ each. (Choice liquors, of course, may cost a little more.) The average mixed drink in a bar costs 30¢-40¢, a beer 20¢.

Meat: quality is improving fast and modern butcher shops are now offering cuts of meat which almost approach U.S. standards. Elsewhere, all meat is freshly killed and inspected and stamped by a veterinary, then sold fresh. Because the average small town Mexican butcher still has not learned to cut meat, most is sold ungraded so that chuck and porterhouse can often be had at the same price. Only the tenderest cuts are likely to cost more. Since this meat is inclined to be tougher and with more grain than we're used to, most Americans age it in the bottom of the refrigerator and some also add a little tenderizer when cooking. Though this type of meat will never produce a really juicy steak, the result is nowhere near so bad as you may have heard. In fact, when it is roasted in foil you'd hardly know the difference. Hamburger is plentiful everywhere and so are beef, pork, lamb, goat (surprisingly good), mutton and venison in season. Only during spring plowing when most animals are at work in the fields, is there likely to be a shortage. Pork, in fact, *is* equal to ours but we advise buying from shops which guarantee it has been checked for trichinosis. The best beef comes from Chihuahua and the Mexico City area. Veal is the best buy.

Poultry: as with meat, better grades of poultry are rapidly appearing and in large cities, rotisseries are offering fat, ready roasted birds. In smaller towns, all poultry is sold live or freshly killed and is liable to be stringy. Also widely available are wild and tame duck, dove, squab, goose and turkey. Knowledgeable Americans buy a live turkey and fatten it in the backyard. Most poultry sells at slightly below U.S. prices. Eggs are excellent.

Seafood: varies from almost giveaway prices on the coasts to a top of about 60% of U.S. prices. Thanks to government subsidies to encourage fisheries, fresh seafood is flown into cities daily and markets overflow with shrimp, clams, oysters and tropical fish that we consider delicacies.

Vegetables: all temperate and tropical vegetables are available in abundance and range from ridiculously cheap to a top price about 60% less than we're used to paying. In the markets you'll find fresh, crisp artichokes, calabash, eggplant, beans, cabbage, lettuce and just about every other kind you can name plus some you can't. At slightly higher prices all are available in supermarkets, supposedly cleaned, and wrapped in cellophane.

Naturally, prices vary from place to place, from season to season and cost more in a city supermarket than when bought by your maid in a village market. Also, we can't guarantee that a storekeeper charging 50¢ a dozen for eggs this week won't ask 60¢ next week or that you might pay 55¢ when an astute bargainer could get them for 45¢. The best quality always costs more. But here, to give you a *rough* idea of food prices, is a representative list based on supermarket tags and on prices paid *by our maid* in a local market.

Beef filet	50-¢-60¢ lb.
Round steak	40¢ lb.
Hamburger steak	40¢-55¢ lb.
Best chicken	50¢-65¢ lb.
Ham	50¢-80¢ lb.
Bacon	40¢-62¢ lb.
Red snapper	37¢ lb.
Oyster	20¢ doz.
Shrimps	50¢ lb.
Duck	35¢ lb.
Veal chops	43¢ lb.
Cheese, average	40¢ lb.
Turkey, whole	$6-$7
Cabbage	10¢ head
Eggs	50¢-72¢ doz.
Pasteurized milk	18¢ quart
Pasteurized butter	64¢ lb.
Regular coffee	50¢ lb.
Vegetables, average	4¢-7¢ lb.
Lettuce	5¢-12¢ head
Honey	80¢ quart
Avocados	5¢ each
Papaya	16¢-30¢ each
Mangos, best	2¢-6¢ each
Oranges	1¢-2¢ each
Watermelon	20¢ each
Bananas	5¢ lb.
Best pineapples	15¢-30¢ each
Pears	2¢ each

LOYAL, HONEST AND CHEERFUL, Mexican maids are those wonder girls who uncomplainingly work 12-14 hours a day 6-7 days a week and do all your cleaning, shopping, cooking and laundry for an average wage of about $16 a month. Indeed, Mexican maids are so amazingly good that all social gossipers can find to discuss is their *lack* of maid problems. Though some maids *are* illiterate and slow and others unused to American households, the average Mexican maid is often superior to an American maid costing $50 per week.

There are no domestic employment agencies. Instead, you simply tell your friends and make it known you require a maid. And within a day or two, several will have knocked on your door. They're easily found in American colonies where the small but steady turnover of domestic help is already

Doctor Visit—Parts of Body

apéndice	appendix
arteria	artery
barba	chin
boca	mouth
brazo	arm
cabeza	head
cadera	hip
cara	face
cerebro	brain
clavicula	collarbone
codo	elbow
corazón	heart
cuerpo	body
dedo	finger
dedo del pie	toe
dientes	teeth
espalda	back
espenilla, piel	skin
espinazo	spine
estómago	stomach
frente	forehead
garganta	throat
glandula	gland
higado	liver
hombro	shoulder
hueso	bone
intestinos	bowels
labio	lip
mandíbula	jaw
mano	hand
muñeca	wrist
musculo	muscle
muslo	thigh
nariz	nose
nuca	neck
oido	ear
ojo	eye
pecho	chest
pierna	leg
pies	feet
pulgar	thumb
pulmón	lung
rinón	kidney
rodilla	knee
tobillo	ankle

familiar with the requirements of Americans. And even if you can't find a cook who knows American menus, the average Mexican woman is such a born cook that she'll catch on fast.

Some Americans prefer untrained maids. "Then you can train them to suit yourself," one seasoned American housewife explained. "The only snag is that after you've trained a girl, someone else may offer her higher wages to go and work for them. But I've only lost one girl so far. I always treat my younger maids like daughters. There's no master-maid relationship in our house. Our maids enjoy parties as much as we do and never complain about staying up late. But not everyone treats their help like human beings."

Besides general maids, you can hire a skilled cook and if you need them, a house-boy, chauffeur, gardener and children's nurse-maid. With more than one child, you'll generally need two maids anyway, one to cook and shop and the other to wash and iron. But a fulltime children's *nana* is one of Mexico's boons to busy mothers. She'll not only spend her entire day with the children and wash and starch their clothes but, while they're young, also sleep in their room at night. For all this amazing personal service, you'll pay monthly wages like these— wages in brackets apply to topgrade servants in Mexico City only: maids $15-$20 ($33-$40); cook $20-$30 ($40-$55); nurse-maid $20-$30 ($30-$45); houseboy $12-$15 ($20-$35); chauffeur $25-$45 ($75-$90); gardener $22-$30 ($40-$60). Elsewhere, you'll pay the higher rate in larger towns and cities, the lower rate in small towns and villages.

Because domestic help prefers to eat the simple rice-beans-tortillas diet of the *ejido* classes, feeding your servants adds little to your costs. In small towns and villages, al-most all maids prefer to sleep at home. But in larger towns and cities, most homes in-clude one or two maids' rooms with separate baths. Rest assured that their room and board costs little. According to law, a do-mestic employed for more than one month can be dismissed without notice only for theft, disobedience or drunkenness. Other-wise, six months' wages must be paid in lieu of six months' notice. You are also supposed to provide uniforms and shoes and pay medi-cal and dental bills including those for maternity confinements after which your maid is entitled to resume service in your employ. In practice, however, these regulations are seldom if ever observed in smaller towns and villages. And in cities, maids must belong to a union before they can be enforced. Few domestics ever join. One way to safeguard yourself, however, is to hire your maid on a month by month basis. You are, incidental-

ly, also responsible for burying them if they die.

It's smart to demand references before hir-ing any servant. Otherwise, you may find crockery breakage excessive. Have your maid itemize all purchases; otherwise a dishonest domestic could collect 10% or so of your grocery bill. By law, your maid is entitled to 24 hours off each week. But you can always find a baby sitter for 32¢ per half day. If you prefer, you can have a part-time maid do all your cleaning, shopping and laundry at about two thirds the rates previ-ously given. And by the day, a gardener runs from 90¢-$1.50. Brooms, brushes, mops and other household wares are all ridiculous-ly cheap—you can stock a large house for $3-$4.

UTILITIES COST about half as much as at home. Electricity is available everywhere at 110-125 volts with 50 cycles in Mexico City and 60 cycles in most other places. All your appliances will operate on Mexican current with the exception, on the 50 cycle supply only, of American made TV sets, electric clocks, sewing machines, record players and tape recorders. Since appliances cost more in Mexico, most expatriates bring in smaller appliances such as toasters and irons. Even if broken, they can be repaired more cheap-ly than in the U.S. Due to constant enlarge-ment of power stations, current in rural areas is sometimes cut off for a few hours at a time and even in cities it may fail briefly during thunderstorms. But by and large, Mexico's electricity is regular and dependable and your bill will average $4.00-$5.00 monthly, slightly higher if you em-ploy portable heaters during winter. Electric cooking stoves are considered too expensive to be used.

Piped butane gas is available only in a few border towns and in some newly built apartments. In the average home it comes from 15-40 kilogram cylinder costing ap-proximately $2.50 apiece and monthly con-sumption averages $3. Almost all cooking is done by gas and if you can obtain a burner, it is also excellent for heating. Alternatively, oil heaters could be used.

Water bills are either included in the rent or charged at a flat $1 per month. Ice is inexpensive and in larger towns, delivered daily (commercial ice should not be used in drinks). Telephone service costs about 35% less than in the States—but there's a

Doctor Visit—Ailments

agotamiento	neuvous breakdown
ampolla	blister
asma	asthma
ataque del corazón	heart attack
catarro	a cold
el colera	cholera
contusión	bruise
crónico	chronic
difteria	diphtheria
disenteria	dysentery
divieso	a boil
enfermedad	illness
fiebre amarilla	yellow fever
fractura	fracture
gripe	flu
hemorroide	piles
paludismo	malaria
paperas	mumps
presión alta	high blood pressure
quemadura	burn
quemadura del sol	sunburn
reumatismo	rheumatism
sarampión	measles
seno	sinus
sordo	deaf
torcedura	sprain
urticaria	hives
ulcera	ulcer
veneno	poison
varicela	chicken pox
viruelas	smallpox

here apply to the average sized city. Expect to pay more in Mexico City.

MEDICAL EXPENSES are so low that you can travel to Mexico first class, have an operation, recuperate at a plush resort and still come out ahead of having the same operation in your home town hospital. Every drug available in the U.S. is also available in Mexico plus some new ones we don't have. All drugs are strictly government controlled and manufactured to the highest specifications. Many are imported from Germany. And most run from 20%-40% less than in the States (i.e. a million units of penicillin, injected, costs less than $2.50). Numerous items which require a prescription in the States can be bought over the counter in Mexico. Among these are tranquillizers, barbiturates, sleeping pills and certain antibotics. Prescriptions, once given by a doctor, are returned and can be used over and over again.

Every village has a well stocked *farmacia* and those in cities would do credit to any we have. Rest assured you'll have no trouble getting prescriptions filled. Most *farmacias* give a discount for quantity purchases and, of course, they sell such needed items as toothpaste, mouthwash, cosmetics and razor

rub. First, you must be able to speak Spanish to use one. Secondly, phones are hard to get and expensive to install. To have a phone installed you are required to buy some $240 worth of Telefonos de Mexico stock—a blue chip security which yields over 9%. (Tip: most people foolishly sell theirs immediately at giveaway prices. Be on the lookout for these bargains.) Actually, few Americans bother with phones. Maids will always carry messages and in villages—many of which are without phones—this is standard practice. You can always phone the States from the nearest telephone office; during the siesta period you can get through in minutes.

Telegraph service is swift and efficient, messages are accepted in English and costs are about half ours. No collect or COD service is available between Mexico and the U.S. A final small item you may encounter in cities is a monthly fee of about $2 to the neighborhood watchman who keeps an eye on your home while you are out. All costs

Doctor Visit—Symptoms

astilla	splinter
caries	tooth decay
dolor	pain, ache
dolor de cabeza	headache
dolor de garganta	sore throat
dolor de muelas	toothache
doloroso	painful
enfermo	ill, sick
erupción	a rash
escalofríos	chills
espina	thorn, fishbone
fiebre	fever
hinchado	swollen
inflamada	inflamed
llaga	a sore
mareado	dizzy
nervioso	nervous
prenada	pregnant
respiración	breath
sangrando	bleeding
sangre	blood
un tos	a cough
vinagrera	heartburn
vómito	vomit

blades. In fact, you can often obtain imported French cosmetics at very low cost. Typrical prices for Mexican items: toilet soap 8¢, shaving cream 20¢ a tube, oilet tissue 8¢ a roll.

Mexico has first class medical schools and standards are high. Nowhere will you be out of reach of a Spanish speaking doctor who can, at least, attend to emergencies. At all retirement colonies and in larger towns, you'll find English speaking doctors and specialists (lists available from American consulates). Manq have received training in the U.S. or Europe. In tune with the slower tempo of Mexico, these doctors will give unlimited time to your case. There's no rushing you through to get on to the next patient. Thus diagnosis and treatment are often superior. You'll find well equipped clinics and laboratories galore and costs at all are low. The average doctor visit will set you back $2.50-$3, a half hour consultation with the average specialist won't run much over $4.

There are excellent hospitals in most cities and in many smaller towns. Topping the list is the American British Cowdray (ABC) Hospital in Mexico City but others like Guadalajara's Mexico-American and San Miguel Allende's small modern hospital are just as good. All are equipped with the most modern facilities and are cheerful, bright and well maintained. Many hospitals are staffed by nuns, others by well trained nurses. Yet full costs in a private room run less than staying in most hotels. As this was written, in a medium sized town an attractive private room costs $7 a day and *complete* costs, including room and *all* medications for an appendicitis operation totalled $175; in a larger provincial capital a private room costs $9 and *complete* costs for a gall bladder operation just $350. English is spoken in all larger hospitals.

Both the American Blue Cross and American Blue Shield plans, so we are informed, cover hospitalization for non-permanent residents (tourist card holders) in Mexico. Furthermore, Blue Cross states that it extends benefits for your hospital care or its equivalent to members anywhere in Mexico. Though you might have to pay the bill yourself, they will swiftly reimburse you within the terms of their contract. In addition, hospitalization plans are available in Mexico. Ambulance service is supplied in all parts of Mexico, either through the mu-

nicipal Green Cross or the Mexican Red Cross. Private nurses can be hired very inexpensively (i.e., $20-$30 a month).

Mexico's unhurried dentists also do splendid work at rates well below those charged by dentists in the States. Mexican dentists are world famed for their skillfully made plates and bridgework. The best dentists usually maintain a laboratory in connection with their offices. The same can be said for oculists. Every city has certified oculists with the most modern equipment. Costs are far lower than we're used to. For example, using our own frames, we recently had a complete eye examination and *two* new sets of Zeiss lenses for just $9.

IN MEXICO, a haircut, shave and the finest shoeshine you ever had will set you back under 80¢. First class barber shops charge 50¢ for a haircut, 20¢ for a shave; second class ones 28¢ for a haircut, 15¢ for a shave. A haircut at home in your own patio runs about 32¢. A careful manicure adds about 45¢ more. A shoeshine is 8¢. And no tips are ever expected.

Modern beauty shops cater to women at prices under half those in American cities. You can get a shampoo and wave set from 80¢-$2.50, a permanent wave from $2.

Doctor Visit—Treatment

aspirina	aspirin
compressa	compress
cura	cure
curita	bandaid
dieta	diet
dosis	dose
inyección	injection
emplasto, unguento	salve
gasa	gauze
jarabe	syrup
laxante	laxative
lentes anteojos	eyeglasses
pildora	pill
purgante	physic
rayos ekis	X ray
reacción de la sangre	blood test
receta	prescription
reconocimiento medical	medical check up
tela adhesivo	adhesive tape
vacunar	to inoculate
vacuna	vaccination
vendaje	bandage
vitamina	vitamin
yodo	iodine

Mexican Medical Terms

ambulancia	ambulance
cirujano	surgeon
cita	appointment
clinica	clinic
dentista	dentist
dispensario	dispensary
enfermera	nurse
especialista	specialist
médico	a doctor
sanatorio	sanitarium
veterinario	veterinary

If you don't have a maid, a laundress will do the family wash for around $1. Or you'll find excellent laundries and dry cleaners in every city. Dry cleaning a suit or dress costs 50¢-60¢.

All repair work is cheap and carefully done. You'll find repair shops of every description with the staff ready to work half the night if necessary to get your job done on time. There are good shoe, auto, TV and radio, tailoring and dressmaking shops where any kind of alteration can be done, frequently more satisfactorily than in the States. (Example: a careless American mechanic fitted a new exhaust so badly it rattled all the way to Mexico and finally fell off; a Mexican mechanic reshaped and refitted the pipe, a beautiful job over which he labored most of the day and charged $2.50.)

Between the U.S. and Mexico airmail service and delivery is almost as swift as in the U.S. And provided you use Mexican airmail stationery, it is also cheaper. Between the States and Guadalajara, airmail takes 3-4 days, first class mail 5-8 days and newspapers and magazines about 6-8 days. Domestic Mexican airmail and first class is slightly slower, parcel mail much slower. Occasionally mail goes astray or is irregular or delayed. But we've never lost anything important. Mail is delivered to your home in cities (where it does no harm to give a few pesos to the mailman occasionally); in villages you either pick it up at the Post Office or rent a box for around $4 a year. When first going to Mexico, you can have your mail sent in care of a travel agent, American consulate or hotel or, if you want General Delivery, have it addressed *Lista de Correos* instead. We do not recommend the use of international parcel post.

Mail rates are often subject to change but at press time, rates in *Mexican centavos*

(12.5¢ Mexican=1¢ U.S.) were as follows: ordinary mail, domestic 40¢, to U.S. 40¢; postcards 20¢; registered letters 50¢; special delivery 50¢; airmail 20 grams domestic or 10 grams to U.S. 80¢ airmail postcards, domestic 50¢, to U.S. 80¢; third class mail per 50 grams 30¢. Airmail to Canada is currently the same as to the U.S. Mail from the U.S. to Mexico goes at the usual domestic rates.

For up-to-date international news, the English language *News* is sold in all cities daily. To find out what's happening in Mexico, however, you'll have to read such excellent Spanish language papers as *El Universal* or *El Excelsior*—both of which also carry a page of English language news. All books and magazines can be received by mail free of duty.

GETTING ABOUT is no problem. Because few Mexicans own cars, buses are far more numerous than in the States. A first class city bus ride costs 4¢ in Mexico City, 3¢ elsewhere. Taxis are available everywhere (well, almost) and rats are about half those we'd pay at home. They're called *libres* and you recognize them by their markings or by the *libre* sign, meaning free, shown on the windshield and flipped back when occupied. To hail one in the street, raise your arm and hiss. They are also found at taxi ranks called *sitios*. In cities, taxis are either metered or they display a published tariff. If you don't see either, ask the price immediately and bargain it down. Bargain for all longer runs. The usual reduction is 30%. Rates are the same regardless of the number of passengers. In Mexico City, you can ride at still less cost by jitney cabs which charge around one peso per seat.

For longer distance travel, there are buses, trains and planes. Splendid first class intercity buses operate all over Mexico with reserved seat accommodation at roughly 1¢-1½¢ a mile. You book your seat in advance at the terminal of the bus company you will travel by. Since distances in Mexico are tremendous, and rest stops not too frequent, most seasoned travelers take along a lunch box as the Mexicans do. Stops are made only at scheduled towns and on a through ticket, no intermediate stopovers are permitted. Thus to reach out of the way places, you may have to ride for short distances on the rather colorful second class buses.

Paralleling bus services from Mexico City to Cuernavaca, Taxco and Acapulco and to the Bajio cities are fast *turismos* or jitnies, charging slightly more than buses. Since baggage space is limited and legroom no more than in the average car, we frankly prefer the first class buses. For a complete guide to Mexican bus and turismo services, pick up a copy of *Guia de Transportes Aereos y Autotransportes de Mexico,* on hand in most hotels and travel agencies or available for about $1 by mail from Apartado Postal 8929, Mexico 1, D.F.

Other than on the run from Laredo to Mexico City, Mexico's railway equipment is slightly inferior to that of American roads. Nonetheless, improvements are constantly being made and you certainly won't suffer when you can go first class with Pullman berth for a little over 1¢ a mile. A private compartment costs about $3-$4 extra.

U-Drive cars are for rent in Mexico City, Guadalajara, Monterrey, etc. For a Chevrolet, you'll pay $50 a week plus 9¢ a mile which, shared among 4 people, means a full week of touring for about $30 apiece. For a couple, European rental cars are a better deal. Try Volkswagen Rents, Hamburgo 135 or Alex, Havre 28, both in Mexico City. Too, chauffeurs are inexpensive.

Mexico's air services enjoy a splendid reputation. Some airports are superior to ours. Inter-city services are frequent, fares lower than in the U.S. Besides the widely advertised inter-city flights, servies by smaller planes link almost every point in Mexico. In fact, you can point to any spot on the may and chances are you can reach it very inexpensively by small charter planes flown by veteran bush pilots.

If you visit Mexico without your car, you'll have no trouble duplicating our retirement tour (described later) by Mexicos excellent public transportation.

PARTIES ARE POPULAR in all retirement colonies. Take one we recently attended in Ajijic. Twenty guests were invited and during the evening, 40 others drifted in and out. A three piece mariachi band played for dancing. Other guests sat here and there in earnest discussion. For serious conversation is still valued here. Drinks were on a serve yourself basis from a table groaning with bottles of everything but whisky and a small bathtub full of punch. Later, barbecued

goat kid was served before a blazing fire of piñon logs. For an hour, jazz fields took over the *mariachis'* instruments. Then an American girl gave a magnificent repertoire of Elizabethan ballads. Few guests left before 2 A.M. At home, such an event could not be staged for under $150. But with Mexico's low cost liquor, food and servants, the host's expense hardly exceeded $30.

Regardless of income, every expatriate can enjoy the evening cocktail hour and other entertainments are within reach of every purse. Movie seats run from 16¢-32¢, drive-ins 80¢ a carload; ringside seats at the frequent boxing and wrestling matches are 60¢-80¢; and a good seat at a play, concert, ballet or opera performance can be had for 96¢. We've spent an evening in a first class night club for under $2 apiece. For the more active, there are sports clubs charging around $4 for membership and levying monthly dues

Barber-Beauty-Cosmetics

afeitada	a shave
afeite, cosméticos	make up, cosmetics
barniz (or esmalte)	
para unas	nail polish
bigote	moustache
borla	powder puff
crema de limpair	cold cream
crema de rasurar	shaving cream
crema para la cara	face cream
colorete	rouge
corto de pelo	haircut
corto	short haircut
regular	regular haircut
ganchito	hairpin
gargarizmo, antiséptico para la boca	mouthwash
hoja de rasurar	razor blade
imperdible	safety pin
lapiz de cejas	eyebrow pencil
lapiz labiac	lipstick
lima para las unas	nail file
loción de resurar	shaving lotion
loción para los manos	hand lotion
pasador	bobby pin
pasta para los dientes	toothpaste
peluqueria	barber shop
permanente	permanent wave
rastrillo, razura	razor
redicilla	hair net
rimel	mascara
rubia	blonde
salón de belleza	beauty shop
triguena	brunette

of $1.60 per family. And at the top of the scale are swank country clubs with swimming pools, golf courses, tennis and social life at which annual dues run about $240 per family or $12 per person by the month. Then you'll find the more familiar Lions, Rotary and other service organizations all of which welcome American members. Homier still are the American Legion groups, active in the largest cities, and American Societies—patriotic, charitable and social organizations through which, for a few dollars a year, you can quickly get to meet all the most desirable American families as well as many educated Mexicans.

Spanish speaking Catholics can attend church anywhere in Mexico and even Protestants enjoy the more colorful cathedral ceremonies. Otherwise, you'll want to know that only in the largest cities and retirement colonies are you likely to find special English language services. These include both Catholic and Protestant. Most Protestant churches give non-denominational services open to all Protestants and their ministers are often missionaries. Members of other religious groups such as the Mormon, Jewish and Christian Science faiths are likely to find services only in the three largest cities.

If you enjoy classical, jazz and Mexican folk music, you'll find your radio a rich source of entertainment. Until you learn fluent Spanish, the commercials will pass by unnoticed. With an antenna, almost any set will bring in American stations after dark and with a short wave set, you can bring in good music from all over the world.

In short, there is no lack of entertainment. Due to lower costs, most retirees enjoy a far higher level of social life than they could do at home. Loneliness is next to impossible. Outside cities and away from beaten tourist tracks, when two Americans meet in Mexico they stop and speak. To make dozens of new friends quickly, head for one of the smaller retirement spots like San Miguel Allende, Chapala or Ajijic. We utterly defy anyone to be lonely in these.

All these places boast a *public* social life in which any likeable American is welcome. By this, we mean that people entertain as much *outside* their homes as they do inside them. Immediately you're recognized as something other than a tourist, you'll quickly find yourself in the swim. (This cannot be done in four days; it can be done in 14.

Hence you simply cannot get to know any town in a mere few days and any judgments based on such short acquaintance are invariably incorrect.) Readilgy found friendship is one of Mexico's intangible attractions which critics are all too prone to overlook. Worth noting, however, is that as you move up to larger, more fashionable and expensive retirement spots so does acquaintance become less easy, public life becomes more private, and snobbery and military protocol increase. (Example: in villages retired American sergeants and generals hobnob together, in fashionable resorts they sit at separate tables.)

American colonies in Mexico range from that of the huge group of American business families in Mexico City to groups of half a dozen couples at tiny, virtually undiscovered village resorts. Today, almost every attractive Mexican town or village has its small American colony. What creates this phenomenon? Undoubtedly, colonies grew out of the newness and strangeness of Mexico. Americans found themselves thrown together by the social, cultural and language barriers they encountered. As we've just said, the smaller colonies are an admirable solution to the loneliness often experienced by retirees in American towns. Within them, you are insulated from the foreignness of Mexico. In fact, life in the largest colony is like living in the States with a Mexican backdrop. You can open a dollar bank account, find an American style home through an American real estate agent, enjoy English language radio and TV programs and read an English language newspaper, deal with an American stockbroker who has a direct line to New York, send your children to an American high school or U.S. accredited college, shop at Sears and Woolworths, join all-American bridge and garden clubs and be asked to contribute to the Junior League Community Chest. Furthermore, life in the Mexico City colony can cost as much as, and sometimes more than, if you lived in the States.

With social life led by the Embassy and composed of well paid business and executive couples, the average retiree finds himself unable to keep up with the Mexico City colony. Some couples who live outside Mexico City do join in the colony's downtown clubs and social life. Some even manage to meet the very aloof old timers. Frankly, however, we find the Mexico City colony too much like

Lineal Measurement and Distance

2.54 Centimeters	1 inch
30.5 centimeters	1 foot
100 centimeters	1 meter
1 meter	3.2 feet
1,000 meters	1 kilometer
1 kilometer	.62 miles
1.6 kilometers	1 mile
3.2 kilometers	2 miles
4.8 kilometers	3 miles
6.4 kilometers	4 miles
8 kilometers	5 miles
50 kilometers	31 miles
100 kilometers	62 miles

Thus 100 kilometers an hour equals 62 mph

---

home and too expensive. With all due respect to the American Legion, Lions, Rotarians and Shriners—all of which have sizeable Mexican memberships—we feel much more at home in the international flavor of such organizations as Cosmopolitan International or the International Club.

In other colonies, the closer you get to the heart of Mexico itself, the cheaper and often more enjoyable life becomes. Mexicans are invited to the colony's social activities. And those Americans who attain fluent Spanish become progressively integrated with the Mexican population and live, as you might say, on the fringe of the colony. The most self-sufficient sometimes leave the colony and set up housekeeping in an all-Mexican village. Invariably, they are soon joined by others seeking unspoiled charm and lower costs. And a new American colony is formed.

Following the pattern of Gresham's Law of Resorts, so called by Cleveland Amory who concluded that resorts were first discovered by artists followed in their turn by good millionaires, then by bad millionaires, Mexico's new retirement colonies were mostly discovered by artists or pioneering Europeans. Following them come several people of character who often find themselves able to live like millionaires. Then come those who would like to live like millionaires but who arrive too late to snap up the bargains. Often quite bohemian in its early days, the colony gradually assumes more mature overtones. Old adobe houses are turned into charming villas. Delicatessens appear. Prices slowly rise. The artists leave. The villagers become more prosperous. And eventually life resembles that of a small Florida retirement town with a Mexican background.

Since few Americans care to pioneer, established colonies are, for most, the ideal place. But you *must* choose the one that is right for you. Within Mexico, you can find every shade of climate from tropical to alpine, from rain forest to rainless desert and a variety of environments from cities offering bonanzas to sports lovers, to those rich in art and culture where sportsmen are bored or art colonies where you can be a sinner or a saint (or a remittance man, oddbody, alcoholic or divorcee seeking fun) and nobody cares. Time after time, we met do-nothing types in San Miguel Allende who should have been in Chapala; and in Chapala industrious, creative folk who should have been in San Miguel.

To select the place which comes closest to perfection for you, make a list of all the requirements you desire and match them with the data given in Part II for Mexico's most popular retirement towns and resorts. A couple from Florida, for example, wanted: 1. a climate like Florida's but with warmer winters; 2. good sports fishing and clear water for skindiving; 3. beaches for shelling and driftwood collecting; 4. good reasonably priced air connections to Florida. They found all four in Cozumel Island off the cost of Yucatan. We also very strongly recommend your taking the tour of retirement towns described later. Most couples planning to retire in Florida tour the entire state first and actually look over more potential retirement spots than exist in all of Mexico. But in Mexico, they simply head for a single retirement spot they've heard about and totally ignore others which might be far more suitable. Our advice: look them all over first before deciding which is your own personal paradise.

THE PERILS OF PARADISE. Nowhere on earth will you find absolute perfection. California has its earthquakes, smog and taxes; Florida its bugs, hot summers and humidity. Mexico, too, has its drawbacks—we've already mentioned a few of the more minor ones. We shall not bother to go into an analysis of the pros and cons of retiring in a distant town or state, for this applies as much to moving to a new part of the U.S. as to moving to Mexico. (For a complete review of this subject, read *Where to Retire on a Small Income*, $1.50 postpaid from Harian Publications, Greenlawn, New York.)

86

But before you become starry eyed about getting away from it all in Mexico, consider what you are getting away to. There's usually a price to pay for everything. Among drawbacks that we personally class as minor ones are dust storms, noise and insects. To you, however, these might be strong objections.

In most desert regions, dust storms occur in spring. If you come from Dust Bowl regions or New Mexico you'll find them less bothersome than in the U.S. Yet they do exist. Flies buzz around the dirtier public markets and some get in your house. They are worst in the rainy season. Occasional scorpions, large spiders, centipedes and roaches ride in on loads of firewood. Mosquitoes and sandflies are not unknown and *jejenes* are sometimes a nuisance on the coast. As a resident of Florida, though, we find insects less troublesome in Mexico. Nevertheless, for you, they might be worse.

Noise seems inseparable from the Mexican scene. A typical fiesta day in a village opens with a battery of fireworks at 5 A.M. followed by the usual crowing roosters and at dawn, band parades through the streets. Tolling church bells add their crescendo at regular intervals. In the distance are blaring radios, occasional sound trucks in the streets and loudspeakers in the plaza. From time to time, trucks and buses roar through the streets. And the quiet of the nights is punctuated first by the roars of an outdoor movie, then by the barking of dogs and at intervals through the night, by the almost human cries of burros. This is about the worst compound of noise you can expect. In modern subdivisions and in the better residential sections of larger towns, comparative quiet can be found.

What might be described as Mexico's biggest drawback are the precautions you must take to safeguard your health. Before coming down for permanent residence (not a vacation) we most strongly urge you to be vaccinated and to take shots for typhoid and paratyphoid A and B, tetanus and cholera. These shots can be taken on arrival in Mexico at less cost than in the U.S. Henceforth, you can then forget about these tropical diseases. For jaunts into torrid, tropical regions a malaria prophylactic such as Aralen will keep you immune. Typhus, we might add, is rare in Mexico as are many of the virus allergies and infections so common in the States.

Useful Travel Terms

aduana	customs
aeropuerto	airport
avenida	avenue
baul	trunk
billete	ticket
bordos, topes, tumulos	built-in bumps to slow traffic
botones	bell boy
calle	street
calzada	boulevard
camarera	chambermaid
camino	road
camión	bus
cantina	bar
carretera	highway
cerrado	closed
cuarto sencillo	single room
cuarto para dos personas	double room
demora	delay
desvio	detour
entrada	entrance
equipaje	baggage
estación	station
ferrocarril	railway
funcionario	an official
gerente	manager
guia	guide
horario	time table
ida	one way
ida y vuelta	round trip
limpiabotas	shoeshine boy
maleta	suitcase
mesero	waiter
migración	immigration
mozo	porter
no hay paso	dead end
propina	tip
salida	way out
sanidad	health inspection
se prohibe fumar	no smoking
tren	train

A toilet may be called bano, doblevesé, escusado, gabinette, lavabo, lavatorio, modoro, retrete, sanitorio or servicio. Ladies' rooms bear the sign Damas, Majeres or Senoras; men's rooms Caballeros, Hombres or Senores.

These simple precautions will guard you against all health hazards but digestive disorders. Dysentery is not nearly so prevalent as most people imagine. Nine-tenths of the so-called dysentery incurred by tourists is due to overindulgence in rich food and drink, too much tropical fruit (many are mildly l̤a͟ e), over extertion at high altitudes and to drink laxative mineral water or to new minerals contained in drinking water. Mexicans, by the way, experience similar effects when visiting the States.

But let's face the facts. Both the common and relatively harmless bacillic dysentery and the more rare but serious amoebic dysentery can be contracted from drinking impure water. Brucellosis or undulant fever can be contracted from unpasteurized milk and dairy products. Other types of intestinal blitz can come from eating uncooked vegetables or raw fruits which are not peeled. And through poor refrigeration or lack of it, you *can* incur a mild case of food poisoning.

In practice, among residents who know the score, these ailments are relatively rare. A simple set of rules safeguards most seasoned expatriates from all but an occasional mild bout of bacillic dysentery. In any event, modern medicines will squelch dysentery in a few hours. Recommended are Donnagel or Diodoquins (available through prescription in the States at about $1.50 per six ounce bottle) and Neotracina, Sulfasuxidina, Cremomycin or Sulfatracina—all available over the counter in Mexican pharmacies. Blackberry brandy is also very helpful. Should you get a touch of entero-colitis, a combination of Jarabe Hillem and Cetamicil will soon have you right. And if you accidentally contract mild food poisoning—symptoms are like dysentery but accompanied by fever —Kaopectate is a swift working remedy.

To avoid these annoyances, Americans drink only purified water (delivered to your door in 5-gallon jugs called *garrafones* at 12¢-16¢). They train their maids to soak all unpeelable fruits and vegetables to be eaten raw—celery, lettuce, strawberries etc.— in a solution of hydro-chlorazone pills for at least 30 minutes prior to eating. They make sure maids boil all other vegetables for a full 30 minutes. And they train their maids to wash their hands after visiting the toilet and to add a chlorine solution to the washing up water.

Once set up, these precautions are really no drawback at all. But you cannot afford to lower your guard, even for a single meal. Use only pasteurized milk and dairy products (produced at modern dairy plants). Do not eat pork which has not been inspected for trichinosis. Outside your home, eat only in clean looking, obviously well run restaurants. These are not necessarily the most expensive.

If you have any doubts, drop an iodine or hydro-chlorazone pill in your waterglass and let it stand before drinking. Wipe the top of all beverage bottles carefully before drinking from them Drinking water is pure in Monterrey and claimed pure in Mexico City. Elsewhere, never drink tap water; don't even use it for brushing your teeth. Use the bottled water supplied in flasks instead. Ice, of course, can be just as impure as water. Take it only in homes or in first class bars and restaurants.

When traveling, stick to hot meals of well cooked foods. Soups and coffee are safe, especially with fresh canned cream. But outside first class restaurants, avoid raw salads, potato, cream and egg salads, all cream, custards and dairy products, and cold fish and meats. Eat only hard, well cured cheeses. Forced to eat sometimes in primitive Indian villages, we invariably take only hot, fresh tortillas, eggs and thick skinned fruits which we peel ourselves. We have yet to suffer the slightest reaction. Bottled beverages are sold everywhere and most appear to be safe.

Follow these simple rules and you can live as healthfully in Mexico as in the United States. Once acquired, these habits become second nature. Few expatriates consider them drawbacks. From this viewpoint, therefore, Mexico does *not* present any serious health hazard. There is, of course, no substitute for sensible precautions such as having your nursemaid given a chest X-ray, serology and a check up for intestinal parasites. But there is certainly no reason to be fearful about your health in Mexico. For further reading, we suggest pamphlet FS 2.2:T69/5/961 *Health Information for Travel in Mexico* available for 5¢ from the Superintendent of Documents, Washington 25, D.C.

DRIVING IN MEXICO is the supreme motoring experience on the North American continent. Highways are good, traffic light, there are plenty of hotels, motels and restaurants in all price brackets, gas stations and repair shops exist in all cities and the scenery is truly magnificent. To enjoy it best, however, there are a few things you should know.

Make sure your car is in top condition, especially the brakes, battery and cooling system. Carry an efficient jack and tools, spare fan belt, condenser, points and fuses. Repair shops, called *talleres mecanicos* are numerous but often short on spares for newer cars. Mexico's standard 32½-foot wide highways (the newest are wider) are well paved but with an abrasive surface hard on tires. Older highways are sometimes bumpy with, occasionally, small chug holes and broken shoulders. Thus you'll find six-ply tires or puncture proof premium types best (at that, we drove thousands of miles researching this book on 4-ply tires with tubes). Personally, we always have our car reverse flushed before entering Mexico. For overheating is easily caused at high desert altitudes. (Tip. brush the butterflies off your radiator each day.) Truck drivers will cheerfully help if you get stuck and though they may ask no reward, a tip of 10-15 pesos is customary.

Drive carefully and don't drive at night. There are animals, pedestrians and bicyclists on the highways. Around the corner may be a walking funeral procession, playing children, a washout, a stalled truck or a line of rocks across the road to mark a detour. Always give right of way to commercial vehicles at narrow bridges or to a passenger car if the driver flashes his lights first. Road signs are in Spanish but the same shape as at home; hand signals may mean anything. In cities, watch for numerous one way streets marked by green *Transito* arrows. At intersections, red arrows marked *Preferencia* must be treated as stop signs. Khaki-clad traffic policemen direct traffic at the busiest intersections: stop when the policeman's front or back is towards you; go when he turns sideways. The maximum highway speed is 60 m.p.h., in towns and villages from 18-25 m.p.h.

Highways are not so well marked as ours. If in doubt, simply say to someone the name of the *next* town on your route. If you're headed for it, he will say *si*, if not *no*. Routes through cities are often puzzling. Best bet is to hire one of the small boys who hang around gas stations to guide you out of town. One peso plus 50 centavos for his bus fare back is adequate. Avoid like the plague those unauthorized guides or touts who station themselves on the outskirts of cities and offer to drive you through or to a hotel which they represent. Use of the horn is forbidden in Mexican cities. At traffic signals, simultaneous red and green lights indicate "turn left only."

Fill your gas tank at every opportunity. Stations close early, are far apart and sometimes sold out (a house coiled round a pump means "out of gas"). Two kinds of gas are sold: the 90-octane Gasolmex from green and

Parts of your Car

acumulador, bateria	battery
anillos de los pistones	piston rings
arranque automático	self starter
automovil, coche, maquina	car
bocina	horn
bujia	spark plug
cajuela	trunk
camara	inner tube
carburador	carburetor
cilindro	cylinder
correa de ventilador	fan belt
diferencial	differential
distribuidor	distributor
eje de las ruedas	axle
embrague	clutch
engranaje	gear
faro	light
filtro	filter
freno	brake
generador	generator
guardafango	bumper
limpiador de parabrisas	windshield wiper
llanta	tire
mechanismo de la dirección	steering gear
parabrisas	windshield
pistones	piston
radiador	radiator
tueda	wheel
tubo de escape	exhaust pipe
las velocidades	transmission

white pumps corresponds to our high test and costs 30¢-33¢ per gallon; the 82-octane Supermexolina from red and white pumps corresponds to our regular and costs 24¢-27¢ a gallon. Oil is available in all SAE numbers. You can choose from Mexolub, a good inexpensive Mexican oil; the better Pemex Sol, Pemex Sol Dorado or Pemex Sol Special, all sold at gas stations; or canned American brands sold by private oil dispensaries. Prices run from 30¢-60¢ a quart, possibly more for premium American brands. Glance at the pump to make sure it reads zero before your gas is pumped and tip the boy who cleans your windshield and inflates your tires from forty to sixty centavos. A car wash costs 24¢, a grease job 64¢. It's advisable to watch an oil change to ensure that your old oil is not put back. Sanborns border insurance stations issue current reports on crooked gas stations and other minor rackets.

Parking meters have yet to appear in Mexico. Instead you will find parking areas guarded by uniformed *cuidadores.* Tip them about what you'd put in a parking meter with a one peso minimum. Always keep your car locked *especially the hood* and never leave valuables visible inside. Don't leave your car on city streets at night. Inexpensive garages exist everywhere.

If you're going to be in Mexico more than a month, cancel your American insurance policy the moment you cross the border. Few if any American policies cover you in Mexico. To be covered you will need a Mexican policy. All companies charge the same rates but some give better service. The best companies include Anglo-Mexicana, La Azteca, Tepeyac, La Commercial, La Provincial and America General. To save time at the border you can buy your policy by mail from Allen Lloyd, Aptdo 1470, Guadalajara, Jal., Mexico. Or you can buy it at the border. From our experience we can highly recommend Sanborns insurance agencies which exist on the American side at most border towns and which supply clients with many valuable free services as well as road logs, stickers and up-to-the-minute highway information sometimes superior to that obtainable from the AAA.

Individual policies vary slightly from company to company but all offer two principal types: 1. the more costly short term tourist policies which, for a minimum of $7.50, insure you on a daily basis which can be as low as 32¢ a day; and 2. the far more economical resident policies available for a minimum period of 90 days. For example, a 90 day policy costs 28% less than on a daily basis, a 180 day policy 49% less and an annual policy 70% less. Worth knowing is that annual policies may be taken out for any period over 90 days and the unused balance in excess of 90 days can be refunded. Thus you can insure yourself for shorter periods at the low annual rate.

Don't overinsure yourself. For liability 50,000-100,000 pesos is entirely adequate in Mexico and 60,000 pesos is ample for property damage. We also recommend partial deductible collision insurance rather than full coverage (which is usually available only on policies running over 35 days). The most economical deductible rate is that based on 2% of your car's valuation. For example, if your car is worth 20,000 pesos, the deductible amount is 400 pesos or $32. As

Useful Driving Terms

aceite	oil
aditivo	valve additive
averia	breakdown
engrasar	to grease
estacionamiento	parking space
gato	jack
grua	wrecking truck
libra	pound (tire pressures)
llanta baja	flat tire
luz de trafico	traffic light
manometro de aire	tire gauge
multa	a fine
pensión de coches	overnight garage
pinchazo, punzada	puncture

proof of the adequacy of such coverage, damages of $4,000-$8,000 are the legal limit which a Mexican court may award. In a wreck in which we ere involved as passenger in a friend's uninsured car, our friend wrecked the entire front end of a truck and destroyed its cargo of flowers, knocked the corner off a house, slightly injured a pedestrian; he was fined for driving the wrong way up a one way street and had to pay a lawyer to straighten it all out. For all this havoc, the total bill (back in 1956) came to $97 for everything. (Don't consider this as a recommendation to drive without insurance. For uninsured drivers all accidents are treated as criminal cases, involve time consuming legal complications and if anyone is really hurt, you go straight to jail. Whereas if you are insured, your local agent will quickly straighten matters out, settle claims and have your swiftly on your way.)

When buying insurance, note such points as that theft insurance covers only theft of the car not accessories and that most companies allow 400 pesos for towing charges and give a 10% discount for annual policy renewals if no claims were made in the previous year. Trailers must be insured with your car and add about 50% more. By and large, a new car costs about $100 annually to insure. We pay only $50 a year for an older car—less than we pay in the States.

Which leads to yet another economy. Nobody bats an eyelid if you drive a ten year old car in Mexico. You won't be looked down on if you drive an older model. Because labor is cheap, repair costs are low. And since most Mexican cars are also old, mechanics actually have a better stock of spares for older cars. Insurance rates on older cars are lower, too. Thus by keeping your present car for Mexico, you can save several thousand dollars in a decade.

Typical costs for 12,000 miles of annual driving run about $375 for average weight cars, $300 for lighter ones and this includes insurance and maintenance but *not* major repairs. In larger towns, you'll find well equipped agencies for all American and most European makes. And there are excellent Mexican tires such as Goodyear Oxo, Goodrich, Euzkadi and General Popo plus, if you prefer them, cheaper recaps.

First introduced in 1960, Mexico's "friendly favor fleet" of green and orange Tourist Patrol trucks cruises every important highway four times a day. Each is equipped with a radio, a mechanic and English speaking driver and their aim is to help motorists free of charge. Whatever your trouble, they'll fix it or they can supply you with spares, gas or water at cost.

More about driving: for cars like the Mercedes Benz that operate on diesel fuel, you can count on finding good diesel fuel throughout Mexico at just 10¢ a gallon. Now a caution: always check the denomination of your bill when paying for gas. If you give a 50 peso bill for 20 pesos worth of gas, the occasional crooked attendant will swear you gave him only a ten peso bill and will ask for ten pesos more. It pays, also, to check your own oil dipstick, to examine oil cans to make sure it has all been poured into your car, and to count your change carefully. Finally, veteran Mexican motorists always advise carrying *two fully mounted spare tires.*

A RETIREMENT TOUR OF MEXICO. As we've said before, this book is not a travel guide. And since for touring you *do* need a travel guide, we recommend as the best and most completed available *Mexico and Guatemala by Car,* also by this author and available for $1.50 postpaid from Harian Publications, Greenlawn, New York. Assuming you'll be armed with this book, we shall not go further into the ramifications of touring. Suffice it to say you'll find costs along the tourist highways a little higher than those in spas and retirement spots. Along the road, expect to pay $3-$7 double for overnight accommodation and around $9 daily for meals for two. Try to fit your eating hours into Mexican schedules: breakfast 8-10, lunch 2-4, and dinner 8:30-10:30. Most tourist eateries do,

however, provide meals at familiar American hours. There's no need to patronize deluxe hotels. Oftentimes, a less expensive, well run place is as well located as a more expensive one. Spring and fall are the best seasons to tour, Easter Week most crowded. Advance reservations are advised in Mexico City, Monterrey, Cuernavaca, Taxco and Acapulco if you go there. Too, you won't find tourist guides much help for retirement. The rest of the information you need you'll find in *Mexico and Guatemala by Car* along with a complete run down of all recommended overnight accommodations, restaurants, routes and sightseeing.

The tour outlined below is a circular itinerary and you can pick it up at any point, follow it complete around and return to the border by the same or by another route. Depending on where you cross the border, the point at which you join the tour will be from 761 to 1,084 miles south. En route, you have a choice of four approach highways and while traveling along them, you should stop to look over these potential retirement towns. The approach routes are: 1. Highway #85, a scenic mountain route from Laredo or Brownsville to Mexico City where you pick up the tour— look over Zimapan, a village with a good retirement hotel. 2. Highway #57, a fast level route from Laredo or Eagle Pass to San Miguel de Allende where you pick up the tour—look over Saltillo and San Luis Potosi. 3. Highway #45 from El Paso to Guanajuato where you pick up the tour— look over Durango, Zacatecas and Aguascalientes. 4. Highway #15 from Nogales along the Pacific Coast to Guadalajara where you pick up the tour—look over Alamos and Tepic.

Starting from Guadalajara, your retirement tour then goes like this (spas mentioned in brackets make excellent overnight or rest stops; the most attractive retirement towns are in italics); from *Guadalajara* to *Chapala, Ajijic, Jocotepec,* Jiquilpan, *Uruapan.* Patzcuaro, *Morelia* (San Jose Purua spa), *Valle de Bravo,* (Ixtapan de La Sal spa), *Taxco, Cuernavaca* with side trips to *Cuautla,* and *Tepoztlan,* Mexico City, *Tequisquiapan, Queretaro,* Celaya, *San Miguel de Allende, Guanajuato* (Comanjilla spa) thence via Abosolo spa back to Guadalajara. This tour can be comfortably accomplished in 21 days allowing you ample time to look over each of the more important retirement spots.

With more time, we advise adding this extension from and back to Mexico City. Leave Mexico City for Puebla, *Oaxaca,* and *San Cristobal Las Casas* in Chiapas. Backtrack to Juchitan and continue of *Vera Cruz.* From Vera Cruz you can return to Mexico City either through a) *Jalapa,* or b) by way of Cordoba, *Orizaba,* (Tehuacan spa) and Puebla. This tour would add a further nine days, making a month for the entire itinerary.

SUCCESSFUL RETIREMENT in Mexico means capitalizing on what Mexico *already has,* not trying to turn it into another United States. As one *simpatico* retiree states: "When I see Mexican *filete* selling at 50¢ a pound, I have *filete* for dinner; I don't buy imported American turkey at $2 a pound. If people want everything just as it is at home, why don't they stay there?" Anyone who erroneously attempts to import an American style of pushbutton luxury to Mexico is going to pay through the nose.

To live inexpensively in Mexico means making the best of what *Mexico* offers. It means living in a Mexican designed home built of Mexican materials, furnishing in Mexican furniture and Indian art works, and living on Mexican foods and Mexican liquors. What matter if your kitchen *does* look like an American kitchen of the 1920s? *You* are not expected to work in it. Nor need you. The whole idea behind Mexican living is to free yourself *entirely from chores.* Mexican living leaves housewives completely free of household tasks. You can enjoy gardening without any of the toil or the everlasting weeding and mowing. Mexico gives you instead *the maximum amount of time to spend in living.* The result is a way of life which combines the more desirable 20th century conveniences with the prestige and leisure of a Spanish aristocrat, the luxury of servants and the opportunity to enjoy rich and stimulating activities.

If Mexico still does not sound as if it's for you, *then don't go.* Although we'd like to see you enjoying life across the border, frankly it doesn't make one iota of difference to us. We have no car insurance, no real estate, no hotel rooms to sell. All we sell is the information in this and other books. And if this information can save you from unsatisfactory retirement in Mexico then we shall feel that the work involved was well and truly justified.

Mexican Financial Terms

acción	stock
accionista	stockholder
agencia	agency
agente	agent
ahorros	savings
banco	bank
bolsa	stock exchange
bolsista	stockbroker
bonos	bonds
caja fuerte	a safe
cambio	money exchange
cheque	check
compania de seguros	insurance company
estampilla	stamp
fecha	date
firma	signature
giro postal	money order
impuesto	tax
interés	interest
inversión	investment
invertir	to invest
oficina	office
oficial	officer
palabra	word
por ciento	per cent
portafolio	briefcase
préstamo	loan
seguro	insurance
seguro contra incendios	fire insurance
seguro de vida	life insurance

Chapter VII

HOW TO HAVE
AN EXECUTIVE'S VACATION
ON A SECRETARY'S BUDGET

Is YOUR WALLET too anemic to pay $20 or more daily at a winter resort hotel in Florida or Arizona? At winter resorts in both states hotel rates soar, apartment rents double and a flat 20% is tacked on to everything else. Despite this, there is no guarantee of warmth.

Yet there's no need to envy friends who go south for winter. You can do far better on much less. During these same winter months, Mexico's beach resorts bask in almost unbroken tropical sunshine. Vera Cruz on the Gulf is farther south than Honolulu and Acapulco on the Pacific is south of Jamaica. There hasn't been a frost on Mexico's lower Pacific Coast in a hundred years and the occasional midwinter northers of the Gulf Coast are far less severe than Florida's. Both coasts have warm winter weather, both have beaches to equal the finest in Florida and rates at both are half those charged for comparable accommodations at American resorts.

It's hard to believe but you can spend a month at a choice of first rate Mexican resort hotels facing palm-fringed tropical beaches for well under $7 a day. Some charge less than $5.50, three whopping meals included daily, of course. With a few exceptions, there are no crowded beaches and there are no parking meters and no bumper-to-bumper driving to reach these resorts. You can choose between gay resorts with night life or you can loaf at quiet get-away-from-it-all spots where you can lie in a hammock while you sip milk spiced with rum from a freshly plucked coconut.

By and large, rates at Mexico's beach resorts are half those charged in Florida during winter. But, remember, luxury hotels still cost money and you'll pay $16 a day for a hotel which in Miami charges $32. So choose a hotel, and a resort, that fits your budget. Then you'll find that you too can afford to spend the winter far from ice and snow in a setting so exotic that even those of your friends who went to the Bahamas or Jamaica will turn green with envy.

But Mexico's climatically ideal resorts don't stop at beaches. If you prefer, you can stay at a winter desert resort at prices half those charged in Arizona. And when your friends head north to find summertime coolness in New England or Canada, you can find a still cooler vacation for much less at Mexico's high altitude resorts.

Whichever you want, here to help you choose is a rundown on Mexico's beaches and on winter and summer resorts inland. You'll find the actual resorts described, together with recommended accommodations, in Par II of this book.

MEXICO'S BARGAIN COAST is the Gulf of Mexico, a semi-discovered crescent of white and brown beaches rimmed by jungles and running from the Texas border to the British Honduras frontier. Virtually undiscovered Edens dot the entire coast, all have an unmistakable Caribbean flavor and even in the smallest, nights are made romantic by *serena-* *tas* and marimba bands. Starting from the Rio Grande in the north, the coast of Tamaulipas consists of wide clean beaches backed by calm lagoons. Some resorts are so remote they can be reached only by local air taxis. Hotels are modest and so are prices. Quite attractive is Lauro Villa Beach at Matamoros just across the border while

Tampico's La Barra and Miramar Beaches are popular all year. To really get away from it all and enjoy a low cost Mexican style vacation you might try such spots as Pikio, Las Gaviotas, Ritz and La Pesca, also El Tordo Beach near Aldama, accessible only by air. However, hotels leave much to be desired.

Moving south, hard packed surf beaches extend for miles along the coast of Vera Cruz. Ideal resorts are: Tuxpan, with 25 miles of white beach; Tecolutla, an idyllic spot with excellent beaches, swimming and shelling; Nautla, undeveloped but with both beach and lagoon bathing; Vera Cruz city, a bright, musical, colonial port with good beaches at Mocambo and Boca del Rio; and Coatzacoalcos which, though boasting fair beaches, suffers from cloudy skies and heavier rain. Cloud and rain also mar the Tabasco Coast. In Campeche state, the island town of Ciudad del Carmen, despite its shrimp boom, is a flavorful escapist spot; and Old World Campeche now boasts a first class resort hotel. Small resorts dot the Yucatan Coast but the beaches are not outstanding. Round the corner in Quintana Roo, however, are two of the most delightful unspoiled island resorts in the Caribbean—Isla Mujeres and Cozumel. Like the inaccessible, resortless coast of mainland Quintana Roo, both have flawless white beaches and transparent aquamarine seas.

THE LUSH, LAVISH Pacific Coast is the nearest thing to paradise this side of Tahiti. Long white beaches, jungles, waterfalls and lagoons line this versatile shore. Surf is practically unknown in the Gulf of California, dangerous undertow is rare and from Mazatlan to Acapulco the coast looks more like the South Pacific than does Tahiti itself. The waters are perfect for swimming and the brilliant pageant of underwater life makes snorkeling irresistible. Unfortunately, many of the most unspoiled and beautiful resorts—often shaded by broad banyan trees—lack acceptable hotels. But from October to May, those which do have good accommodations become a true paradise. Because of the hotter, damper summer weather, rates take a substantial drop from June through September. Even so, many knowledgeable people enjoy vacationing during these bargain months by choosing hotels on hills where the cool sea breeze blows day and night.

Tipping in Mexico

As a general rule, you should tip for all services rendered. Where you would give 50¢ in the United States, give 4 pesos in heavily touristed areas, 3 pesos in less touristed areas and 2 pesos off the beaten track. Otherwise, give 15% on tourist circuits and 10% elsewhere. Here is a suggested tipping scale for a medium priced American Plan resort hotel.

Bartender: 1 peso, when served.

Bellhop and room service: 1-2 pesos per call.

Chambermaid. 2 pesos a day or 16 pesos a week.

Checkroom girl: 2 pesos, when served.

Doorman: 2 pesos if performing a service.

Guide: 10 pesos per full day.

Head waiter: 5 pesos per day or 25 pesos per week.

Lounge waiter: 10%-15% of bill, when presented.

Mariachis: bargain for 1 peso per song per player, or less.

Porters: 1 peso per bag, maximum of 5 pesos.

Waiter: 2 pesos per meal or 10%-15% of bill.

Watchman: 1 peso per hour, maximum of 3 pesos.

Plan to tip hotel staffs at the end of your stay. Or if staying longer than a week, once a week. Most restaurant waiters pool their tips so that you can, upon inquiring if this is done, place your tip with the headwaiter. In all cases, you'll find it cheaper to tip *at the end* rather than by the day, by the drink or by the bag. When staying for a month or more at a nonluxury hotel, you can substantially reduce your tips. At village posadas 4%-5% of your bill is often adequate. Never tip less than 50 centavos. In plush Mexico City or Acapulco hotels you should slightly raise the above scales to conform with 15% tipping practices. If in doubt, always tip! When staying as a guest at a private home, it is preferable to give the maids a small present of candy, clothing or jewelry rather than a cash tip. Always carry plenty of small change, preferably in bright, new one peso coins.

Starting from the California line, Mexico's first two resorts are Rosarita Beach and Ensenada just south of San Diego. Both are enjoyable all year but rather overpriced. Thousands of miles of almost inaccessible white coral sands rim the Baja California peninsula but apart from fishing resorts, the only two good beach resorts are La Paz and San Felipe. On the mainland coast, prices stay rather high until you pass south of Mazatlan. Expensive Guaymas has rosy beaches and lush Mazatlan offers exceptionally attractive white beaches. Tropical San Blas has both surf and lagoon bathing (but 'ware insects). For a real beachcombing vacation, Nayarit has numerous beach resort villages such as Chacala, Los Corchos, Novillero Beach and Miramar, but to date most lack satisfactory hotels.

Forested coves with beaches by the hundred line the magnificent tropical Jalisco coast. Here are such beauty spots as Puerto Vallarta, accessible only by air and dry season jungle bus—Mexico's most charming and picturesque fishing village; Barra de Navidad with its steep, sloping beach on an indescribably beautiful half moon bay; and such beachcomber resorts as Yelapa and Tenacatita which have simple accommodations and Chamela Bay which does not. Moving into tiny Colima, we find the colorful old port of Manzanillo with rocky bays, sandy beaches and good hotels and the completely Mexican beach resort of Cuyutlan, famed for its periodic 60-feet high waves. Farther south, the coast of Michoacan is, if anything, even more strikingly beautiful than Jalisco's. But to date it remains completely undeveloped. Only at Playa Azul is there even primitive accommodation. Crossing the Rio Balsas into Guerrero, we soon come to Zihuatanejo, a true escapist Eden on a dark blue bay with a natural setting superior to that of even Acapulco and at least one good hotel. Idyllic coves and breathtakingly beautiful tropical beaches continue to line the coast down to the big resort of Acapulco, Mexico's Miami Beach. South of Acapulco, the coast continues almost inaccessible to the Guatemala border. Only at Puerto Angel (see under Oaxaca) and at the pleasant beach of La Ventosa near Salina Cruz can the coast be reached by road.

FOR AN INEXPENSIVE winter desert resort we'd suggest Ajijic, Chapala, Cuernavaca, Oaxaca, Tepoztlan, Uruapan, Valles and Victoria among other places. At somewhat higher cost there are also Alamos and Hermosillo. Also offering warm inland winter vacationing much like that of Central Florida are such places as Villa Juarez, Pue., Merida, San Andres Tuxtla, Ver., and Tecate, B.C. Tho escape summer heat after July 1, our choices would be Aguascalentes, Ajijic, Chapala, Cordoba, Cuernavaca, Durango, Ensenada, Guanajuato, Ixtapan, Jalapa, Mexico City, Morelia, Orizaba, Pachuca, Patzcuaro, Puebla, Queretaro, San Jose Purus, San Miguel Allende, San Cristobal Las Casas, Taxco, Tehuacan, Toluca, Uruapan and Valle de Bravo. For a quiet, atmospheric honeymoon we'd suggest—in season and depending on how romanically and authentically Mexican you prefer your setting: Acapulco, Cuautla, Cuernavaca (or Lake Tequesquitengo), Cordoba, Fortin, Guanajuato, Guaymas, Ixtapan, Jalapa, Manzanillo, Mazatlan, Morelia, Patzcuaro, Puerto Vallarta, San Jose Purua, San Miguel Allende, Tecolutla, Tehuacan, Tepoztlan, Uruapan or Vera Cruz.

FOR A QUIET, restful vacation or even semi or permanent retirement, consider toning up at one of Mexico's salubrious spas. Most are located in the republic's central volcanic belt at altitudes of 3,000'-6,500'—the climate range of perpetual springtime—and are ideal all year. Doctors are in attendance at the handful of really large spas and you can choose from tranquil do-nothing inns to resort hotels with round the clock entertainment. In the Bajio country, costs are astonishingly low and here, too, you can spend a winter desert vacation at a spa for much, much less than in Arizona. Several well recommended spa hotels charge only $5-$6 daily with all meals and a choice of several swimming pools. And you could, if you liked, retire in these spa hotels and live better on less than at any American retirement hotel.

Worth knowing is that though the spas still provide valuable therapeutic treatment, these days they are largely patronized by people simply wishing to keep fit. For example, a Turkish bath costs only 40¢ and when not free to hotel guests, a spa bath runs 16¢-40¢ and a massage costs a bit more plus a 40¢ tip. Probably, however, you'll want to choose a spa for some particular ailment (or you may want to retire near a small spa beneficial to an ailment you have). So here is a list of ailments or parts of the body for which various spas claim beneficial treatment.

Bone ailments: Comanjilla, San Jose Purua.

Circulatory ailments: Cointzio, Comanjilla, Cuautla, Ixtapan, La Caldera, Ojo Caliente, Penon, San Jose Purua, Taboada, Taninul, Tehuixtla and Topo Chico.

Diabetes: Cuautla, San Jose Purua, Taninul, Topo Chico.

Digestive ailments: Agua Azul, Cointzio, Cuautla, Lourdes, Ojo Caliente, San Jose Purua, Taboada, Taninul, and Topo Chico.

Heart ailments: Cuautla, San Jose Purua.

Kidney ailments: Comanjilla, La Caldera, Lourdes.

Liver ailments: Cointzio, Lourdes, Penon and Tehuacan.

Nervous ailments: Agua Azul, Comanjilla, Cuautla, Ixtapan, Lourdes, Ojo Caliente, Taboada and Tehuacan.

Rheumatism, arthritis: Agua Azul, Comanjilla, Cuautla, Ixtapan, La Caldera, Ojo Caliente and Taboada.

Skin ailments: Comanjilla, Cuautla, Ojo Caliente, Taboada, Taninul and Tehuixtla.

Sterility: Comanjilla, Ixtapan, La Caldera, Penon and San Jose Purua.

All spas are described in Part II, some under the name of the nearest city. To help you locate them: Agua Azul is near Puebla; Cointzio near Morelia; Comanjilla near Leon; La Caldera (Abasolo) near Irapuato; Lourdes near San Luis Potosi; Ojo Caliente near Aguascalientes; Penon near Mexico City; Taninul near Valles; Taboada near San Miguel Allende; Tehuixtla near Cuernavaca and Topo Chico near Monterrey. There are many others, of course, and they're all described in a free booklet entitled *Mexico's Spas* obtainable from the Pemex Travel Club, Juarez 89, Mexico City.

Mexico also has at least two American style health resorts which specialize in dieting. The first is the big Rancho La Puerta, described under Tecate in Part II (Region 1) of this book. The other is the Rio Caliente S.A. Health Spa, Apartado 1187, Guadalajara. This spa charges $44-$53 per week for an overall health program to correct living habits based on the Lytton-Bernard papaya diet. The Rio Caliente spa is also site of a small housing development of retired American health seekers; newcomers are welcome to join. (Another Natural Hygiene health and retirement resort recently opened at Cuernavaca. Write: Villa Vegetariana, Cerritos 5-A, Cuernavaca.)

For a dude ranch vacation, we'd suggest Rincon del Montero Guest Ranch, Parras, Coah. For $18-$20 a day a couple can occupy a cozy bungalow, enjoy three excellent meals and unlimited riding. Rancho El Morillo, Aptdo 304, Saltillo, Coah., located on a picturesque old hacienda near Saltillo, charges only $6-$8 a day per person with meals and you pay for riding separately. Equestrian enthusiasts should also write to Escuela Ecuestre, Aptdo 185, San Miguel de Allende, Gto., an expensive but top caliber riding academy.

TRAILER LIFE IN MEXICO, unknown a few years ago, is fast becoming popular. But parks still fail to measure up to their United States counterparts and for some years hence we predict you will have to be fairly self-sufficient. Thus our advice is to stick to the main highways. For hauling a trailer into Central Mexico, the fairly level highways #45 and #57 would be our choice though #15 isn't too bad and large trailers *have* been taken up #85. Trailer park rates average $1.50 per night or about $17 a month. Cities with recommendable trailer park accommodations at press time were Acapulco, Aguascalientes, Cuernavaca, Durango, Ensenada, Guadalajara, Guaymas, Hermosillo, Linares, Manzanillo, Matehuala, Mazatlan, Mexico City, Navojoa, Oaxaca, Ciudad Obregon and Tepic.

For more detailed information and practical advice, write Publications Division, Mobile Homes Manufacturers Association, 20 North Wacker Drive, Chicago 6, for their free publication *Mexican Adventure by Travel Trailer.* Campers and trailerites should also buy *Mexico Auto Camper and Trailer Guide* by Cliff Cross, available for $2.95 from Sanborn's Insurance Office, McAllen, Texas. A free booklet *Camping in Mexico* is also available from the Helite Trailer Company, Lodi, Calif.

Undoubtedly, as new parks open, conditions will improve. Meanwhile, you can if you wish, park by the roadside or on beaches. Camping is almost totally undeveloped, though most ranchers will permit you to camp and there are plenty of ideal sites at off-the-beaten-path resorts. (Caution: camping or trailer parking by the roadside is not recommended because of thieves.)

ABOUT HOTELS. Generally speaking, Mexico has two classes of hotels: ultra modern and deluxe hostelries which are relatively expensive; and old fashioned, run down colonial era places which are cheap but unsatisfactory. Because most tourists patronize the best deluxe hotels they seldom discover Mexican atmosphere and return mistakenly convinced that Mexico is no longer a bargain.

What they do not know is that between these two extremes are a comparatively few really outstanding and superior second class hotels which offer comfort, character, charm and good food at second class prices. Finding the names of the best and most expensive hotels is no problem. Any travel guidebook will direct you to these overpriced, underserviced tourist palaces. Instead of taking this easy way out, our purpose in this book is to recommend the *best buys* in Mexico's resort hotels. Not all our recommendations are confined to superior second class hotels. For those with more to spend, we recommend best buys among first class and even deluxe hotels. But the majority of our recommendations are for best buys in superior second class hosterlies. And many of these are ideally suited as retiement hotels. (Incidentally, if you come across any we haven't named, we'd appreciate a postcard telling us about it and directed to Hotel and Restaurant Inspection, Harian Publications, Greenlawn, New York.)

Naturally, a hotel could run down after our inspection but by and large, all the hotels we recommend have purified drinking water, clean restaurants and hot water day and night and all have private showers and toilets. Many also have elevator service and such facilities as barbershops or barber service in your room, valet service, bars, cocktail lounges, swimming pools and English speaking staffs. But remember this is Mexico and your hotel room will be furnished in Mexican style. That means tiled floors with perhaps a rug or two and with far less of the plushy carpets and velvet drapes common in the United States. Beds are generally, but not invariably, comfortable (in small hotels try them beforehand). Tub baths are relatively rare. Plumbing sometimes breaks down and all experienced hotel guests carry a flat type sink stopper to replace washbasin plugs which are frequently missing. Outside deluxe hotels, fans and air conditioning are also rare, though by the same token they are seldom needed. At all high altitudes in winter, make sure your room has heat or a fireplace. Offsetting such minor drawbacks will be the true old fashioned hospitality you will find along with splendid service, multi-course meals and, often enough, historical atmosphere and charm.

In addition, most cities have small modern hotels which in their early years of operation are often good buys. There are also comfortable pensions, many run by Europeans, and private homes where you can board with a middle class Mexican family. All hotel rates are posted behind the door of each room. But this doesn't mean that hotel managers are not susceptible to bargaining. Reservations are advised everywhere during Easter Week, at beach resorts December to February and in July and August, at weekends in cities within 200 miles of the border and always in Mexico City and Cuernavaca. Expect to pay much higher rates for your hotel in Mexico City. There are few bargains to be found in the capital.

It's Cheaper in Mexico

A Missouri couple were planning to spend their two weeks' vacation in California for which they set aside $280. They were also planning other expenditures during the next few months, for which they had been told these were the costs: new glasses $40, a dental bridge $200, a tailored worsted suit $175, car repairs $140, Christmas gifts $40, medical examination and treatment $90, furniture $120 and a dinner service $120. Together with their vacation, their total planned expenses amounted to $1,205.

A friend suggested they vacation in Mexico instead and do their shopping at the same time. Since Guadalajara is roughly the same distance from Missouri as California, they drove there instead. These were the actual prices they paid for their two weeks' stay in Guadalajara and for their other purchases: vacation $175, glasses $15, dental bridge $85, suit $90, car repairs $65, gifts $17, medical costs $35, furniture $55 and dinner service $60—a total $597 or a saving of $698 . . . almost exactly half of what the same items would have cost in the States.

Part II

Directory of Retirement Spots, Spas, Resorts and Sports Centers
The Climate of Mexico

TRAVEL GUIDES designed for transient tourists are fond of calling Mexico the Land of Many Climates. Quite correctly, they point out that altitude determines three grades of temperature—tropical, temperate or cool—that a general season of brief afternoon showers covers most of the country from June through September and that Mexico can be visited in any season. All this is perfectly true and quite adequate for someone moving on from place to place. But since this book is designed for someone staying in *one* place—for a vacation, a sojourn, or perhaps a lifetime— we propose to delve more deeply into the subject of Mexico's climate. In fact, we may become a trifle scientific—an approach we don't think too technical for anyone seeking the perfect climate in which to retire.

Mexico lies between the latitudes of 32.40 and 14 degrees North and is bisected by the Tropic of Cancer. Essentially, it is therefore tropical. As I write this in latitude 20° North, my desk is slightly south of Honolulu, Hongkong, Mecca and Central Cuba. I am well south of such notorious hot spots as Calcutta, Delhi, Suez, Cairo and Washington, D.C. Yet the temperature here at 4 P.M. in late July is a cool 69°. Six months later, in January, the mercury will read a balmy 61°. Though my desk stands well inside the tropics, I omitted to mention that it was also located at an altitude of 5,000 feet. Add together the eternal summer of the tropics and the eternal winter of high mountains and you have that amazing compromise true of most of Mexico—eternal springtime.

A cross section of Mexico looks like an M. On both coasts are low costal plains called *tierra caliente* for their true tropical climate. Back of them rise the high sierras, giving rise to cool alpine regions known as *tierra fria*. Then at lower altitudes between the mountains lies the *mesa central* with such a delightfully temperate climate it is fondly called the *tierra templada*. These gradations of temperature are common to *all* of Mexico wherever the land is high enough to make them true.

The *tierra caliente* or hot country lies between sea level and 3,000' and has a mean annual temperature of 77°-88° rising occasionally in summer to 100° or even 105°. Delightful as a winter resort area from December to February and not uncomfortable from October through May, it is nevertheless rather too hot and humid in summer for optimum comfort. Tropical lightweight clothing is indicated at all seasons plus sunglasses and thick-soled shoes for walking on sun-roasted beaches. A light sweater is useful in midwinter. Above 2,000', ordinary summer weight clothing will suffice in winter.

The *tierra templada* or temperate highlands range between 3,000' and 7,000' with a mean average temperature of 60°-77°. Here, brusque temperature changes are rare, the seasons blend imperceptibly and throughout the year, the climate remains supremely livable.

The *tierra templada* may be further subdivided into the low and high plateau. The low plateau between 3,000' and 4,500' has a yearly average temperature of 77° with warm but comfortable summers (average May temperature, 85° by day).

Particularly where mountains to the north block winter winds, cold spells are rare and winters warm and balmy. At 4,500' the climate is well nigh perfect. The high plateau between 4,500' and 7,000' has a yearly average temperature of 70° with slightly cooler summer (average May temperature, 82° by day). Particularly where mountains do *not* block winter, cold spells stabbing down from Canada sometimes send the mercury plunging into the chilly 40°s and winter nights (and days) can be snappy.

For the low plateau, late spring weight clothing is suitable; for the high plateau, late summer and fall weight. In both sweaters and jackets are welcome evening wear and in midwinter, you'll appreciate a light topcoat.

The *tierra fria* lies above 7,000' and nowhere does the mean annual temperature exceed 62°. For those who do not mind the altitude this country is as livable as San Francisco. The predominance of summer resorts testifies to the comfortable summer climate. Winter days are cool and nights can be really cold—so cold that Indians sleeping outdoors sometimes freeze to death. Here, late spring and fall weight clothing is a necessity at all seasons: wool or gabardine suits, sweaters and tweeds with medium weight topcoats are required throughout the year. Take careful note of the altitude of any city you plan to visit at over 7,000'. It will be much cooler than you think. In winter, plan to stay only at establishments which provide heat or fireplaces and try to reserve a room (or rent a home) with southern exposure.

Thus does altitude govern the temperature throughout Mexico. Controlling the climate over most of the republic are the wet and dry seasons. The September equinox sees the end of the rainy season, leaving the country green, fresh and cool. Ideally, mid-October through mid-November are the months to visit Mexico. After November, the countryside dries out, turning brown and dusty. But flowers still bloom in constant profusion. In mid-winter, jacaranda and poinsettia fleck a countryside flooded with sunshine. Automobiles can venture over remote back roads and buses get through to the most isolated villages. Small harmless whirlwinds accompany the spring equinox and herald the arrival in late February or March of a week or ten days of changeable, often rainy weather. Then it becomes drier and warmer. April and May are the dustiest, hottest months for travel. In mid-June, the clouds pile up and the first refreshing showers arrive. Parched foliage bursts out all over, landscapes turn a vivid green and flame vine pours over walls and gardens. Summer mornings are invariably clear. Later in the day, towering clouds gather overhead and between 4 and 7 P.M., a short, sharp deluge cools the air. Seldom does the rain last longer than an hour. Far from proving inconvenient or depressing, the showers are stimulating, even exhilarating. During these months, Mexico's *tierra fria* resorts are packed with Texas cars. By September, the rains have eased off. A final day or two of rain may accompany a hurricane passing up the coast. Then it's all over and the skies stay clear for the ensuing eight months.

These combinations of altitude and season give to Mexico six distinctly different climates. They are shown on the map in Fig. 4. Within each numbered belt approximately the same *pattern* of climate exists. You find essentially the same climate and vegetation in all three areas marked 4 on the map—in the Yucatan, around Vera Cruz and along the south Pacific Coast. Although temperatures are still determined by altitude, within each numbered region, the pattern of climate and season is almost identical. The remainder of Part II is therefore arranged by these same climatic regions. Resorts and retirement towns are listed under the respective climatic region in which they belong. The same pattern of climate applies to all places within each region. Because no towns of any importance exist in the high alpine climate of the western sierras marked M, this section has been omitted.

ADDING MORE LIFE TO YOUR YEARS. Anyone who has read Huntington's *Mainsprings of Civilization* and similar books is aware that the burden of fighting cold and freezing weather brings an early death to thousands of elderly sufferers from arteriosclerosis, diabetes, chronic nephritis and other ailments that affect us after 50. In the United States, summer heat waves also take their toll of oldsters. Many of their lives could have been prolonged had they been spent in a region of eternally warm sunshine with plenty of fresh air, fresh fruits and freedom from wet feet, heart strain, colds and chills. As authors Jaqueline Berke and Vivian Wilson advise in their excellent book *Watch Out for the Weather:* "take the best that cold weather can give you till you reach middle age and then forsake it for the relaxation you can find farther south."

What is the optimum climate for life after 50? That depends on your temperament and health. For an elderly person in good health, the ideal climate is one where you can spend every day outdoors if you wish, where sunshine is abundant but varied by occasional cloudiness and where weather changes are frequent but moderate. It is also one where the daytime temperature seldom exceeds 85°, night temperatures do not fall below 55° and the relative humidity averages about 55%-60%. *The climate of Central Mexico comes closer to meeting these conditions than any place in the continental United States.*

Storms which worsen and irritate many nervous and digestive complaints are almost non-existent. For most of Mexico, the skies are cloudy half of the time and together with the usual wide desert range of daily temperatures, this provides just the right amount of stimulation free of all extremes. For example, the average hourly temperatures for Guadalajara are: 7 A.M. 57°; 9 A.M. 61°; 11 A.M. 68°; 1 P.M. 73°; 3 P.M. 76°; 5 P.M. 74°; 7 P.M. 72°; and 9 P.M. 67°. And Guadalajara's relative humidity averages exactly 60%.

Extensive research by the Instituto Nacional de Cardiologia in Mexico City has proved that altitude alone will not affect your heart at elevations below 10,000'. However, if you already have a serious heart disorder, a degenerative disease or are extremely nervous, you should consult your physician before deciding to live at over 5,000'. Otherwise, you will rapidly adapt to the altitude. Although at first you may feel tired, breathless and experience minor digestive upsets, within a few days the hemoglobin content of your blood will change, your respiration rate will pick up and you will swiftly find yourself acclimatized. It is, of course, wise not to retard this process by heavy eating or drinking or strenuous exercise. Other hazards? No pollen indeces are available but Mexico has ragweed to some extent everywhere. And mild earthquakes occur occasionally. Major tremors were felt in 1909, 1937 and 1957 but of recent years, damage has been no greater than in California.

Now, point by point, let's review other factors affecting Mexico's overall climate and your health.

Cloudiness: on the *mesa central*, the south is cloudier than the north in summer; in winter, the situation is reversed. The Gulf Coast is cloudier than the *mesa central*. Least cloudy part of Mexico is the northwest desert area of Region 1 where Yuma and Guaymas report the least overcast skies in Mexico. On the Pacific Coast, summer and fall are cloudiest and this cloudiness decreases from south to north.

Fog: dense fogs such as those of the northern U.S. are almost unknown. The fogs referred to in climate statistics throughout Part II are due to radiation. These fogs form in the early hours and usually disappear soon after sunrise. Nevertheless, in our statistics, any day with radiation fog is considered a foggy day. Most of these fogs occur December through February, particularly on the *mesa central* and in valleys opening to the Gulf. Fogs are rarer on the Pacific Coast, especially south of Mazatalan. The northern half of Mexico experiences more radiation fog than the southern half.

Humidity: is highest on the Gulf Coast (85%), lower on the Pacific Coast (78%), and lowest on the *mesa central* (55%). Everywhere, you'll find a great variation during the day, since humidity varies with temperature and is highest during the cool early morning hours and lowest in the warmer late afternoon. On both the Gulf Coast and *mesa central*, the humidity is lowest in March and April and highest in August and September. Everywhere during the rainy season, however, you will encounter occasional calm, rather humid days which on the coasts become sultry and oppressive.

Rainfall: is heaviest on the Gulf Coast and on the eastern slopes of the Sierra Madre Oriental, particularly where the mountains slope up steeply from the coast. Thus rainfall varies from almost nil at the head of the Gulf of California to 156" annually at Teapa in the rain forests of Tabasco on the Gulf of Mexico. Along the eastern half of Mexico, the last rainy regions are those in the dry shadow of the Sierra Madre range. On the *mesa central,* rain decreases from south to north so that the northern border states receive a bare 15"-20" annually and Sonora-Baja California only 6"-12". The cool Pacific Ocean is responsible for the low rainfall throughout the peninsula of Baja California which, in the center, is almost rainless. Along the Pacific Coast, rainfall increases from less than 10" in the upper Gulf of California to a maximum of 54" around Acapulco, then decreases gradually south. Because the waters surrounding the Mexican mainland are warm, rains provide little cooling effect on the coasts.

Seasons: mountainous regions apart, Mexico has no real winter. Elsewhere, summer and winter are much more alike than in the United States. With the exception of northern Baja California, winters are almost entirely rain-free, the atmosphere crystal clear, the purity of air remarkable.

Temperatures: since the sun is overhead in southern Mexico by April, in central Mexico by May, the hottest month for most of the republic is May. There are exceptions: July is hottest in northwest Mexico and in extreme south Mexico. By July, no coastal city except Ensenada is reporting mean temperatures of under 80° and the hottest coastal months are August and September. By contrast, January is the coolest month in central Mexico and February on the Pacific Coast. Daily temperature ranges are least on the coasts, highest in the arid northern deserts. In February at 6,100' in Chihuahua, the daily temperature ranges from 6° to 70° —a difference of 63° in a matter of 8 hours. In high mountain valleys in Region M, freezing temperatures may occur nine months of the year.

Thunderstorms: are most common June to September on the *mesa central* where they occur around 5:30 P.M., often with considerable lightning. Thunderstorms, however, are far fewer in Mexico than in Florida. Unless accompanying northers, they are almost unknown from Novermber through March.

Winds: most of Mexico lies within the belt of warm, easterly trade winds. These winds strike the Gulf Coast bringing heavier rain to the coastal plain and eastern slopes of the Sierra Madre Oriental. During winter, the trades blow almost continually on the Gulf Coast south of the tropic. In summer, they dominate almost the entire Gulf Coast. The high range of the Sierra Madre Oriental blocks their ingress inland, however, and on the Pacific Coast the prevailing winds are northerly or northwest.

Breaking this pattern from November through February are cold, gusty northers whose influence is felt the entire length of the Gulf Coast and to some extent on the plateau. In fact, extratropical cyclones crossing the Rockies bring occasional winter rain to the dry northern desert. There are two types of northers: dry northers which, on the Gulf Coast are usually preceded by a hot, sultry *surada* or southerly wind, bring cold, dry weather with clear skies; and wet northers, which are genuine cold waves, bring cold, moist, windy weather with cloudy skies which may last several days and leave snow on the mountains.

Nonetheless, the usual Gulf Coast conditions are steady, cooling trade winds with light land and sea breezes and thunder squalls May though September. On the Pacific Coast, light land and sea breezes are the rule from January through April with strong but brief *chubasco* squalls May through September. From May through December, gales are not uncommon on the Pacific Coast.

From June to November, both coasts of Mexico are subject to hurricanes, infrequent in any one locality but nonetheless destructive. Pacific Coast hurricanes are generally smaller in area than those of the Gulf. As in Florida, warning is given by radio and, in fact, any outdoorsman can easily predict an approaching hurricane by the long sea swell, falling barometer and brilliant red skies at sunset and sunrise. From most coastal points, anyone with a car can swiftly retreat to safety in the interior.

A daily weather forecast for the entire country is given in English in the Mexico City *News.* We should emphasize also the importance of microclimates when choosing a place to retire. Mexico's irregular topography produces innumerable local variations in climate. Places like Lake Chapala, Taxco and Cuautla—sheltered by mountains to the north—are invariably warmer in winter than other places open to northers. And the temperature on one side of a coastal bay may be 10° hotter than on the other side, depending of course on the prevailing wind.

Apart from these factors, you can multiply the finest day you've ever known by 365 and apply it to any place in any of Mexico's five populated regions. Mexico boasts an unequalled sunshine record and on the plateau, at least, humidity is slight. Brief afternoon showers refresh the countryside from June through October; the rest of the time, the skies are almost cloudless, the atmosphere wine clear and bracing, the climate dry and free of all extremes.

ABOUT PLACES AND HOTELS. This is not a guide to every place in Mexico. Part II is a directory to Mexico's best retirement spots and to resorts, spas and sports centers where you'll enjoy spending your entire vacation or a longer stay. Throughout, emphasis is on your *staying in one place,* not in touring and moving around.

Therefore, the hotels listed as Best Hotel Buys under each place were selected as the best buys for a *longer stay* (say a week or more). Although most also take overnight guests, they are not necessarily recommended as convenient overnight stops. The fact that most *are* best buys is based on their reduced rates for stays of a week or more. Most, but not all, offer a reduction of about 10% for a week's stay, 15% off by the month, 20% off for three months and 25% off by the year. These reductions also vary among individual hotels.

It must be understood that to date no such thing as a full scale retirement hotel exists in Mexico. Our "retirement hotels" simply happen to be ordinary Mexican resort hotels that are also aply suited for retirement. Most offer lower rates and superior food, service and comfort to the so-called retirement hotels of the United States. In some of our listings, we term as "retirement hotels" those hotels most suitable for retirement.

To cater to all tastes, we have attempted to recommend best buys in more than one

Temperature Equivalents

The Centigrade thermometer is used in Mexico and compares with the Fahrenheit scale thus:

C°	F°
37	98.6
35	95
30	86
25	77
20	68
15	59
10	50
5	41
0	32

To convert Fahrenheit temperatures over zero to Centrigrade, subtract 32 from the number of degrees, add 10% and divide by 2. (Example: 68°F—32=36+3.6 or 4 for ease =40÷2=20°C). To convert Centigrade temperatures over freezing to Fahrenheit, multiply by 2, subtract 10%, then add 32. (Example: 15°Cx2=30—10%=—3 =27+32=59°F.).

---

price category. Following the name of each hotel is an abbreviation (i.e. *Hotel Vega,* I. *Casa Reina,* M. *Hotel Regis,* E.). These mean:

I Inexpensive.
M Medium priced.
E Rather expensive.
VE Very expensive.

Because many hotels have a range of room rates, from inexpensive to medium, etc., we frequently use the abbreviation I-M etc. All rates were checked shortly before publication but naturally no guarantee can be made that they will not be raised later and our price indication must therefore be considered as an approximate but not infallible guide.

Region 1. Low Latitude Desert

LYING UNDER the rain shadow of the Sierra Madre Oriental, this is Mexico's true desert—a region characteristic of the Sahara, the Colorado Desert of the U.S., or the great Australian Desert. Desert conditions are less extreme in the east, where the plateau of Chihuahua resembles central Arizona, but in the west, the Sonora Desert and Baja California are extremely arid and dry. In the east, scattered mesquite, greasewood, cactus and yucca dot the plains while alfalfa, cotton and trees thrive on irrigated bottom lands. In the west, some areas are as barren

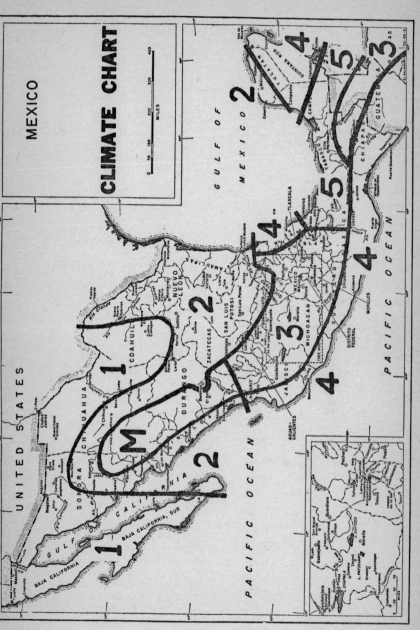

Figure 4. Climate chart of Mexico.

Books on Mexico's Climate

For further reading, we recommend these publications, in addition to complete weather maps:

Climatologia de Mexico, Publication 19 of Instituto Panamericano de Geografia e Historia, Mexico D.F. (1946).

Climate of Mexico, Monthly Weather Review Supplement 33, U.S. Department of Commerce.

Atlas Climatologico de Mexico, Tacuba D.F. (1939).

Catalogo de Publicaciones, Direcction de Geografia y Meterologia, Secretaria de Agricultura y Ganaderia, Avenida Observatorio 192, Tacubaya, D.F., Mexico. Publishes catalog of weather maps and books and also large scale maps of Mexico.

---

as the moon yet under irrigation, the desert produces rich crops of cotton, citrus, dates and winter vegetables.

The seasons: cool, dry, calm weather heralds the fall with frosty mornings common in the eastern mountains; elsewhere, Indian summer weather prevails, ideal for outdoor sports. Winter is surprisingly cool: from November to March frosts are common in the west; the east is still cooler and wide open to northers; freezing temperatures occur in the Chihuahua mountains October through April and sometimes snow lies 12" deep. Occasional winter storms can bring rain, especially in northern Baja California. Spring sees a return of the cool, dry, calm weather of fall; after March, Baja California and Sonora become very warm though frosty mornings still persist in the mountains of Chihuahua. Summers are hot everywhere: Baja California and Sonora experience very hot and dry weather with, from May to September, maximum afternoon temperatures exceeding 100°. Even in the cooler eastern region, 100° afternoon temperatures are not uncommon June through August and in June, heat can be overpowering in Chihuahua's low valleys. Though infrequent in the west, sporadic afternoon thunder showers cool the hottest days (i.e., on 27 days at El Paso, Texas, 13 at Yuma, Arizona, and 7 at Guaymas) and sea breezes ameliorate the heat along the Pacific Coast of Baja California.

A phenomenon of this region is the cooling effect of the Pacific Ocean, which brings a Mediterranean climate to the immediate northern coast of Baja California. For ex-

ample, the climate of Ensenada resembles that of San Diego, California.

As Mexico's sunniest region, the western area boasts an almost incredible record of over 90% of possible sunshine, the eastern area 80% or more. Guaymas, in fact, reports cloudiness only 27% of the time and a bare 32 cloudy days each year. Yuma, in Arizona, has only 14% of cloudiness. And as to days with early morning radiation fog, Hermosillo has none, El Paso and Yuma have one annually, Mexicali 5 and Guaymas, on the coast, 65.

Irregular rainfall is characteristic of this arid region. The eastern area reports some rain on 57 days annually, most as afternoon thunder showers July to September. Southern Baja California also receives some rain in these months. The western area reports a meager 3.4" annually, most falling in August and, in northern Baja California, in December.

Almost throughout Region 1, the mean annual temperature exceeds 64° with a wide range in both annual and daily temperatures. Both land and air heat rapidly in the sun and cool rapidly after dark when th mercury quickly drops to comfortable levels. Hermosillo, for example, reports temperatures as low as 34° in winter, as high as 100° in summer and a growing season of roughly 350 days.

Conclusion: summer, fall and winter are ideal for outdoor sports and other pursuits. For permanent living, the best areas are the northwest seacoast tip of Baja California around Ensenada and for those to whom a dry desert climate appeals, the eastern plateau area. Climate here resembles that of El Paso, Texas, a popular U.S. retirement spot for which the following climatic data applies and which gives you a good idea of the climate in neighboring Mexico, El Paso, Texas, 3,170' Average temperatures: annual 64°, annual maximum 76°, annual minimum 51°, coolest month January 45°, warmest July 82°, highest ever 106°, lowest 2°. Relative humidity 41%. Rainfall 9" annually falling on 50 days, most in July. Mean wind velocity 8 knots. Days per year with light fog 1, dense fog 1, gales 28, thunder 27.

ENSENADA, B.C. Alt. 10', pop 50,000. A bustling, busy, neon-lit boom town resort sandwiched between surrounding hills overlooking turquoise Todos Santos Bay. Out of town on the heights of Chapultepec, the charm of Ensenada is evident in the sweeping panorama of the city, harbor, breakwater, Todos Santos Bay and Islands and the headland of Punta Banda. Despite the myriad ultra-modern hotels, motels and night clubs and the touristy gift shops on Avenida Ruiz, this is undoubtedly a beautiful spot with lots to recommend it. The old rambling Riviera Hotel dominates eight miles of wide sand beach and the harbor is dotted with fishing boats at anchor. Nearby are several picturesque villages and new developments with beaches, boats and resort accommodations. They are: Rosarito Beach overlooking the Coronado Islands; San Miguel village, a shady new development with hillside homes and excellent fishing; and Estero Beach, 7 miles south, with more motels and gift shops. Making this area more attractive is its bland Mediterranean climate, excellent all year. Data: Feb. 56°, May 63°, Aug. 70°, Nov. 61°; annual average temp. 61°, rainfall 13.24". (Other data for San Diego, California, 65 miles north: relative humidity 75%, cloudiness 40%; days with rain 47, light fog 30, dense fog 19, thunder 3.)

Expensive by Mexican standards, the Ensenada area is nonetheless attractive for retirement and is inexpensive in a trailer. A deluxe housing project and country club lood down from the hills and all modern conveniences are available. Bothersome are the ubiquitous red clay mud after rains and some flies and mosquitoes. There are good fishing and hunting and night clubs with floor shows. Within easy drives are the thermal resort of San Carlos, the former Russian colony of Guadalupe and numerous small beach resorts ideal for trailer retirement.

Best Hotel Buys: *Bahia,* VE. Swank, deluxe resort hotel. *Villa Carioca Motel,* M. At north end near sea. *Quinta Papagayo,* M. Quiet oceanside resort. *Villa Marina,* M. Bayfront resort on First Street. South of Ensenada are *Hamilton Ranch,* Santo Domingo; *Meling Ranch* and *Santa Maria Sky Ranch;* all rather expensive and accommodating hunters, fishermen and vacationers.

GUAYMAS, Son. Alt 26', pop 35,000. Only 260 miles south of Arizona and on one of the world's most beautiful mountain girded harbors, lies this popular sailfishing resort and shrimping port. A ridge terminating in Cabo Haro divides the town proper from the resort section on Miramar Beach. Built round the beautiful landlocked harbor, white-walled Moorish style houses cluster along the shore while behind them stand the twin-spired 18th century church of San Fernando and the interesting Palacio Municipal. Superb rosy beaches face the cobalt bay ringed by lush accommodations and harsh desert foothills. Flowers drench this peaceful beauty spot in winter, when Guaymas enjoys its best climate. Data: Feb. 66°, May 78°, Aug. 87°, Nov. 72°; annual average temp. 76°, maximum 85° minimum 68°, highest ever 117°, lowest 46°. Relative humidity 59%, raifall 10", cloudiness 27%. Days with rain 39, cloud 32, strong winds 43, fog 62, thunder 7.3.

Though very American and rather expensive, Guaymas is ideal for a long winter vacation or even for retirement. There are excellent trailer parks. At the big Posada San Carlos layout with its residential club development 14 miles northwest of town, you can lease a beach lot and build a home for $8-15,000; or you can lease a superb beach trailer lot for $440 annually. Guaymas offers good seafood, a good hospital, abundant social life, safe drinking water, excellent gardening and riding, tennis and a gun club.

Best Hotel Buys: *Guaymas Inn,* E. Comfortable modern motel. *Rubi,* M. In town near harbor, fair but pleasant. *Motel Armida,* M-E. On highway, pool, gardens, good food.

HERMISOLLO, Son. Alt. 750' pop 80,000. A building boom is transforming this former colonial town into a very pleasant and prosperous ultra-modern city. Surrounded by date and citrus groves, and clean, smart, well paved and up-to-date, this state capital has been given a new look by the lofty white university and by streets of chic shops and busy factories on the outskirts. Yet numerous trees and flowers, narrow old streets and such beauty spots as Parque Madero still form a quiet background to the frontier flavor of the booming outskirts. Despite the bustling activity, we feel Hermosillo still has much to recommend it for a winter desert vacation. From November to May the climate is pleasantly mild and dry. Data: Jan. 60°, April 73°, July 90°, Oct. 79°; annual average temperature 76°, maximum 100°, minimum 34°; rainfall 12.7".

Costs are not remarkably low but you may be able to rent a house in the attractive Colonia Pitic section or you can stay in a hotel or trailer park for less than on the coast. There are excellent shops, a large, fabulously well stocked fresh food market, a modern hospital and clinic and a country club with golf, bowling, tennis and swimming. For amusements, you'll find movies and a theater, riding, hunting and fishing and numerous local points of interest. About 65 miles west by car is the small beach fishing village of Puerto Kino with excellent but undeveloped ocean fishing and, just off-short, curious Tiburon Island, home of the primitive Seri tribe.

Best Hotel Buys: There are no resort hotels but you could probably make a satisfactory arrangement with such medium priced hotels as the *de Anza, Femar, Laval* or *San Alberto.* We'd also check the *Poseda Mexico* in Colonia Pitic.

LORETO, B.C. Pop 1,500. Once the capital of Baja California, this delightful village slipped into oblivion until an airline began landing there in 1951. Even now it is inaccessible by car and time has all but passed by Loreto. aBcked by cactus covered mountains and surrounded by date groves, the sleepy village clusters round the plaza near the restored Mission of Nuestra Senora de Loreto. Unspoiled and utterly charming, it overlooks the beach and the shimmering Gulf of California. There are a small hospital and several nearby missions. But that's all. In addition to some of the world's finest fishing, you can visit offshore islands where there are sea lions, ride and explore for lost mines, treasure and ruined missions and you can hunt. A wonderful get-away-from-it-all retreat.

Best Hotel Buys: *Flying Sportsmen's Lodge,* M-E. Fine beach cottage resort. *Casa Garayzar,* I. Pleasant guest house.

PUERTO PENASCO, Son. A colorful fishing village and beach resort 66 miles south of Arizona and popular with weekending Arizonians. Fish canneries and warehouses surround the boat-filled harbor and there is good bathing from a wide white beach. Clams and crabs can be taken on the flats and within easy reach are the Kino Missions. A pleasant vacation and fishing spot near the border.

Best Hotel Buys: *Playa Hermosa,* M. Cottages in garden near beach; *Penasco,* I-M.

TECATE, B. C. Alt. 500', pop 6,000. Home of the Tecate Brewery, 32 miles from Tijuana. Nestled in a nearby valley is North Ameri-

ca's largest health resort, a unique vegetarian spa and school of scientific living in the guise of a *rancho.* Recommended if you're overweight and desire stimulating and intellectual activity and helpful personal counseling.

Best Hotel Buys: *Rancho La Puerta,* Tecate, California, I-E. America's largest health spa for rest and weight reducing; health baths, swimming, riding, symposiums, etc.

Region 2. Low Latitude Steppe

IN THIS semi-arid region which curves across northern Mexico from southern Baja California to the Gulf and across to northern Yucatan, evaporation everywhere exceeds precipitation. This is a land of thorny bushes, acacia and short grasses on which sheep, goats and cattle graze. Wheat is raised in damper sections and in the irrigated Lower Rio Grande Valley, citrus and truck crops thrive.

Fall is quite dry, bone dry on the Pacifis Coast. During winter, dry offshore winds keep the Pacific Coast dry and though ideal as far south as Mazatlan, occasional cold spells may be felt. Inland, the plateau in winter resembles the U.S. in fall. On the Gulf Coast from November to February, several northers will bring strong winds, cloudiness, rain and a substantial drop in temperature. Invariably at some period each winter, Tampico reports a low of 30° and a topcoat is appreciated. During spring, a week of equinoctial rains in late February or March may break the uniform dryness of the Pacific Coast, which, towards the end of spring, is accompanied by heat. Northers definitely cease in the plateau and Gulf after April and fine weather is guaranteed. Summer brings tropical conditions to most of Region 2 with maximum temperatures of 100° almost universal June through August. Heat, rain and humidity attain their peak on the Pacific Coast July through September when extremes of 104° are not uncommon. Inland, May through July sees temperatures as high as 94° after which the rains, which fall from June 2 to October 1, bring soothing relief. Hot, dry, calm periods are characteristic of the Gulf Coast until the rains begin with heavy downpours in June.

Bright skies are a feature of Region 2. On the Gulf and plateau skies are clear 50% of the time (most Gulf cloudiness is confined to winter) and on the Pacific Coast

60% (ranging down to 35% at Culiacan). Days with fog vary from 20 on the Gulf to 100 on the Gulf coastal plain, 32 on the plateau and 9 on the Pacific (118 at Culiacan). Relative humidity ranges from 70% on the Gulf to 65% farther inland, 49% on the plateau and on the Pacific Coast from 55% in the north to 75% in the south.

Rainfall varies widely from year to year and most rains are brief. Heaviest rains occur on both coasts July through August. Average rainfall for the Gulf Coast is 40" falling to 23" and 18" on the plateau and averaging 25" on the Pacific Coast but only 5.7" at La Paz in Baja California. Thunderstorms occur most frequently on the plateau, less frequently on the Pacific Coast and least on the Gulf Coast (i.e. Chihuahua 36 days annually, Culican 21, Tampico 17). Because of the uniform climate, tempered by ozone flowing down from the sierras, the Pacific Coast is considered healthful for throat and lung diseases.

The climate of northern Yucatan closely resembles that described for the continent. Merida reports an average cloudiness of 56% with 43 foggy days annually. Hot, dry, calm periods occur May to August but sea breezes soon spring up to relieve the oppressive heat. In fact, with a winter average temperature of 60°-75° and a summer average of 75°-95°, Yucatan is seldom unbearably hot. From May though September, thunder storms lasting two to three hours supply most of the area's 28" average rainfall. At all seasons, the wide daily temperature variation ensures cool nights. Throughout winter, Yucutan is warm and balmy. Relative humidity averages 75% and thunder storms occur on eight days annually.

Conclusion: both coasts offer ideal resort weather for outdoor sports in fall, winter and spring. For those who like the climate of South Florida or that of the Lower Gulf Coast of Texas, the coasts of Tamaulipas and Yucatan offer similar living conditions with superior winter weather. At higher altitudes inland, the northern plateau offers similar living conditions to those of Region 3 but with somewhat cooler winters.

ALAMOS, Son. Alt. 1,350', pop 5,500. Over four centuries old and once a rich silvermining capital, Alamos nestles in the Sierra foothills 33 miles by paved road east of Navojoa. Scores of decades ago, wealthy

Clothes

In most retirement colonies and at resorts, everyone lives in cottons and sandals. In the sophisticated cities, however, you are expected to dress more formally. Here, women's slacks, shorts and halters are definitely out. Dark colored suits are preferred. Though formal wear is seldom required, always bring a black dinner jacket in case you should need it.

---

colonists built a city of splendid palaces and luxurious mansions, elegant Moorish arcades and flower bordered patios. Then after the Mexican Revolution, silver mining was abandoned and Alamos became a mellow ghost town. After World War II, Americans began moving in and buying entire, half crumbling palaces for $400-$1,400. With cheap Mexican labor, they restored the once great houses of Alamos. Later on, the *pueblo* was declared a National Monument. Within a mile of the plaza, no facade may be altered, no gas stations, plate glass windows, neon signs or motels installed. The result: neat and clean once more, Alamos retains all its quiet atmosphere of dignified peace. Often called the Taxco of Sonora, it remains a dreamy cobblestoned village of graceful 2-300-year-old buildings where anyone who enjoys the creative arts can work in a setting exuding serenity and all the antiquity of yesteryear.

The view from the old jail on a hill overlooking Alamos reveals the town lying in a valley rimmed by purplish hills. Wild fig trees shade the plaza and its trim, painted bandstand. Overlooking the plaza on the south is the massive twin-spired church; on the west the restored Almada Mansion, now the Los Portales Hotel; and on the east and north neatly restored colonial mansions with colonnaded arches. Winding cobbled streets lead off through more rambling adobe palaces, most occupied by American retirees and all neat and spic and span. Yet still-crumbling ruins add beauty and charm to the 16th century flavor which permeates every inch of this bewitching, unmodernized retirement retreat.

Recommended in the dry season for arthritis and respiratory troubles, Alamos basks in a warm, dry, sunny semitropical climate from October through June. Summer days are hot and some Americans leave in July and August.

Only a day's drive from the border, this restful town has drawn a sizeable permanent colony of discriminating *yanquis*—an unusually high type of American who, seemingly, have created a favorable impression without in any way affecting the Old World customs of the aristocratic Spanish-Mexicans or the gentle, friendly attitude of the Yaqui-Mayo Indians and *mestizos*. Undoubtedly, much of this stems from the work of Mr. William L. Alcorn, who pioneered the restoration. Most restorable ruins have now been refurbished and though living can be inexpensive, it is no longer so low as in earlier days.

Partly this is due to the palaces being bought and sold by various Americans. Each adds improvements and about $3,000 or more to the price. Most palaces with swimming pools now bring $15,000-$18,000. Others, however, sell for considerably less and, especially between May and October, some may be rented. Taxes are still microscopic. Food is slightly higher due to transportation costs but Alamos now has a supermarket and fresh seafood is also inexpensive. Yet most residents feel they can still live better for less than at home. Outside the coastal leasing zone, Alamos property can be owned by *inmigrados* and *inmigrantes*. The only drawbacks are the hot summer days (cooled by afternoon thundershowers) and occasional dry season water shortages.

There are a good trailer park, small bank, market, several drugstores and an emergency hospital. Nearby Navajoa has good doctors and dentists and a fairly good hospital. In Alamos, old crafts have been revived, local leatherworkers produce some of Mexico's finest, cheapest products and there are still good buys in colonial antiques of every description. Naturally, both leather furniture and antiques are widely used as a background to gracious living.

You'll find plenty of social activity with regular Spanish classes for retirees and a movie theatre. Other popular pastimes are duck hunting, fishing in the Gulf of California 40 miles distant, desert horseback rides, visiting the Regional Art Museum and antique hunting, rock hunting around old mines and smelters, botany and birdwatching (both excellent), swimming in Cuchujaqui River, searching for buried treasure with mine detectors and browsing through the ancient cemetery and other atmospheric old landmarks like the colonial prison, market, hospital and slaughterhouse. There are also easy trips to the nearby pottery village of La Uvulama, the smelter of Aduana and working tungsten mines.

Best Hotel Buys: *Los Portales,* M. Small, friendly colonial hotel with roof garden; reasonable monthly rates for hotel retirees.

DURANGO, Dgo. Alt. 6,300', pop 70,000. The salubrious, sunny climate of this modern health resort qualifies Durango as a potential retirement town. Located on a plain surrounded by purple blue Sierra foothills, the city's focal point is its dignified and gracious Plaza Principal, flanked by the domes and facade of an ornate Tuscan style cathedral, a plateresque sagrario and an elegant church. Streets are wide, well paved and dotted with islands of palm trees and flowers. The banks of the Tunal River form a favorite promenade while small, inviting parks are everywhere. All is neat, orderly, well kept and up-to-date. Cool winter nights and summer days are a feature of the mild, temperate climate. Data: Mar. 60°, June 72°, Sept. 67°, Dec. 54°; annual average temp, 63°, maximum 76°, minimum 50°. Relative humidity 55%, rainfall 19.3", cloudiness 44%. Days with rain 113, frost 13, snow 3, clear skies 163, fog 5.5, hail 1.3, thunder 24.

Tidy, friendly and prosperous with a strongly Castilian flavor, Durango has considerable merit for retirement or as a cool summer retreat. There is no large colony yet. The city has good shops and all modern conveniences. Scorpions are the only noticeable insect pests. There are riding and hunting nearby, Sunday morning band concerts in the plaza; and on the outskirts, attractive spa springs rich in beneficial iron.

Best Hotel Buys: *Posada Duran,* M. Small well run colonial inn near plaza. Other hotels such as the *San Luis, Del Valle, Casa Blanca* and *Roma* as well as a trailer park, offer possibilities for retirement.

LA PAZ, B.C. Alt 39', pop. 30,000. In a region of long sweeping beaches and rocky promontories and surrounded by truck farms, this white sportsfishing capital lies on low hills sloping down to blue La Paz Bay. Sheltered by a mile-long sandbar, white hulled yachts and fishing boated fleck the bay before the broad curving, palm-lined Malecon—a bayside boulevard flanked by modern and colonial buildings—which serve La

Paz in place of a central, social plaza. Behind, in town, the rose pink mission looms over the plaza and from the roof, one can view this compact, clean and peaceful subtropical town. Big trees shade streets lined by large white houses with pink and blue borders and high, barred windows. Despite the cars—brought by the new ferry from Mazatlan—Victorian charm still lingers in this one time pearling port. Frigate birds and pelicans soar overhead and 1½ miles north is the superb sandy bathing beach called Coromuel.

A trifle humid in the mornings, the unfailing Coromuel sea breeze invariably springs up by noon and keeps La Paz dry and healthful. Data: average temps., annual 75°, maximum 84°, minimum 65°. Relative humidity 67%, rainfall 5.7", cloudiness 39%. Days with rain 17, fog 18, thunder 6.

Apart from its stupendous fishing, La Paz offers all year warm water swimming, snorkeling and skin diving with magnificent underwater scenery, shell and clam hunting and concerts, dances and *serenatas* on the Malecon twice weekly (incidentally, among the Paceños there are said to be five women to one man). Its isolation raises living costs but La Paz can be recommended as a quiet winter resort. Real estate costs are inexpensive and small estates are cheap and rentals are available at the Brown's. You'll also find a small American colony already well established.

Best Hotel Buys: Los Arcos. M. Cottage resort, Mexican decor. *Mission La Paz,* M. A fair colonial inn. *La Perla,* M. A town hotel with sidewalk cafe on bay. Other hotels in La Paz are the Los Cocos and *Guaycura,* both M, and the *Yeneca,* I. To the south are these fishing resorts: *Bahia Las Palmas,* M. Small, quiet, restful, at Bahia de Palmas. *Casa Fisher,* I. Pleasant guest house at San Jose del Cabo. *Rancho Buena Vista,* E. Near Los Barriles. *Hacienda Cabo San Lucas,* E. Near bay and beach at San Jose del Cabo.

MAZATLAN, Sin. Alt. 17' pop. 95,000. A leisurely town on a peninsula of fanciful rock formations, this shrimp and sportsfishing port is also a popular beach resort. Seen from the mountains, Mazatlan unfolds in its lush, spectacular setting. Soft beaches rim the tortuously-twisted peninsula and islands full of exuberant vegetation dot the blue-green bay. Ultra-modern resort hotels crowd the

half moon esplanade on narrow Olas Atlas Beach. But the town proper and its seaport lie behind Paseo del Centenario, a promenade brightly lit at night. Pink and white houses lead back to the shady Plaza de La Republica, flanked by slender, gold tiled cathedral towers and the inevitable *Palacio Municipal.* And reaching away on either side are more idyllic beaches and coves, and lagoons that are a teeming fantasy of wild bird life. Smart money built the hotels and this civic minded community is exceptionally spic and span. But Mazatlan retains all the dreamy, lazy flavor of a tropical Pacific port.

Though rather hot in summer and windy at times, heat weaves are unknown and the highest temperature on record was only 92°. Data: Jan. 67°, Apr., 70°, July 81°, Sept. 79°; average annual temp. 74°, maximum 78°, minimum 70°, lowest ever 52°. Relatime humidity 77%, rainfall 34", cloudiness 39%. Days with rain 79, fog 19.5, gales 16, thunder 29.

Despite its accessibility, Mazatlan is not expensive. During summer, very reasonably priced rentals can be engaged for the following year, there are no insect problems and no tropical diseases. Community life is easy to enter into and the populace live for pleasure. Mazatlan overflows with seafood at giveaway prices. Besides superlative fishing there is excellent swimming at Playa Sur, Playa Norte and Las Gaviotas and you can skin dive, play golf or tennis, enpoy breathtaking sunsets from a horsedrawn carriage, picnic on the islands, and water ski. For gaiety, you'll find hotels with dancing, cafes with bands and bars like O'Brien's on the hill. There are movies, wrestling, Sunday band concerts and bullfights in season. The Balboa Sports Club is open to members of similar clubs. And preceding Lent, all Mazatlan lets down its hair at the big Mardi Gras.

Our rating: OK for retirement if you don't mind the summers (there are modern villas on the hills and good trailer parks). Fine for quiet vacationing October through May and a terrific bargain June 15-October 15 when hotels slash rates up to 30%. Not expensive any time if you stick to M-priced hotels, avoid seafront rooms and take a double room with full American Plan by the week or month. (For rentals, see Sra. Ramirez at Vigie Apts.)

Best hotel buys: *Belmar,* M. Comfortable, elegant older oceanfront hotel with swimpool. *Freeman,* M. Modern skyscraper hotel with attractive roof garden. *Milan* I. Budget hotel in town near cathedral. *Playa Mazatlan,* M. Three miles north on private peninsula and beach at Las Gaviotas. *Joncol,* I-M. Comfortable budget hotel. At higher prices is *Mendoza's Hosteria,* at lower prices the *Avenida* and *Central.*

MERIDA, Yuc. Alt. 50', pop. 170,000. Down in Yucatan—home of the mysterious Mayan civilization—this spotless colonial city makes a wonderful winter sojourning base. Called the Great White City for the twice annual calcination applied by law to all houses, Merida is a progressive and antiseptically clean city of beautiful parks and gardens, ancient Franciscan churches and Moorish arches. Center of social life is the Plaza de La Independencia—shaded by laurels and dotted with S-shaped "love" seats—and dominated by the great cathedral and the historic Casa Montejo. Here, after dark, graceful *mestiza* girls in magnificently embroidered Mayan *huipiles* or blouses stroll with handsome men wearing pleated *guayaberas.* But this is the center of old Merida. On the outskirts lies a new city of broad paved streets, fine homes, boulevards and parks.

Ideal for vacationing from October to May, Merida also has attributes as an all year retirement spot for those who do not object to hot summer days. But the almost constant breeze tempers the summer days. Data: Feb. 74°, May 82°, Aug. 81°, Nov. 75°; average annual temp., 79°, maximum 88°, minimum 69°. Relative humidity 68%, rainfall 36", cloudiness 67%. Days with rain 151, fog 44, gales 11, thunder 9.

Costs are as low as in the Bajio country and long term sojourners may rent large and elegantly furnished Spanish-Moorish homes for $60-$80 a month, smaller ones $40-50 and small unfurnished homes for permanent residence for $20-$30. There are beautiful homes in the modern northern residential section. And if you care to refurbish them, you can rent enormous haciendas standing in sisal or coconut plantations for $30-$40 a month. Merida has a country club, good shopping, a big central market with good buys in sisal products and tortoise shell, and a wide choice of low cost seafood, superb honeys and venison steaks. Domestic help is cheap, the women excellent cooks. For really low cost living, $100 a month should cover all costs for two in such outlying villages as Uman or Valladolid.

Within easy reach of Merida are the great dead Mayan cities of Chichen Itza, Uxmal and Kabah with temples and pyramids dating from the 5th century and if archeology is your hobby. Merida has a fine historical and archeological museum. Evenings, you can loaf to caressing tropical music on the zocalo and on Sundays there are concerts by a first class band. By day you can swim at nearby beaches, and for the evening there are gay night clubs like the Tulipanes at an underground *cenote.* Merida also has good movies, baseball, Turkish baths, a university and a pre-Lenten carnival which rivals that of New Orleans. Nowadays you can reach Merida by road, a drive of some five days from the nearest U.S. entry point.

Just over an hour to the north lies the modern seaport and beach resort of Progresso. Dotted with summer homes, the beach runs for miles. Used only in July and August, these houses may be rented unfurnished for the rest of the year . . . for just $20-$30 a month. Here you could spend the winter in a climate as warm as that of Florida. Or for something really different, you might sojourn on a coconut ranch which takes guests. For all information and travel in this area we recommend your using the services of Yucatan Trails Travel Agency, Calle 62#482 in Merida.

Best Hotel Buys: *Del Parque,* M. Cheerful, modern downtown hotel. *Posada Aleman,* I-M. Pleasant small hotel with garden. *Alfonso Garcia F.,* M. Suburban hotel with swimming pool, garden and restaurant. (For a long term budget stay, you may prefer to live with a Yucatecan family, your meals furnished or not, as you wish.) At Chixculub is: *Los Cocoteros,* I. Modest but pleasant seafront hotel. All hotels have soqourning possibilities.) Merida has a good trailer park.

SALTILLO, Coah. Alt 5,175', pop 80,000. Within a few hours' drive of the Texas border lies this colonial city which, despite its textile mills, retains all the dignity and charm of its Spanish traditions. Twice weekly *serenatas* to band music are held on the plaza below the richly carved facade of a towering churrigueresque cathedral. From the plaza, streets wind off past fine colonial homes with long barred windows and out to more modern suburbs with broad boulevards and modern homes. The site of several colleges and the cultural center of Northern

Mexico, Saltillo's scholarly atmosphere extends to tranquil Alameda Park, a shady retreat with trees, benches, walks and lakes where scholars congregate to relax and think.

Due to its high, dry, cool summer climate, Saltillo is a popular summer resort. During winter, sheltering mountains keep out the worst northers but chilly midwinter weather is far from unknown. Data: Mar. 59°, June 72°, Sept. 86°, Dec. 54°; average annual temp. 63°, rainfall 13.6".

Some 400 Americans live in Saltillo. Most report prices as inexpensive. All modern conveniences exist and the big central market is filled with bargains in wool blankets and serapes, pottery, silver and tin. There are bullfights in season, good hunting, golf, tennis, polo, swimming, movies and a university and summer school. For night life and other big city facilities. Monterrey lies only an hour's drive away.

Best Hotel Buys: *Urdinola,* I. An older but quite comfortable hotel. *De Avila,* I. Good small modern hotel. *San Luis,* I. Small, modern, downtown. *Premier,* I. Modern, comfortable. All have retirement possibilities. *El Morillo,* I-M. Traditional guest ranch.

SAN LUIS POTOSI, S. L. P. Alt. 6,300'

pop 170,000. A handful of Americans have discovered inexpensive living in this sedate, colonial silver mining town on the flat, dry northern plateau. Though partly industrial, the city preserves a strongly almost severe, colonial aspect. From the great cathedral on Plaza Armas, the tiled majolica domes of handsome churches rise in all directions. Intricate grillwork and balconies adorn the narrow cobbled streets and tiled Calle Hidalgo, the shopping street, is entirely closed to traffic. On the outskirts are attractive residential sections with modern homes. Clean and untouristed, this hospitable city lies within a fast day's drive of the border.

Fairly cool in summer and comparatively warm in winter (but with nippy nights) SLP offers an attractive climate. Data: Feb. 59°, May 70°, Aug. 67°, Nov. 59°; annual average temp. 63°, rainfall 14.4".

Retirees already here report low rents on a wide choice of fine older homes, all modern conveniences at low cost and very good shopping with local bargains in *rebozos,* pottery and inlaid wood. There are movies, an interesting Regional Museum of Art, a wealth of colonial architecture and considerable social activity including an active Rotarian branch. Within easy reach is the splendid spa of Lourdes, beneficial for ulcers, kidneys, liver and varicose veins; and the smaller, less elaborate Ojo Caliente.

Best Hotel Buys: *Balneario Spa Lourdes* (36 miles to south), I. A fine spa resort hotel, formerly a hacienda. Swimming, tennis and numerous games. Fine for retirement. In SLP with retirement possibilities are the: *La Paz,* I. Older but quite satisfactory. *Napoles,* I-M. New and central. *Progreso,* I. Older but comfortable family style hotel with pleasant rooms. *Colonial,* I-M. Good downtown hotel. Others are the new *Concordia, Filher* and the older *De Gante,* all M. For rental apartments, ask at the Dormac Restaurant.

TAMPICO, Tamps. Alt. 15', pop 135,000.

On the north bank of the Panuco River, several miles from the Gulf, this thriving prosperous oil port is best known as tarpon fishing headquarters for the Gulf of Mexico. Mixed in with modern progress are the inevitable touches of old Spain and Tampico, with its imposing cathedral and municipal palace, has more interest than most tourists suppose. A harbor full of tankers and the big oil refineries of Madero are offset by the advantages of two fine beaches and such traditional customs as the *serenatas.*

Sea and mountain breezes cool the hot summer days and for permanent living, Tampico's climate compares favorably with that of Texas' Padre Island beach resorts. Data: Mar. 71°, June 82°, Sept. 81°, Dec. 67°; average annual temp. 76°, maximum 82°, minimum 68°. relative humidity 78%, rainfall 50". Days with rain 123, fog 28, strong winds 14, thunder 17.

A comfortable sojourning haven from October till April and within a day's drive of the border, this reasonably priced city offers retirement possibilities to the fishing-minded couple to whom south Florida's climate appeals. Rentals are normally available, both permanent and seasonal, and there are smart shops, markets loaded with inexpensive seafood, good restaurants and every modern convenience. Since seining was stopped, the fishing has been good and you'll find modern movies, a chic country club, several night clubs, numerous social clubs and TV, baseball, golf, tennis, boxing matches and bullfights in season. With a boat, there are interesting river trips to take, including that to the seafood picnic spots in neighboring "old town." Too, Tampico has the usual pre-Lenten Mardi Gras. Four mile long Miramar Beach offers fine surf bathing and La Barra Beach is attractive.

Best Hotel Buys: *Imperial* M. OK, well run. *Inglaterra,* I-M. Big, central, modernized, comfortable. *Rivera,* I. Large, clean downtown Mexican style hotel. *Mundo,* I. Modern, downtown. *Tampico,* I. Roomy older central hotel with good food.

TOPOLOBAMPO, Sin. A friendly, unspoiled fishing village on a bay 12 miles from Los Mochis. Fishing and skindiving are excellent—a splendid escapist retreat!

Best Hotel Buys: *Yacht Motel,* M-E. Spotless rooms, good food.

VALLES, S. L. P. Alt. 300', pop 25,000. A coffee center in the fertile Huastecan lowlands, sun drenched Valles is a popular winter resort just a day's drive from the border. Here you will find a warm winter climate, hunting, fishing, birdwatching and other outdoor activities and inexpensive resort hotels. Not far away at Tamuin are interesting pre-colonial pyramids and frescoes. Valles has a good trailer park.

Best Hotel Buys: *Covadonga,* I. A good 2nd class bungalow style resort hotel with sulphur swimpool, gold and fishing in 100-acre tropical grounds. *Taninul,* M. An attractive country spa resort hotel on a 1,400 acre estate. A good buy!

Region. 3. Tropical Highland

SHARING THE CLIMATE of all tropical plateaus ranging from 2-6,000' and higher, Mexico's central plateau duplicates the famed eternal springtime found in East Africa. After having travelled all over the world,

Health Foods in Mexico

Mexico abounds in natural, unprocessed foods. Old fashioned mills sell natural, home milled flour. Most fruits and vegetables are organically grown and markets overflow with papaya, tropical fruits, citrus, peas, beans, tomatoes and vegetables. Eggs are large and rich. Top grade yogurt and cottage cheese are widely available; so are untoasted wheat germ and unheated honey. Mexico is such a treasure trove of natural, unadulterated foods that health food stores are unnecessary and the country is a Utopia for the natural hygienist.

thousands of retired American service officers have settled here, firmly convinced that this *is* the world's best retirement climate. Few have been disappointed. Here they have found soothing, restful weather in which days and nights are of almost equal length. "It's like living in June all year," one ex-U.S. Marine colonel says. "Choose a lower altitude if you like it relaxing, a higher altitude if you prefer a tonic, bracing air. It's mild all year, never too hot or too cold and with just sufficient seasonal variation to break the monotony. For my money, this *is* the world's most perfect climate."

Though rainfall is light and irrigation required for agriculture, this region is considered the granary of Mexico. There are grasslands and forests and coffee, bananas, cacao and citrus flourish. Wheat grows on the higher slopes, sheep and cattle graze on the plains. Only along the semi-arid border with Region 2 does vegetation become sparse.

The seasons come and go almost unnoticed. Fall, like spring, is dry and bracing. Winter is equally dry with unending clear skies broken only by the brief cold drizzle of an occasional norther or by several days of steady rain during the spring equinox. Occasional frosts occur at high altitudes in midwinter and fires are needed from December to February (October to March at higher altitudes). In early June, the dry warm spring gives way to brief but almost daily afternoon thunder showers and the temperature stays in the high sixties. High altitude resorts like Patzcuaro and Morelia fill with people fleeing the lowland heat. Most residents find the rainy season enjoyable though a few mentioned occasional dampness and mildew on leather. Magnificent cloud effects combining lightning with gorgeous sunsets are a feature of late summer evenings. On the subtropical Pacific slope, June is the wettest month and though hot in the sun, the shade is always cool. Here, however, humidity is high enough to be uncomfortable.

Although the mean temperature of some months falls below 64°, it never drops below 44°. Seasonal temperature ranges are small but sufficient stimulation comes from the appreciable daily range. As in all desert regions, the land heats swiftly by day and cools rapidly after sundown. Despite the fact that the Pacific slope valleys can become quite hot in May, there are never any heat waves—the mountains are always cool. The average temperature is 63°, average high

74°, average low 50°. The warmest month is May, the coolest December and January.

During winter on Lake Chapala we have seen the sun shine ceaselessly from dawn to dusk for 90 unbroken days. Actually, some sunshine is experienced over the plateau on some 350 days each year. Cloudines exists about 47% of the time, foggy days average 21 and thunder occurs on an average of 34 days each year. Relative humidity is 60%, rainfall 30" annually, some of which falls on some 105 days each year. Storms are rarely experienced.

The entire plateau constitutes one of the world's most healthful regions. Many Indian tribes dwelling here are noted for their longevity. By and large, at altitudes below 6,500', the climate is beneficial for arthritis, rheumatism, hay fever and sinusitis. At altitudes above 6.500' it is not recommended for pulmonary diseases or sinusitis and may lead to over-excitation and irritation of nervous fatigue and digestive or kidney trouble—if you already have one of these ailments. The southern region of Chiapas, in which is the retirement town of Las Casas, resembles the central region with the exception that the rainfall is slightly higher and some can be expected throughout the year.

Conclusion: for people over 50, this *is* the ideal retirement climate. Thank carefully however, before deciding to forsake the springtime mildness of altitudes under 6,500' for the perpetual autumn coolness of those at higher altitudes.

AGUASCALIENTES, Ags. Alt. 6,222', pop 130,000.

Fertile orchards, vineyards and fighting bull ranches surround this colorful and well-planned old-new state capital. Built over ancient catacombs and full of pleasant little parks, Aguascalientes is a neat, quiet town of handsome trees, domes and churches. You'll always find a few Americans on the *portales*-lined Plaza de Constitucion. But there is no large colony, a fact which dumbfounds us for though untouristed, this quietly busy and far from sleepy town is one of the most attractive retirement spots in Mexico.

The climate is magnificent, as mild and benign as that of California's choicest retirement towns and a good deal sunnier. For generations, the city's residents have been noted for remarkable longevity. Data: Feb. 58°, May 72°, Aug. 67°, Nov. 64°; annual average temperature 63°, rainfall 22.5".

The handful of Americans report living costs as among the lowest in Mexico. There's a big new subdivision with all utilities, home sites are available on two nearby lakes and you can raise excellent citrus and grapes and other garden produce. In this thermal region, tap water is hot and presumably pure, there are good hospitals and clinics, Sears and Woolworths, and good schools, drugstores and libraries. Local markets offer bargians in beautiful drawn linen blouses, baby clothes and tableware and in handsome pottery, leather goods and custom made tiles.

Moreover, Aguascalientes boasts five thermal spas with swimming pools in town and 15 others nearby, all beneficial for health. Activities range from fishing, swimming and boating on nearby lakes to riding, hunting, exploring the archeological zone of La Quemada and visiting local fighting bull *ranchos*. Each spring a rich folklore festival is held with bullfights, dances, parades and art exhibitions, another in fall. Our rating: a smaller edition of Guadalajara, the most overlooked bargain retirement town in Mexico.

Best Hotel Buys: *Francia,* I. On the plaza, retirement possibilities. *Paris,* M. A well run, well furnished hotel on the plaza.

COMANJILLA, Gto. Alt. 5,450'.

Six miles up an unpaved road off Highway #45 between Leon and Silao is one of Mexico's greatest bargains. The white stuccoed Hotel Comanjilla lies surrounded by 48 suphuric, carbonated medicinal springs, all chemically different and recommended for arthritis, rheumatism, circulatory ailments and high blood pressure. You can swim in the large pool and drink the waters. Hot spa water is piped into every bathroom in the hotel and the rates for a twin bedded room with three good meals daily are ridiculously low. There are pleasant gardens, tennis, billiards and riding and the Bajio cities are all within easy reach. The climate is mild and exhilerating. Data: Feb. 60°, May 72°, Aug. 68° Nov. 61°; annual average temperature 65°, maximum 79°, minimum 72°. Relative humidity 56%, rainfall 25.3", cloudiness 53%. Days with rain 118, frost 1, fog 42, strong winds 8, thunder 40. Our rating: an ideal get-away-from-it-all retreat, top value as a retirement hotel.

113

Best Hotel Buys: *Balneario de Coman-jilla* (Apartado Postal 111, Leon, Gto). I. Excellent accommodations and good international cuisine. Attractively low rates for permanent retirement.

CUAUTLA, Mor. Alt. 4,200', pop 12,000. A picturesque subtropical mineral spring resort in the lush and verdant Vale of Cuautla. Clean, inviting and unhurried, it offers a tranquil small spa town setting just 90 minutes by car or bus from the theatres and restaurants of Mexico City. Not too many Americans have discovered this little Eden yet; hence prices are much lower than in neighboring Cuernavaca.

Bleak, sharp mountains frame the Vale of Cuautla, a patchwork of silvery streams, rice and sugar plantations and quaint, colorful villages dotted with the unique *coscomates,* huge thatched jogs used for storing corn. Around Cuautla, the countryside becomes more fecund and luxuriant. A gently flowing river divides the town in two: in the modern northern half is a single street of shops, the hotels and an extensive, animated Sunday market where blue costumed Indian women sell good buys in pottery and baskets. South of the river is the old Indian farming community of San Jose, still brimming with character despite the many sleek summer homes. Cuautla is delightfully picturesque: huge mango trees shade the uncrowded flower-lined streets and the river caresses manicured lawns and orchards of tropical fruits. Its proximity to Mexico City draws a sizeable weekend family trade plus some wealthier folk whose smart homes line the Cuernavaca road. At one time a fashionable colonial spa, Cuautla today is a sleepy, soothing, languid garden spot, uncrowded on weekdays and absolutely ideal for relaxing retirement.

Sheltered from northers by the gigantic bulk of Popocatepetl, Cuautla basks in a superbly mild subtropical climate slightly warmer than that of Cuernavaca. Only two months are really hot. The other months are perennially sunny and comfort perfect. There are no winters or brusque changes. The tonic-laden air is recommended for nerves and bronchitis and you'll need a light blanket every night. Data: Feb. 70°, May 77°, Aug. 74°, Nov. 70°; average annual temp., 72°, rainfall 25.5".

Top draw here are the famed sulphur springs of Agua Hedionda, 2½ miles south or five minutes walk across the river. For a nominal fee you may enjoy the entire facilities. The healing waters pour from a rock into a series of oversized Olympic swimpools bordered by a terraced landscaped hill complete with picnic grounds, a modern restaurant and a health building lined with murals by Olga Costa. All are spotlessly clean, modern and ultra-efficient. The waters are beneficial for rheumatism, diabetes and disorders of the heart, lung, liver, kidneys, nerves and circulatory system.

A typical day begins with a morning of sunning and swimming at the spa followed by an afternoon nap, perhaps a cool afternoon dip in one of several swimming holes and quiet relaxation in the public gardens or on Sundays, at the plaza band concert. The only evening recreation is the movies and practically everyone is asleep by 10 P.M. You'll find pleasant country walks and good riding trails and within easy bus or motoring distance, a wealth of conquest and pre-conquest ruins. A score of interesting towns lies nearby including Oaxtepec, the spa of Montezuma I, the charming little spa of Atotonilco and such towns as Yecapixtla, Amayeca and Atlatlahucan, all rich in early baroque churches and convents and ideal for painting.

All costs are very reasonable. There are scores of small resort apartments, cottages and bungalows for rent and economical *pensions* galore.

Best Hotel Buys: *Vasco,* I-M. Attractive resort hotel with swimpool, golf, gardens and quite good food. *Quinta Erica,* I. Small but rambling hotel in beautiful garden with good German cooking.

CUERNAVACA, Mor. Alt. 5,080', pop 60,-000. A fashionable health resort, Cuernavaca is superbly located in a smiling, well protected valley below a horn-shaped ridge of wooded hills. To appreciate it fully, you must stand in the arcade of the Palacio Cortes (dating from 1530). Behind you, bold mammouth Diego murals depict the conquest and revolution. In front, you look straight at the immutable snow capped peaks of Popocatepetl and Ixtaccihuatl. Mountains and flowers form the city's backdrop. Large country estates surround Cuernavaca. Closer in, rambling high-walled villas cover the breeze swept hills. Smaller houses with pink, blue and yellow pastel walls and red tiled roofs crowd into town. Many boast swimming pools and tennis courts and their foliage would do credit to a botanical garden. Every residential section is embowered in trees and flowers. Tropical vines run riot over homes of steel and glass and purple bougainvillea pours over noncommittal facades which screen charming old colonial homes with massive walls, stone columns and beamed ceilings. Never before have you beheld such a tantalizing, warm, green town.

Nearer at hand, the severe castellated walls of colonial churches peek through more walls of luxuriant vegetation. Tree-shaded streets wind down through canyons and ravines to the town's three central plazas. If it's a Sunday evening or a Thursday afternoon you'll hear the strains of band music from one plaza. The second, adjoining, is fitted as an *al fresco* theater. The third is the Jardin Morelos. Two are flanked by chic, cosmopolitan sidewalk cafes where retired Americans sit sipping Cafe Espresso Capuccino. From this central zocalo shop-lined Guerrero Street leads down to the busy market overflowing with palm furniture leather, straw work, sandals and pottery— all valuable attributes to living the good life here.

Chosen first as a resort by Aztec emperors, Cuernavaca has also been the favorite retreat of Cortes, Maximilian, the silver magnate Borda and a host of diplomats, celebrities and movie stars. Landmarks left by the famous include the Pyramid of Teopanzalco —a major archeological site, the great pinkish red Palacio Cortes, the imposing weather beaten rose colored cathedral begun in 1529 and, across the street, the rambling horticultural Jardines Borda with its mirrored pool where the Empress Carlotta bathed among roses in the soft Cuernavaca night air. Despite the growth, the widened paved streets and the weekend crowds, Cuernavaca abounds with ancient relics. History was written on every street corner. *But outside the residential sections, new industry and frenzied building is definitely beginning to spoil the city's traditional charm and the traffic can be maddening.*

Otherwise, Cuernavaca is one of Mexico's most charming towns . . . for Mexicans a salubrious Cinderella, for Americans a symbolic tomorrow's tomorrow of rest and relaxation. In 1949, a bare 60 Americans and a handful of European refugees formed its international colony. Today, the number exceeds 400. Barbara Hutton's estate stands beside those of retired statesmen and business tycoons. Thanks to the new superhighway bringing Mexico City within an hour's ride, Cuernavaca has become a weekend suburb of the capital, a sophisticated international playground—without, fortunately, destroying its original charm and colonial splendor. Still incomparably beautiful, there's a young alive freshness about the place that Cuautla lacks. Attuned to smart modern living, it reminds you of Capri and like that island Eden, retains its own special flavor. A single street still leads down to the old section, a mixture of crooked cobbled streets, ancient churches, native craft shops and picturesque old iron-grilled homes.

"Liking it is a matter of taste," an American retiree said. "It's not a place to take in your stride. Yet it's small enough so that eventually you meet everyone. Regardless of the few night spots on the *zocalo,* most residents entertain at home. Stay here a while and you'll receive invitations to a garden party, lunch or golf. But you can't jump right into our social life."

Sheltered from northers by a mountain ridge, Cuernavaca lays claim to Mexico's most perfect climate. And not without justification. Winters are brisk, spring dry and warmer, the summer rains come mostly at night and fall is well nigh perfect. Every day is sunny with a gentle daytime breeze. There's a nip in the morning air and you'll need a blanket every night. Its soft southern exposure gives Cuernavaca the perfect outdoor climate. Data: Feb. 67°, May 74°, Aug. 68°, Nov. 67°; average annual temp. 69°, rainfall 41.5".

"Life can be as expensive as you want to make it," our retiree friend went on. "Rent controls your expenses. Rentals *are* higher here but out of season you'll find plenty of furnished apartments and a good supply of houses, both furnished and unfurnished. A typical furnished house rents at $128 a month. Others are cheaper. Plush places with swimming pools cost more. Many people dress fashionably and mix with the smart set. Others like me wear old clothes and enjoy ourselves on little. Every morning, you'll find a hundred of us at coffee on the *zocalo.* I've furnished my home in a rich combination of colonial and Indian style, all bought inexpensively in the market. You can get anything in Cuernavaca. There are supermarkets, smart stores, a fine hospital, good restaurants and two first class movie theaters. For evening social life some of us join in the dances at hotels. Yes, Cuernavaca *is* more expensive but scores of us are enjoying it on a comparatively small income."

Americans send their younger children to one of two private English language schools; their older children attend the American School in Mexico City. Land for building is plentiful. Typical of new home prices were those of several smart new subdivisions offering modern two bedroom places from $10,000 complete with lot and all utilities. A good housing agent is Mr. Albert Abkarian, Pasaje Caballero, Guerrero 104.

Activities run the gamut from a bridge club and Women's International Club to religious groups who present occasional concerts and plays, an attractive nine hole golf course (25 pesos daily), riding, art galleries, bingo in the square, weekly wrestling matches, nightly dining and dancing in hotels and pleasant walks. You'll also find a tennis club, bookstores, and cultural and recreational courses at the University of Morelos. Enthusiasts find an abundance of interesting fauna, flora and archeology. And near at hand are such pleasant places as San Anton Falls and San Antonio potters' village, the tree-shaded picnic spot at Balneario Chapultepec, the seven lakes of Zempoala National Park, the pyramid of Xochicalco and the caves of Cacahuamilpa, Cuautla and Tepoztlan (described elsewhere), and, four hours down the road, Acapulco.

Thirty-two miles or half an hour away and at a warmer, dried 2,300', Lake Tequesquitengo is practically a suburb of Cuernavaca. Here is a region of fertile tropical valleys strewn with picturesque ruins, lies an artificial lake surrounded by smart hotels and summer homes in breathtaking modern designs. A trifle too warm (av. 79°) for permanent retirement, Tequesquitengo is nevertheless one of Mexico's loveliest lakes. Nowadays it has blossomed into a smart resort dedicated to water sports (a shade too watery perhaps, for in 1959 it rose and flooded one hotel and hundreds of boat docks and garden terraces). Nonetheless, you'll find it ideal for a visit or a winter vacation based on fishing, sailing, water skiing and skin diving. Nearby are the bathing spas of Las Estacas and Tehuixtla, the latter famed for its sulphurous mud baths and the air-like transparency of its water filled Devil's Cave. There are new subdivisions in the area.

Caution: living costs in Cuernavaca are as high as those of Mexico City.

Best Hotel Buys (Cuernavaca): *Capri*, I-M. Attractive retirement hotel overlooking *barranca,* all rooms with glassed terrace, beautiful gardens, mature recreations, inexpensive long term rates. *Casa Arocena,* M. Small, quiet, central, family run posada, attractive rooms, swimpool. *El Buen Retiro,* M. Retirement health resort, central in beautiful grounds, swimpool, excellent food and service, special long term rates. *La Joya,* I-M. Mexican style resort hotel with swimpool, garden, solarium. *Quinta Las Flores,* M. Pleasant small inn near golf. *Villa Galeano,* M-E. Attractive downtown inn, tropical patio, comfortable rooms, good food. *Casino de La Selva,* M. Pleasant bungalow resort with pools. *Quinta La Ortejina,* I. Homey downtown inn. *Quinta Rosa,* I. Good unpretentious pension on old Route 95 south. *Posada Casona,* I. Economy inn, downtown.

(Tequesquitengo) *Vista Hermosa,* E. Fine old Cortes hacienda built in the 16th century and brimming with charm and modern comforts, stupendous swimpool. One mile from lake, excellent for Sunday lunch outing. Expensive but an experience!

CUITZEO DE HIDALGO, Gto. Twenty minutes by paved highway west of busy Irapuato lies one of Mexico's best and cheapest spas. Ringed by verdant mountains and set in towering palms and flower gardens is a modern spa hotel, the Balneario La Caldera with all inclusive rates less than one third those you'd pay in the United States. There are five swimming pools—one Olympic sized—filled with sulphurous, radioactive waters soothing and beneficial for a general tone up and well recommended for high blood pressure, muscular rheumatism, sciatica and certain kidney and digestive ailments. Each hotel room has a terrace and its own private spa bath and most have picture windows. Located in the heart of the balmy, spring-like Bajio country, La Caldera is within easy reach of such interesting cities as Guanajuato, Irapuato, Leon, San Miguel Allende, Salamanca and Celaya and is wholeheartedly recommended for a long healthful vacation or permanent hotel retirement.

Best Hotel Buys: *Balneario La Caldera,* I. Excellent modern spa resort hotel, all outdoor sports, games and pastimes, and riding. A top buy: monthly rate for retirees!

FORTIN DE LAS FLORES, Ver. Alt. 2,743', pop 5,000. In the exotic center of Mexico's largest flower growing region—where orchids grow wild—this mountain resort lies in a supremely beautiful setting of Old World Mexico perfumed by the lush prodigality of flowers. On clear days, the great peak of Orizaba floats above the rooftops and all around are coffee plantations, citrus groves and sugar cane farms. In spring or fall the climate is ideal but copious summer rains and humidity and occasional midwinter northers preclude our recommending Fortin for retirement. Data: Feb. 64°, May 72°, Aug. 70°, Nov. 64°; annual average temp. 67°, rainfall 88". Nonetheless, for a lazy, warm and refreshing vacation it cannot be beat.

Best Hotel Buys: *Posada Loma.* I. Small bungalow resort with swimpool in floral gardens. *Yola,* I. Inexpensive hotel in town.

GUADALAJARA, Jal. Alt., 5,200', pop 900,000. Home of tequila, *charros, mariachis* and the Mexican hat dance and the second city of Mexico, this thriving, gay, dignified metropolis occupies a plain in the broad, mountain-rimmed Valley of Atemarac. Called the "City of Aristocrats" and the "Dresden of Mexico," Guadalajara combines modern civilization with the charm of old Spain. As a stronghold of Castilian pride, emphasis lies on bold male gallantry and beautiful women, folk songs and dances and the customs and charm of colonial Mexico. The perfumed older suburbs along Avenida de Vallarta are draped in blue jacaranda and purple bougainvillea and are full of sumptuous residences of wrought iron gateways and flower-filled patios. Indeed, old Guadalajara is a truly Moorish city of ornate facades and heavily studded doors. Surrounding the great downtown cathedral are four of the finest plazas in Mexico. Unlike other cities, Guadalajara has not converted its plazas into parking lots. The parking lot lies under the plazas.

Without destroying its Spanish character, Guadalajara has been thoroughly face lifted. Avenida Juarez, the main street, resembles that of an American city. Here is the New Mexico of functional apartment houses, tall office buildings and gleaming walls of glass. Here are modern supermarkets and up-to-date movies, good restaurants, cafes and theaters and ultra modern subdivisions. No wonder Guadalajara boasts the largest single retirement colony in Mexico.

If your retirement plans involve life in the pleasant suburbs of a large cultured city, you cannot do better than choose Guadalajara. The benign climate is mild and dry all year, never hot and seldom cold. Data: Feb. 61°, May 72°, Aug. 68°, Nov. 61°; annual average temperature 66°, maximum 79°, minimum 54°. Relative humidity 60%, rainfall 38", cloudiness 50%. Days with rain 107, fog 7, strong winds 26, hail 2.6, thunder 10.4.

In short, Guadalajara gives you most of the benefits of Mexico City and none of the drawbacks. Unlike towns on the Acapulco circuit, Guadalajara's prices are not killing the tourist goose that laid the golden egg. You can live in the city or in such delightful suburbs as Chapalita, Jardines del Bosque or the Country Club and once settled in an inexpensive rental, living is no more costly than in the Lake Chapala villages and possibly less. The most deluxe, ultra modern unfurnished apartments command a *top* rental of $90 a month, the average modern 3-bedroom unfurnished home about $75 and 2-bedroom furnished homes around $65. Hundreds of ex-Army and Navy couples are paying no more than $35-$40 a month for a modern unfurnished rental. A good supply of rentals, both homes and apartments, is usually available and new homes sell from $10,000. There's an English language real estate agent (Mexa S.A., at Vallarta 2835) and, usually, many vacancy ads appear in the newspaper *El Informador* and in the *Colony Reporter* or *Guadalajara News Week.*

A great educational, art and medical center, Guadalajara gives you every modern convenience against an unhurried background rich in the poetic qualities of the city's nostalgic past. A brief rundown of facilities would include: laundromats, an excellent bus service, modern supermarkets and dairies, big banks, an American school; the modern Mercado Libertad jammed with bargains in handblown glass, pottery, hide covered furniture and leather goods, copper and silver, and textiles; and amazingly modern shops. Here are Woolworths and Sears and such superbly stocked department stores as Faviers. You can dine in an American, French or German restaurant and the markets overflow with fresh seafood flown in daily. There are English speaking doctors, dentists and specialists galore, several hospitals including the finely equipped Mexican-American, a huge new medical center, scores of clinics and laboratories and big drug stores open 24 hours. There are boxing and wrestling matches at the Arena Coliseo, bullfights, the first class Benjamin Franklin Library and half a dozen English language bookshops; lectures, Spanish classes and conversational evenings at the North American Institute; at least five first class movie theaters and one drive-in, and the fine Guadalajara Sports Club with membership at around $4 and dues of under $2 a month per family . . . for which you get an Olympic sized swimming pool, dances and tennis. Here, too, is the American Society of Jalisco through which you'll meet worthwhile people and also the Rotarians, Lions and American Legion.

Then there's the inexpensive Degollado Theater where the Guadalajara Symphony and visiting European artists perform, as well as touring opera, ballet and drama. Out at the Country Club you'll find a first class 18 hole golf course, swimming pool and clubhouse with a handsome social salon overlooking La Barranca. Membership is rather steep but the outlay is worth it—for it puts you right at the top of Guadalajara society. There are non-denominational English language church services, twice weekly band concerts and *serenatas* in the plaza, three horseback riding associations, an interesting museum of arts and crafts, scads of art exhibitions including the famous Orozco Museum and soccer, tennis, polo, swimming, rodeos and *charreadas*. You'll find an active YWCA, a month long state fair in December, TV, a free music library, baseball in the Central Mexican League, sulphur spa baths out at La Barranca, and the delightful (and free) Sauza Casino. Name almost anything else but first class night clubs and Guadalajara has it. Barra de Navidad on the Pacific Coast is a bare five hours' drive and Puerto Vallarta just an hour by air.

Worth looking over, too, is the neighboring Tonaltecan pottery town of Tlaquepaque, four miles out. In this picturesque village and summer retreat for Guadalajara's wealthy families, a sizeable expatriate colony has discovered large older homes—some like palaces —with suprisingly inexpensive rents. Strike up a conversation with those retirees who frequent the central arcaded plaza, El Parian.

All of this, mind you, lies within a forty minutes' drive of the Lake Chapala resorts. Here is one place in Mexico where you can enjoy almost all the amenities of America.

Guadalajara is also home of Mexico's first retirement village, a 300-home develop-

ment for Americans complete with medical plan, clubhouse and recreation center. Write for details to Centro de Vivienda para Retirados S. A., Aptdo 1797, Guadalajara. Also worth subscribing to is the weekly newspaper of the expatriate colony. Called *The Colony,* it's available at $4.50 per year from Juarez 211, Desp. 512, Guadalajara.

Best Hotel Buys: *Guadalajara,* I. Small, modest, central, colonial type. *Morales,* I-M. Comfortable Spanish colonial type, central, good food. *Nueva Galicia,* I. Modern and cheerful, a good budget hotel. *Roma,* M. Downtown commercial hotel, good food. *Francis,* I. At Maestranza 35, pleasant hotel in old monastery. There are also *pensiones.*

GUANAJUATO, Gto. Alt 6,081', pop 34,-000. Tucked away like some fantastic Shangri-La deep in a gorge of the vast Sierra Madre range, this colorful state capital clings to the hillsides in rows of crooked streets and in houses of white, old yellow and terra cotta tones. As you approach the city through Marfil Canyon, it appears quite small. But the winding main street leads on through seven plazas while cobblestoned *callejones* wind up the steeply-tilted hillsides. Some streets are so narrow that only one person can pass; others are so steep they are stepped; and still others cross on bridges overhead. Great beamed houses with iron-grilled balconies line streets lit by Old World coach lanterns. Plazas, palaces and churches abound. Still unspoiled and relatively untouristed, Guanajuato waxed fat on its silver mines for centuries and has been steadily mellowing since 1554. Today, its unique community pride keeps it prosperous and clean. In fact, you are fined if your *criada* has not swept the street outside by mid-morning.

From the Pipila Statue high above, Guanajuato unfolds like a glistening Moorish citadel, an effect created by its early day Andalusian miners so that now it resembles Granada or Córdova. You note the stark, bone dry mountains dotted with ruined haciendas and the sharp, bald summits that rise wild and striking above the city. Guanajuato looks upwards to the ghost mining village of La Valenciana and down to the abandoned mining town of Marfil. Mine shafts still honeycomb the city's foundations. Looking straight down at last, one perceives the jumble of cool garden plazas, tiled domes, ancient towers and the sea of red tiled roofs, patios and arches that is Guanajuato today.

Your eye catches the great white castle-like university, the Victorian-Edwardian Teatro Juarez and a sprinkling of smart modern homes. Everywhere, charming old stucco houses with heavy studded doors and wrought iron balconies pile up the hillsides around patios of brilliant flowers.

You have just viewed one of Mexico's most beautiful colonial cities. In picturesqueness, Guanajuato rivals Taxco. Every corner holds an artistic treasure, charming vistas unfold at every turn. You'll find corners that are severe and forbidding, others brimming with Spanish arrogance and beauty. For time has stood still in this story book town. Though only a few hours from Mexico City, its isolation has preserved its medieval Arabesque flavor; its horse and buggy atmosphere is almost untouched.

Definitely temperate in climate and cool at all seasons, sunny Guanajuato's sole drawback is the risk of winter cold. Data: Feb. 60°, May 71°, Aug. 66°, Nov. 60°; annual average temp. 64°, rainfall 29.6″

Drawn by its quaintness and antiquity is a small but growing permanent American colony. For $60-$65 a month, these teachers, artists and writers have rented charming old homes with beamed ceilings and balconies. Other couples prefer the more modern homes. One Harian reader reports living in a nine room home fully furnished right down to an electric refrigerator, gas stove, kitchen utensils, linen and silverware—all for $60 a month. Advises he: "Get here well before June or after October to avoid our summer tourist renters. All costs are low and several couples have furnished their homes with amazing buys in locally made homespun fabrics, yellow-brown pottery, chic ceramics and antiques. There are modern shops and book stores, movies and a surprisingly clean, orderly and up-to-date market. Yet Guanajuato preserves all the slower tempo, the graciousness of life as it was lived in older days."

Accent is on quiet retirement. If you're an artist, photographer or historian, you'll find endless fascination. Among Guanajuato's churches are three of the most ornate in Mexico and the city overflows with historic buildings such as the romantic old Teatro Juarez, the grim Alhondiga de Granaditas—now a museum, the Pantheon with its catacombs and mummies, and scores of other marvelous churches. Then there's well preserved Marfil, a complete but roofless abandoned city and one of the largest ghost towns on earth, a small part of which has been settled by American expatriates. The hills invite walking and riding and nobody misses the twice weekly *serenata* to band music in Jardin de La Union—a plaza that might have been a stage set of the early 1800s.

Most retirees are quiet, culturally inclined folk who enjoy the series of medieval Cervantes plays performed annually on the streets, the numerous symphony concerts and art exhibitions, and the opera and drama held at the opulent Teatro Juarez. Dominating life is the enormous university which, provided you speak Spanish, offers cultural facilities of every kind.

Best Hotel Buys: *Posada de La Presa,* I. Small informal inn, homey and comfortable. *Posada de Santa Fe,* I-M. Comfortable colonial style inn, well run and up-to-date.

HUASCA, Hgo. Alt 6,200′. If you'd like to stay at a real Mexican hacienda, just 25 miles from Pachuca you'll find Mexico's fabulous Hacienda San Miguel Regla, the massive medieval home of Count Regla, now owned and operated as a country hotel by the Pan American Doctors Club. Two hundred years old and enclosed by immense walls, all rooms have a bath and fireplace and there is an outdoor heated swimpool, nine hole golf course and all outdoor sports. Our rating: one of the most unique, atmospheric and unforgettable vacation retreats in Mexico.

Best Hotel Buys: *Hacienda San Miguel Regla* (Huasca, Hgo.), M-E. Reservations essential, write or phone ahead.

IXTAPAN DE LA SAL, Mex. Alt. 5,850′, pop 3,000. A picturesque spa in a setting of tropical flower gardens and beautiful mountain scenery, Ixtapan consists of two parts: the older white village of Ixtapan de La Sal which is easy on the pocket book and the new model city and plush spa of Nueva Ixtapan which is considerably more expensive. Even so, costs are still under those you would pay in the States and few Mexican spas can compare in elegance and luxury with Nueva Ixtapan. Broad boulevards lead to handsome residential sections of modern 2-3 bedroom homes which can be purchased from $7,000 and which have built-in furniture. Eventually, this will grow into a 250-home development complete with supermarket, hospital, golf, park and social club—all designed for the

American retiree. Every spa treatment is here from luxurious onyx Roman baths to a health center with scientific massages. There are three attractive public swimming pools, 20 private baths and more being built, all spouting therapeutic radioactive thermal waters recommended for rheumatism, gout, lumbago, high blood pressure, circulatory ailments, nervous breakdowns, insomnia, faulty metabolism and sterility. Although all spa and sports facilities are free at the Hotel Ixtapan, budgeteers-in-the-know stay at smaller hotel-pensions in Ixtapan de La Sal and pay separately for the spa baths, mud treatments, golf, riding, tennis etc., as they require. The temperate climate is exhilarating. Data: Feb. 67°, May 75°, Aug. 68°, Nov. 66°; annual average temp. 69°, rainfall 41". Don't overlook this chic but secluded retirement spot.

Best Hotel Buys: *Bungalows Lolita*, I. Small homey pension, reduced rates for retirees. *Ixtapan, VE.* Exclusive luxury resort hotel in beautiful landscaped grounds, all spa and sports facilities included in rates. *Kiss*, E. New, modern, comfortable. Good budget pensions are *Posada Don Manual, Hotel Ideal* and *Sra. Gadd's.*

LAKE CHAPALA, Jal. Alt. 5,000'. In three dreamy towns 37 miles south of Guadalajara on Lake Chapala—Mexico's largest lake—live several hundred American retirees, writers and artists, the largest non-urban American expatriate colony on earth. A mountain range to the north protects the three lakeside *pueblos* from winter winds but neither short cold spells nor occasional rainy days are entirely absent and heat is essential on winter nights. Yet scores of Army and Navy men concur it is the world's best climate. Of this area, Terry said: "in benignity and ouright healthfulness it is perhaps not excelled by any other area in the Americas." The temperature ranges from 65°-80° by day and 55"-75° by night, slightly lower in midwinter. Best described as a perpetual Indian summer, from October through mid-June Lake Chapala is considered beneficial for asthma, sinusitis and rheumatic ailments. June to October is like spring, October to March is dry and bracing, April and May are warm but seldom hot. The clear, dry purity of air is responsible for the magnificent panoramas seen from the *pueblos*. The great lake seventy miles long and twenty miles wide is rimmed on all sides by purple mountains. And despite its murky color and the floating patches of water hyacinths, it glints like silver in the almost perpetual tropical sun.

From east to west and linked by a paved road, the three popular retirement villages are Chapala, Ajijic and Jocotepec.

CHAPALA. Alt. 5,022', pop 6,000. At the end of a fast paved highway straight into Guadalajara, this gay, bright,, musical lakeshore resort lies at the foot of sloping mountains. Here for decades, the wealthy of Guadalajara have owned magnificent villas; the Hotel Villa Monte Carlo was formerly the country house of Porfirio Diaz. *Mariachis* stroll the broad, tree-lined main street and retired Americans by the score loaf on benches in the plaza, now called Gringo Square. You'll discover Chapala as a storybook Spanish town of red tiled roofs, shady flower-splashed patios and cozy lakeside bars and beer gardens. Its first foreign resident was D. H. Lawrence and here also, Tennessee Williams is reputed to have written *A Streetcar Named Desire.* Weekending Guadalajarans crowd its small beach and pretty *mestizas* stroll the promenade planted in flamboyant flame trees. West along the shore, magnificent villas line the lake.

Nowadays, several hundred retirees and a handful of writers and artists have their own Chapala Society—a civic and service organization which holds monthly dinners and can help you get located—and a sporty 18 hole golf course and country club for which membership costs $125 or dues of $7 per month (daily green fees are $1.25 plus 35¢ per round for caddies). A new Yacht Club has been formed and there are sailing races on Sundays. You can swim in a choice of two pools, one of which is sulphurous and beneficial for rheumatism (there are also private spa baths). Birdwatching is rewarding in winter, there are easy trips to beautiful Juanacatlan Falls, to nearby lake villages and to islands on the lake, and Protestant church services are available. Chapala has good local doctors, three well stocked drug stores, two small supermarkets and all the facilities of Guadalajara are a bare forty minutes away.

Older homes rent furnished at an average of $65-$85 (but $100-$125 in winter). Yet two miles west on the paved road to Ajijic is a real discovery in Mexican retirement. Chulavista is an attractive American style country club development in a natural amphitheater overlooking the lake. Here a two bedroom home with lot begins at under $8,500, an average home $9,750 and others run up to a top of $18,000. Standard 65' x 100' lots are $2,800, others up to $8,000. Here you have excellent pure water, good zoning, no straying animals or noise and paved streets and sidewalks. There are a motel with pool and a nine hole golf course and good restaurant. First class buses pass the door and also link all Lake Chapala villages with Guadalajara. Significant of Chapala is the number of ex-Army and Navy officers retired there, a situation which has led to the recognition of military ranks and protocol. Although Chulavista is no longer inexpensive, several other subdivisions offer lots and homes at lower cost and there are normally a number of small furnished apartments at $60 a month.

Best Hotel Buys: *Country Club Arms*, M. Small, clean and modern with rooms, suites and apartments by the month. *Holiday Motel*, M. Attractive resort motel with good food at Chulavista. *Nido*, I. An unpretentious budget hotel in town, O.K. for retirement.

AJIJIC. Alt. 5,030', pop 3,500. An ancient Tarascan fishing village, Ajijic nestles on the lush shores of Lake Chapala beneath a steep, green and esthetically contoured mountain range. Its forbidding exterior makes first impressions disappointing. Unpretentious adobe homes line the narrow, cobblestoned streets; dogs, poultry and cattle wander around; nut brown Indians squat outside the *cantina;* a loudspeaker in the plaza blares out raucous music. Nine out of ten tourists look and leave. But be guided by that old maxim: "You can't always tell from outside." You notice the neat, trim plaza with its well painted bandstand, the picturesque fishing nets strung along the shore. What lies behind those bare adobe walls? Inside are white patios lush with flowers, well equipped art studios and the comfortable homes and apartments of Ajijic's 300 permanent American residents.

Years ago, a retired British engineer seeking a Utopia discovered this garden spot and built himself an impressive lakeshore home fronted by an acre of color-splashed blooms. After World War II, veterans studying in Guadalajara found they could live well here on their G.I. Bill payments. Artists moved in, led by several well known modern painters.

Several writers and musicians followed together with a group of enterprising ladies who reorganized Ajijic's dwindling handloom crafts into a thriving industry. With a few exceptions, this group still forms Ajijic's Old Guard. Getting in early, they bought up the choicest lots and homes, secured long term leases on the lowest rentals and today, most of these old timers offer outstanding examples of the way in which the good life can be enjoyed in Mexico on little.

Not a few of these couples, who originally arranged long term leases on simple adobe homes renting at $7.50-$15 a month, are still paying these fantistically low rents and living well on very small budgets. Though the best houses have all been refurbished, much the same can still be done with others. Still other couples have built, some constructing lavish homes costing up to $14,000 and $15,000. New homes are sprouting all around the village and to the west, ultra modern homes are studding a new hillside subdivision.

Unhurried and relaxed with an undisguised atmosphere of easy living and the bohemian background of an art colony, Ajijic has understandably drawn its share of wacky people and for many the flavor was somewhat too disquieting. Nowadays, however, the bohemians are being replaced by a more solid class of citizen. Particularly inspiring are Ajijic's Old Guard, none of whom was ever an eccentric and each of whom has his interests to keep him busy: writing, painting, ceramics or weaving. One artist whose failing eyesight forced him to give up painting inaugurated the colorful Galeria de Arte bar. Authors and others dabble in real estate. None is half so idle as some reports make out. The painters are particularly industrious. But by 7 P.M. most have knocked off for cocktails and later you may see them at the frequent parties.

Ajijic today is a slightly raffish, slightly bohemian rustic village where retirees outnumber the artists five to one. Nevertheless, overtones of its Greenwich Village past continue to lure a handful of bearded beatniks and unstable people whose problems follow them to Mexico. Among this group, threats of suicide as appeals for sympathy once became so common that for a novelty, one Old Guard hostess sent out invitations in the form of suicide notes ending with such comments as "Don't forget to bring the shrimp recipe." Ajijic is still no place for suburban conformists but neither is its non-conformity disquieting. Drinks and gossip are still favorite pastimes but criticism today centers on the unstable electricity supply and the water hyacinths which clog the lake rather than on eccentric people.

Outside the winter season, rentals are in fairly good supply, the village shops well stocked, there are a grocery and butcher and on weekend nights, dances at the Galeria. Almost everyone rides, most couples keep horses and there are plenty of good riding trails.

Best Hotel Buys: *Posada Ajijic,* M-E. A rustic and rambling but comfortable inn with colorful bar. Now well run; the food, service and hospitality are good. Has attractive bungalow units for hotel retirement including meals and all services. *Posada Rancho Santa Isabel,* I-M. Semi-detached modern one room bungalows on spacious lakeside grounds, good food.

JOCOTEPEC. Alt. 5,030', pop 3,000. A few miles west of Ajijic, less publicized and touristed and without a large foreign colony is the picturesque Indian fishing village of Jocotepec, famed for its white serapes and a church with a legendary "immovable" woodcarving of Christ. In spring, the plaza bursts into the yellow and blue blooms of primavera and tabachin trees. Here a handful of Americans—mostly writers and artists—have renovated large, older homes and others have built. So far, nothing has occurred to destroy the quiet charm and slow ancient tempo of its tranquil simplicity. Unlike Ajijic, with its arty gift shops and real estate agents, Jocotepec is pioneer territory and still afflicted with such drawbacks as the noises common to all Mexican villages and lack of any American style activities. Depending on season, large homes can still be leased and renovated and living costs can be kept reasonably low.

Best Hotel Buys: *La Quinta,* I. Quaint rambling village inn, American operated. Good for retirement.

MEXICO CITY, D.F. Alt. 7,350', pop 5,250,000. Ringed by mountains and overlooked by the snow-capped peaks of Ixta and Popo, Mexico City lies on a slowly sinking lake bed in the cool and lofty Vale of Anahuac. The world's tenth largest city and the fourth largest in Latin America, it is also the highest major metropolis on earth. It is the dynamic cultural, intellectual, educational, industrial and administrative hub of Mexico—yet it is not Mexico but a curious half United States, half Mexican admixture with the continental overtones left by Maximilian. Furious traffic travels broad eight laned avenues lined by excitingly modern perpendicular architecture often wedded to colonial relics built by the *conquistadores.* Bauhuas type skyscrapers stand alongside rococo-adorned Victorian villas. Side by side are unbelievable poverty and fabulous luxuries. Elegantly gowned women stroll past fashionable shops while a block away, Indians in from *ejido* villages live in indescribable squalor. There are endless miles of dull streets and slums. Ultra-modern factories dot the outskirts and here and there, one sees the Brave New Mexico transforming slums into *multifamiliares.*

Mexico City is caught in the biggest boom in its history. Flushed with success, it is like Houston or Los Angeles, forever tearing down and building anew. To the incessant clatter of pneumatic drills, street markets are yielding to modern indoor markets and new skyscrapers adding to an enthralling skyline that already includes a 43 story behemoth, the tallest building in Latin America. Why, then, list Mexico City in this book? For three reasons: a) people who have always lived in big cities, may, like an ex-mayor of New York, wish to retire here; b) its cultural facilities and unmatched entertainment are within easy reach of several small retirement towns; and c) whether you live in Mexico or are merely a visitor, a vacation here *in the warmer summer months* is always enjoyable.

You get your bearings at the city's center, the old colonial zocalo flnked by the immense cathedral, various palaces and the national pawnshop. From here, the main drag leads out through shop-lined Madero and Juarez to the broad, handsome Paseo de La Reforma which runs southwest to Chapultepec Park, Mexico City's version of Central Park or the Bois de Boulogne. From the Reforma's eight *glorietas* or circular plazas, broad boulevards lead out to quiet, shady residential suburbs where most of Mexico City's huge American colony resides.

There is no shirt-sleeve Guadalajara climate. At this altiude, the weather is cool-to-mild and exhilarating. Woollen suits are worn all year and topcoats in winter. Heat is required for at least three months annually.

The climate is like eternal autumn and mid-winter northers may bring light snow. However, Mexico City has a high percentage of sunshine and is reputedly good for asthma. Data: Feb. 56°, May 65°, Aug. 61°, Nov. 56°; annual average temp. 60°, maximum 74°, minimum 46°. Relative humidity 58%, rainfall 29", cloudiness 51%. Days with rain 170, hail 9.6, fog 14, thunder 59.3. Unfortunately, however, the capital nowdays suffers from a permanent smog.

All costs are higher than elsewhere but even so you can live for less than in New York or Washington, D.C. Comfortable pensions supply full room and board for under $4 a day and you'll find a wide range of rents from inexpensive unfurnished apartments in old colonias to overpriced penthouses in the swankiest suburbs. Though the American colony is widely distributed among eight or ten suburbs, it has its own schools, clubs and churches and forms a fairly closely knit group. Due to the aggravating traffic, a car is not recommended. Instead, low cost buses, streetcars and jitneys run everywhere. Rentals are listed at the American Embassy and also in newspapers. Frequently required when leasing is the signature of a *fiador* or guarantor. The suburbs are sprinkled with quiet oases, however, and rents are lower farther out. Among the most popular residential areas are: Lomas de Chapultepec near the American School, very bourgeois and expensive; Lomas Hipodromo, modern, set on hills and fairly expensive; Jardines de Pedregal, a colony of flat roofed homes with garden walls, ultra-modern and expensive; Nueva Anzures and Polanco, modern, chic, bourgeois and costly; Coyoacan, an historic colonial suburb, also expensive; San Angel and San Angel Inn, quaintly colonial with beautiful homes behind old stone walls and slightly less costly; Lomas Barrilaco, beyond Chapultepec, somewhat less expensive; and Tlalpam, ten miles out, with beautiful homes at somewhat less cost. There are, of course, many cheaper but less select suburbs and you can, if you wish, even find cooperative apartments called *condiminios*.

Facilities, in brief, would include excellent public transportation; splendid shopping with big department stores like Sears, Centro Mercantil and Sanborns and *supermercados* like the Sumesa chain; loads of toprung doctors, dentists and specialists and excellent hospitals led by the ABC; good private schools, the American School and Mexico City College;

modern markets in every *colonia;* English language newscasts and newspapers and just about every modern convenience.

As mentioned elsewhere in this book, there are several country clubs, sporting clubs and golf courses; all sports and recreations; horse racing in winter; at least nine important museums and art galleries galore; concerts, recitals, ballet and opera in season at Bellas Artes; Mexico's top bullfights; the country's largest Benjamin Franklin Library; swimming at the *albercas* of athletic clubs; folk song and dance performances; excellent movies; jai alai; several TV stations; an American Society and an active bridge club; and a lively cocktail hour and night life galore. Among favorite retiree pastimes are the intensive Spanish lessons at the North American Institute of Cultural Relations; the Tuesday evening bilingual sessions at Villa Jones International Cultural Center; and the absorbing group of museums in Chapultepec Park, among which is the world's largest museum of anthropology. As a visitor, you can obtain current information on all entertainment from the weekly giveaway on hand in all hotels.

There are thermal baths at Peñon and if archeology is your penchant, you'll find a dozen interesting zones within easy reach. Short trips by car or bus take you to Teotihuacan pyramids and the shrine of Guadalupe, the convent of Tepozotlan and the pyramids of Tenayuca, to Texcoco and the villages, to alpine Amecameca and to Toluca, Tlaxcala, Cuernavaca and a dozen other top interest spots. Suffice it to say that whatever your interests, Mexico City can satisfy them.

Best Hotel Buys: rates are astronomical at the usual deluxe hotels recommended in guide books. Concurrent with construction of these impersonal noisy tourist palaces has been erection of dozens of superior second class hotels which offer cleanliness, comfort, quiet and good food at half the price. For permanent residence or a long stay, however, we recommend the city's pensions.

Charleston, M. Small, modern, south side at Queretaro 209. *Del Bosque,* M. In beautiful mid-town residential area. *Emporio,* M. Comfortable downtown hotel with roof garden. *L'Escargot,* M. Pleasant hotel, takes pets. *Geneve,* I-M. Popular budget tourist hotel, well run. *Guardiola,* I. Downtown, older but comfortable. *Lincoln,* M. Nice older downtown hotel with good food. *Majestic,* M. Colonial hotel on zocalo, roof garden, comfortable. *Maria Christina,* I-M. Colonial hotel off Reforma, comfortable with garden and terrace. *Montejo,* M-E. Best buy in first class hotels. *Suites del Sol,* E. Central at Insurgentes Sur 15, fine efficiencies. *Pension Kohler* (Florencia 70), I. Homey downtown pension, big sunny rooms, a best buy! *Polanco,* I. Quiet, near Chapultepec, roof garden restaurant. *Virreyes,* M. In shabby central area but a sound buy! *Ritz,* M. Refurbished with attractive rooms and good restaurant. *Vasco de Quiroga,* I-M. Modern, comfortable and well run. *Casa Chavez* (Florencia 36), I. Good pension. *Maurice,* M. Central, quiet, good food.

MORELIA, Mich. Alt. 6,309', pop 135,000. An old Castilian city that resembles a living museum of Mexican history, Morelia lies against a mountain backdrop in a spot chosen by Spanish nobility as the most attractive in the entire New World. All around, the fertile green valley of Guayangareo forms a floral land of distant lakes, waterfalls and valleys while dairy farms border the city itself. From Mexico City five hours away, you enter the city past a huge 254-arch aqueduct completed in 1789. And you roll through paved streets bordered by majestic, handsomely proportioned pink-hued buildings to Morelia's two central plazas. Here you behold the slim twin towers of Mexico's most famous plateresque cathedral and you climb to the top for a view of the city.

Meeting your eye is a town of broad streets and orderly green parks bursting with trees and flowers. The entire city radiates a warm rose-tinted glow due to the pink trachyte used in its construction. There are stately homes and public buildings on every block and a wealth of quaint old churches, palaces, patios and mansions everywhere. You descend to the two plazas below and linger among the arcades and shops. You feel the history of this ancient university town. You discover an air of dignity and refinement, an atmosphere of leisure and relaxation and you hear of Morelia's magnificent tradition of culture and music.

Here are the soaring baroque belltowers of San Nicolas College, second oldest university in the western hemisphere with one of the world's finest musical conservatories, home today of a magnificent boys choir with golden angelic voices and, as always, a center of intense musical activity. There are modern frescoes in the public buildings and such overpowering sculptures as the Tarascan Fountain supported by three kneeling impressionist figures. You find the city is studded with shady green parks of which the loveliest is undoubtedly the enchanting Jardin de Las Roses. A treasurehouse of exquisite 18th century architecture, peaceful, aristocratic Morelia probably *is* the most attractive and most integral of Mexico's colonial cities. The thoroughfares are so scrupulously clean you could eat off the sidewalks. A city ordinance permits new construction only in the traditional colonial style.

Excellent air drainage keeps Morelia delightfully cool, dry and uniform throughout the year. Blue skies, a mildly warm sun and balmy days are standard weather in every month. With temperatures definitely on the cool side, Morelia is popular as a summer resort while winter nights and mornings are inclined to be nippy. The brisk air is undoubtedly responsible for the city's high energy and cultural achievements and its present fast growth. Data: Feb. 60°, May 69°, Aug. 64°, Nov. 60°; annual average temp. 64°, maximum 73°, minimum 53°. Relative humidity 63%, rainfall 31.2", cloudiness 48%. Days with rain 126, hail 4.3, fog 33.5, strong winds 9.4, thunder 23.

For generations, Morelians have been experts in the art of living. And emulating them today is a small American art colony drawn originally by the summer art school and now swelled by a growing number of retirees including many Canadians. "This is one of Mexico's best retirement towns," a Canadian couple told us. "There are no hills to climb. You can choose between beautiful old houses with gardens in the center or new housing developments on the outskirts where the main expatriate colony is located. As capital of Michoacan, all the Tarascan folk arts are sold in the market and you can furnish your home inexpensively with superb lacquerware, *serapes,* pottery and copper. All costs are very reasonable and many local food and drink specialties like the *ronpepe* eggnog and fruit wines are a definite adjunct to gracious living. Every modern convenience is here and the stores are stocked with the latest merchandise."

For activities, the Canadians listed riding, a miniature golf course, movies, Sunday open air concerts in Jardin de Las Roses, bullfights, swimming and horse races. They also took a weekly motor trip to a nearby town such as Patzcuaro or Uruapan or went down into the tropical fishing and hunting country at Huetamo, an hour away. Also near at hand is the beautiful thermal spa of Zinapecuaro and others at Atzimba, Cointzio and San Jose Purua. For cultural entertainment, there are daily rehearsals of the famous boys choir, the summer school and School of Fine Arts (weaving, pottery, jewelry design etc.) at San Nicolas College and other English and Spanish classes and square dances at the Mexico-North American Institute. Morelia is a Mecca for architecture students: the Michoacan Museum has a fine collection of archeological, zoological, geological, paleontological, historical and ethnographic subjects while interesting churches and sculptures abound. For social life, you'll find country clubs with frequent dances and the sidewalk shops and side streets are endlessly interesting for strolling and walking.

Best Hotel Buys: *Villa San Jose,* M. Splendid cottage resort in Santa Maria Hills, some discount for longer stays. *Acueducto,* I-M. Atmospheric colonial type hotel, pool, good food, long term rates. *La Soledad,* I-M. Atmospheric restored coaching inn, very comfortable, restful patio, 20% annual discount to hotel retirees.

OAXACA, Oax. Alt. 5,100', pop 70,000. A colonial city of weathered green stone, Oaxaca occupies a wide green-gold valley in the sunny Zapotecan kingdom deep in southern Mexico. Your best introduction is the view from Cerro del Fortin hilltop, crowned by the bronze statue of Benito Juarez. Below, you see a colonial Spanish city rich in primitive Indian art and color. The shade of lime sherbet, the jade green stone buildings range out from the *zocalo* to streets of low, pink pastel 16th century houses adorned with great nail studded doors and the most elaborate wrought iron grilles and balconies in Mexico. Almost every street corner seems to have its graceful, dignified church with a carved green stone facade. No wonder they call Oaxaca the "Emerald City." Everywhere, the green stone supplies a verdant air of freshness. Even from this distance you are aware of Oaxaca's exotic flavor, its placid demeanor, its air of antiquity and of being dreamily asleep.

To experience Oaxaca best, you must sit at a sidewalk cafe on the shady *zocala,* haunt of hundreds of frisky squirrels. Here, the past and present go hand in hand: you see Zapotecs and Mixtecs in white costumes and

wide hats and white robed ladies from Yalalag and you hear the babel of tongues emanating from south Mexico's innumerable Indian tribes. Sojourn here, retire here and you'll have unlimited time to enjoy the pageantry of southern Mexico which passes by. Indian life flows around the Spanish heritage like the tide around a rock. Wherever you look, you perceive a sea of bronzed faces and regional costumes galore. For in Oaxaca, Indian and white cultures are closely integrated. The result forms one of the most enchanting places in Mexico.

Stroll the languid streets lined by shady calabash and laurel trees and you'll discover such outstanding landmarks as the massive green facade and tiled dome of the cathedral begun in 1533! the polychrome sculpture in San Domingo—Mexico's finest colonial church; the impressive architecture of Santo Domingo Convent; the beautiful baroque church of La Soledad; and the busy Institute of Arts and Sciences, the university of southern Mexico. Yes, this *is* the real Mexico —Mexico South, the traveler's Mexico. Oaxaca really *is* charming—in a primitive, unspoiled way. This is no place to find night clubs or ballet. But if all you seek is serene beauty and peaceful charm, you'll find that this delightful 19th century city has it in abundance.

Mild all year and free of all extremes or altitude trouble, Oaxaca is a popular winter resort for Americans-in-the-know. December through February brings an unbroken succession of dry, warm, sunny days. And between winter and summer, the average temperature varies by less than 11°. Data: Feb. 66°, May 73°, Aug. 69°, Nov. 65°; annual average temp. 68°, maximum 82°, minimum 55°. Relative humidity 65%, rainfall 26", cloudiness 49%. Days with rain 118, hail 2.2, fog 8.5, strong winds 57.2, thunder 48.4.

A low cost spot, Oaxaca already boasts a sizeable permanent middle aged expatriate colony, most enjoying life on small pensions. You can live simply on half of what you'd spend at home. Though houses are not plentiful and it takes time to find a rental, all real estate costs are low. (Tip: larger houses for rent are more numerous than smaller ones; some neer refurbishing.) Don't come here unless you know you really like Mexico. For anyone who appreciates Mexican mores and folk arts, Oaxaca is a treasure trove.

The market, one of Mexico's most colorful, overflows with hand tooled leather goods, beautiful textiles, *serapes* and distinctive green glazed pottery. If you're an astute bargainer—and you must be in Oaxaca—you can furnish your home with the most fabulous handwoven tablecloths, bedspreads, multicolored pottery, Spanish antiques, brilliant articles of maguey fiber and ceramics in glowing colors—all for the proverbial song. At low cost you can wear beautifully hand made shirts and blouses, skirts or suits. There are tropical fruits galore, Etla boiled cheeses (safe to eat) and, believe it or not, plenty of bookstores with American books and magazines.

Those who do not appreciate this bounty are directed to the statue of Benito Juarez pointing away from the city and apparently meaning. "If you don't like it, you can leave." Most visitors are so enchanted however, they plan to return and retire. Despite the Indian background and primitive flavor, living here is no hardship. "Sure, you can find drawbacks," said one contented ex-New Yorker. "The trip to the border takes three days. You can find dust and dirt and in winter, the water supply is mercurial. Toilets don't always work and plumbers are slow to arrive. The place looks unprogressive and disorderly. Some homes need repairs. But so what? You can live here for half what it costs in Cuernavaca."

Capital of one of Mexico's three most interesting states, Oaxaca is center for many things to see and do. For those interested in archeology and anthropology, there's the Regional Museum of crafts and archeology plus two of Mexico's greatest pre-conquest ruins: awesome Monte Alban, seven miles away on a hilltop overlooking Oaxaca, is packed with 11th century Zapotecan tombs, tunnels, ball courts, pyramids and plazas; and Mitla, 25 miles south with its own museum, is another city of four elaborately carved palaces dedicated to 12th century Zapotecan mortuary rites. Besides these, Oaxaca offers a rich variety of Indian life: people, churches, streets, villages and craft markets for pottery and weaving. Too, Mexico City College has a research center here for archeology and anthropology. Rock hounds find the state honeycombed with gold mines. And three hours away lies the interesting Tehuana isthmus. There are nightly *serenatas* in the plaza with first class military band concerts thrice weekly, concerts on two

other nights by the excellent state symphony orchestra and on the remaining nights by a sweet-toned marimba band. Topping all Oaxaca's folk activities are the elaborate Christmas *posadas* and the mid-July feather dances. For beach or sea fishing, you can visit nearby Puerto Angel (a ten hour trip over a rather rough road), a charming unspoiled beach village on a blue sandy bay surrounded by cliffs and wooded hills. Accommodations are primitive but passable for sportsmen or a short stay. In short, Oaxaca will satisfy anyone who genuinely loves Mexico, who appreciates Indian art and life and who knows how to capitalize on the best that Mexico offers. For those who seek standard tourist amusements, sports, night life, Cape Cod cottages and early American furniture, it simply does not exist here.

Best Hotel Buys: *Francia,* I. Plain, clean Mexican style hotel, large rooms, good food, excellent value. *Rancho San Felipe,* I. Charming converted hacienda taking guests, out of town, reservations needed. *Principal,* I. Currently the best in economy hotels; small pleasant, well run. *Pension Suiza,* I. Comfortable pension with good food. *Monte Alban,* I. Renovated old timer; retirement rates. (Oaxaca has a trailer court.)

PATZCUARO, Mich. Alt. 7,253', pop 15,000. On a mountain slope overlooking island-dotted Lake Patzcuaro is this proud, austere and serene colonial town of hilly, cobblestoned streets lined by white walled, red roofed adobe houses. In the great central arcaded plaza is held one of Mexico's most colorful markets and other plazas adjoin a block apart. Overlooking the town from a hill is the ancient La Colegiata Church and Patzcuaro abounds with colonial mansions, churches, restful parks, fountains and cloistered convents and temples. Just offshore, on Janitzio Island, zigzag walks climb up through a quaint Tarascan fishing village to a gigantic statue of Morelos containing murals by Cuevas and a death mask of the priest himself. Wherever you look, and especially from the heights of El Estribo, Calvary Hill or the Morelos statue, this great 10 x 40 mile lake—one of the world's highest—offers tempting beauty and the town itself retains all the antiquity of the colonial era. Every morning, fishermen go forth in log canoes propelled by round paddles, each loaded with a curious butterfly net. And the women wear the most intriguing blue or red-and-black checkered skirts and satin blouses.

Invigorating and healthful but with crisp mornings and chilly nights, Patzcuaro shares the climate of Mexico City. Data: Feb. 55°, May 61°, Aug. 59°, Nov. 54°; annual average temp. 57°, rainfall 35". Though Patzcuaro is rather too cool in winter for ideal retirement, a foreign colony *has* been established across the lake at Erongaricuaro. For our money, its greatest appeal is as a cool summer resort and an agreeable antidote to tension. Delicious whitefish are sold in the market along with bargains in beautifully designed lacquerware, copper, pottery and embroidered blouses and tablecloths. Nothing is expensive, living attractively cheap. A photographer's and artist's Mecca, Patzcuaro is scene of many colorful aborigine dances and fiestas, an interesting Museum of Popular Art, a UNESCO educational center and a summer school. There is riding, swimming (cool), fishing and hunting, pleasant walks and within easy reach are Tzintzuntzan, Yacatas pyramids, Morelia and Uruapan.

Best Hotel Buys: *Posada de Don Vasco,* M. Comfortable modern hacienda style hotel facing lake two miles out, weekly reductions. *Poseda de La Basilica,* I. Remodelled mansion opposite church, spacious rooms, good food. *Dolatri,* I. Very inexpensive and clean budgeteers' hotel.

QUERETARO, Qro. Alt. 6,042', pop 70,000. Rich in historical associations and colonial charm, this dreamy looking yet busy commercial town has all the antiquity of earlier days. Viewed from the Hill of the Bells where Maximilian was shot, Queretaro spreads out over its gentle valley like a Corot landscape. From the 74 arches of its graceful old aqueduct to shady Alameda Park, you see scores of old churches with a strongly Moorish air and convents, fine old homes, patios, fountains, flower filled parks and plazas. The clean, level streets are lined with handsome colonial buildings and architectural treasures, many revealing the work of Tresguerras.

The climate is similar to San Miguel Allende's but slightly warmer. Data: Feb. 60°, May 70°, Aug. 67°, Nov. 61°; annual average temp. 65°, maximum 78°, minimum 52°; highest ever 97°, lowest 31°. Relative humidity 56% rainfall 20", cloudiness 40%. Days with rain 90, hail 1.7, fog 11.3, snow .1, thunder 33.5.

Despite its attractions, this is virtually untouched territory for American retirees. There is no expatriate colony to push up prices, no heavy American demand for rentals. Here you should find costs as low as anywhere in Mexico. Best part in which to live is the upper part of town towards Plazuela de La Cruz or else on the outskirts. Queretaro has all the facilities you expect of a city of this size including an excellent dentist. Straw articles of every type are ridiculously cheap. There are Sunday band concerts in the plaza, movies and a spa on the outskirts. This is good rock hunting country while nearby are many interesting Bajio towns. Our rating: one of the best Bajio towns for low cost retirement.

Best Hotel Buys: *Balneario El Jacal,* I. Five miles out with spa swimpool, steam baths, gardens; retirement possibilities. *Del Marques,* I. An older modest hotel; good food; good for retirement. *Gran,* I-M. Modernized older hotel.

SAN CRISTOBAL LAS CASAS, Chis. Alt. 7,350', pop 25,000. High in a shining valley rimmed by mountains and primeval forests, this colonial city is home to a small foreign colony who originally came here to study anthropology. For anyone who is interested in anthropology or ethnology or who would enjoy Mexico's richest Indian background, Las Casas is a real discovery. A gem of an old colonial town founded in 1528, its narrow cobbled streets meander past baroque churches and rows of one story whitewashed houses to a vivid market which is trading center for the region's 250,000 Indians. Here, with their roots still in the pre-conquest past, are Chamulas, Tenejapans, Tzotzils and Zinacantan Indians, all dressed in traditional costume and looking like shy gnomes. The medieval town itself is still divided into *barrios,* one for each trade, and Calle Guadalupe is lined by Indian shops.

Untouristed and long isolated, Las Casas has preserved its grilled windows, carved facades and colonial flavor almost untouched. Of course, this is no place to find city conveniences and the climate is cool with chilly nights. But for a summer vacation it really teems with interest. All costs are low and there are bargains galore in leather, pottery, antiques, *serapes,* embroidery and Guatemala style weavings. Fine old houses can be rented inexpensively and there is a surprisingly good city bus service. Anthropological and ethnological studies center around La Cabana research center, there are pagan festivals and weird religious rites aplenty and interesting rides to Indian villages like Zinacantan and Chamula. Our rating: Mexico's best retirement spot for students of Indian life; also recommended for summer vacations with an Indian background.

Best Hotel Buys: *Espanol*, I. Near plaza, quiet, colonial atmosphere with gardens and good food.

SAN JOSE PURUA, Mich. Alt. 4,300'. Poised on the brink of a brown ravine, in a superbly beautiful Tarascan valley, is a deluxe spa hotel, the Balneario San Jose Purua. Viewed from its terraces, the scenic mountain grandeur competes with the turbulent Tuxpan River far below. Surrounding the spa are acres of landscaped park filled with tropical blooms and fruits and the hills are carpeted with flowers. The climate is warm in summer, temperate the rest of the year and seldom does the mercury vary by more than 10°. Data: Mar. 63°, June 71°, Sept. 68°, Dec. 60°; annual average temp. 65°, rainfall 36.7". Insect repellant is useful in summer.

Thermal radioactive sulphur springs supply four swimming pools and endless private baths, all highly recommended for stomach and liver ailments, diabetes, tension, arthritis and nervous and circulatory disorders. A nurse and doctor are in attendance and there are massages and mud baths. Probably Mexico's loveliest spa, the hotel is a series of low, red roofed buildings surrounded by manicured lawns and delightful gardens.

Only a mile or two away but a steep 1,000 feet below is Agua Blanca, a motel-like spa tucked away in an idyllic garden spot beside the river and among tall, tropic trees. Called the Poor Man's San Jose Purua, Agua Blanca is priced right for hotel retirement. You can stay here and use the facilities of San Jose Purua.

Best Hotel Buys: *Balneario San Jose Purua,* VE. A first class spa resort hotel with excellent food, a grotto nightclub, riding, and casino (take a room well away from noisy bowling alleys). *Balneario Agua Blanca* (at Jungapeo, Mich.), I-M. Spa hotel decorated in Tarascan motifs with large, cool, comfortable rooms and country club flavor. Discount to retirees.

SAN MIGUEL DE ALLENDE, Gto. Alt. 6,400', pop 14,500. For a combination of restful, enjoyable living with the added stimulus of hobbies or study, you'll drool over this famous art center of terraced cobblestoned streets and flower filled gardens— all built on a sloping hillside commanding an unobstructed sixty mile view. So purely colonial is this city the Mexican Government has declared it a national monument to remain untouched for posterity. And today it is Mexico's most magnificent example of colonial architecture. Only interiors may be modernized. There are no neon signs, commercialism or plate glass windows. Used as the setting for the movies *Brave Bulls* and *Serenade,* SMA's heaviest industry is serving as an artists' model. For painters it fairly teems with color and composition.

View it first from the Instituto Hotel looking up Moctezuma Hill. Houses of pink sandstone, brick and adobe soar up the hill in geometrical pattern while their red tiled roofs appear to fall cubistically down the hillside. Then climb up among the new American villas to Calle Real and look down. Dominating the town is the pink, multi-steepled "Gothesque" parish church overlooking a set of vertical winding streets, parks, statutes, facades and fountains, many designed by Tresguerras, Mexico's Michelangelo. Shimmering fanciful church cupolas and glazed domes loom over the rooftops and the mellow ringing of church bells adds to the restful, medieval aspect. As you descend to the plaza, you note the Old World lanterns used for street lighting and the magnificently carved doorways, so heavily studded that knocking is inaudible and mailmen blow whistles. Below the parish chuch, the tree-shaded plaza is rimmed by *portales* and prim flagstone walks and decorated with turn-of-the-century iron seats and flower beds with a pink-toned bandstand in the center. In all of Mexico, you will not find a more beautiful plaza.

Not without justification has SMA become one of the world's largest expatriate Yankee settlements. Famous Mexicans retire here too. From all over the Americas come students to study arts and crafts at its celebrated Instituto Allende. From 350-450 art loving Americans permanently share this inspiring, unspoiled town. Down in the plaza ex-Army sergeants, firemen and merchant seamen loll in the morning sun. Not all are artists. But most retirees are more industrious, more creative than the latter day settlers of Lake Chapala. Here idleness is rare. Drink, bridge and gossip take second place to study and retirement hobbies.

The large American-Canadian colony has created a slight air of cosmopolitan sophistication. You can sip Cafe Espresso at a big, new glassed-in cafe off the plaza and you can get an ice cream sundae, hamburger or hot dog if you desire. Originally founded in 1937 by Americans artists seeking a cheaper setting, SMA's colony has since become the escapist retreat of famous entertainment personalities both from Mexico and the United States. Add to these its own residents—many of pedigreed Spanish families—plus the Indian population and you have an idea of the vivacious, festive spirit which finds its outlet in no fewer than thirty fiestas held each year.

The benign climate resembles that of Santa Barbara but is drier, and in spring, warmer. In he clear, invigorating mountain air, blankets are needed every night and from October through February, nights can become quite cold with two or three frosts. Too high for cardiac sufferers, SMA is beneficial for sufferers from sinus, arthritis and rheumatism. Sole drawback is the possibility of brief winted cold snaps. Data: Feb. 59", May 71°, Aug. 67°, Nov. 59°; annual average temp. 64°, rainfall 21.4".

Provided you come outside the crowded summer school season, you'll find rentals normally in fair supply (say a dozen to choose from, mostly apartments). Houses are fewer. Small furnished apartments range from $40-$98, houses when available from $65. Under construction are two new subdivisions: Colonia Arcos de San Miguel overlooking the city from the former ranch of ex-bullfighter Pepe Ortiz; and the Lomas subdivision at the lower end of town. Both offer all utilities, city drainage, cobbled streets and houses for as little as $4,500 plus lot. For $8,900 plus lot, you can build a two story home which would be worth $18,000 in California. Lots sell at $750-$1,500, with the best view sites at $3,000 or more. Other couples enjoy rebuilding ruined palaces.

As hilly as San Francisco, SMA is one place where a car is really useful. With it, you can reach the border and return in 48 hours. Alternatively you can go by bus or train. SMA boasts a modern 25 bed hospital opened in 1957, well stocked drug stores, clinics in two neighboring towns, an excellent dentist and doctors. Water is spring fresh, city sewage efficient. American influence has been responsible for inauguration of up-to-date grocery stores with imported products, a modern butcher and good poultry supply and a fine public library. For bargains in home furnishings, the local market supplies excellent tinwork, pottery, *cambaya* cloth and woven goods and *serapes* and beautiful items of nail-studded leather. There are several good children's *colegios,* a local Spanish language high school and an American run school for younger children ($40 a month).

Center of life is the Instituto Allende, originally the country palace of the Condes de La Canal. Headed today by lean, suntanned Stirling Dickinson, for 11 months of the year it offers English language courses in all the fine arts, Spanish, creative writing and practically every handicraft from lithography to sculpture and photography. Tuition averages $50 a month or $135 per three months for the full program—varied, well integrated and most worthwhile. There is no age limit, no special entry requirements and all retirees who can afford it keep fully occupied throughout the year. Numerous social and cultural activities are tied in including summer drama. Too, SMA also has a splendidly equipped branch of Mexico City's Bellas Artes fine arts school (with regular concerts etc., open to the public) and also a branch of the Academia Hispano Americana language school.

In addition, SMA has movies, concerts, art exhibitions and an Instituto Club with two tennis courts, bowling, fronton-tennis and occasional dances. Riding is popular and there is a splendid hilltop riding school. You can swim at a pool in town or in the Taboada Hot Springs pool several miles out in the mesquite. There are good local duck hunting, TV, fiestas throughout the year featuring *conchero* dancers, Saturday house and garden tours sponsored by the American Ladies Committee of SMA library, American and Spanish movies at the Instituto and lots of *posadas* prior to Christmas. Easy bus or car trips take you to the ceramics center of Dolores Hidalgo, to the pilgrimage monastery at Atotonilco, to Queretaro, Guanajuato and Patzcuaro, and in 3½ hours to Mexico City. Most entertainment takes the form of informal home parties but there is dancing on weekend nights at the Patio Bar, a favorite rendezvous furnished in colonial style with bullfight posters. San Miguel also has a good drama company: the Gallery Players.

To get into the swim quickly, you should enroll at the Instituto and drop into the *Cucuracha* for an evening drink. Our rating: if you want to combine painting, study, friends and hobbies with comfortable low cost living, SMA is the best all around retirement spot in Mexico. Idleness, that chronic plague of Mexican retirement, is virtually impossible here.

Belst Hote Buys: *Casa Sauto,* I. Good Mexican pension. *Colon,* I. Small central hotel. *Colonial,* I. Clean, central, nice patio, good food. *Instituto Allende,* I. Modern, well run hotel in Instituto, magnificent balcony view from all rooms, good food. *Posada de Las Monjas,* I. Central with panoramic roof garden view. *Poseda San Francisco,* M. Traditional colonial patio style hotel in former monastery, cool, quiet and attractive. *Rancho Atascadero,* I. Restored hilltop hacienda, gardens, swimpool, fireplaces, good food. *Posada de La Fuente,* I. Good small downtown pension-hotel.

TAXCO, Gro. Alt. 5,756', pop 19,000. An Italian-like hillside silver smithing village, Taxco definitely *is* Mexico's most arresting and picturesque town. Poised on the polychromed sides of the rugged Guerrero hills, this mountain eyrie pyramids up the slopes in tiers of glistening white houses with their warm red roofs creating a stepladder effect. Almost verical mosaic-patterned cobblestoned streets twist up and down, past buildings with rough, heavy beams and facades of finely chiselled stone. Handwrought iron lanterns light the streets at night and everywhere are ancient doorways, woodwork and grilled balconies spilling over with flowers. There are literally hundreds of vantage points, each with its spell binding view. From any, Taxco appeals like a gigantic, unreal movie set. As a National Monument, its unity of style has been preserved for all time. No modernization is permitted to destroy Taxco's historic integrity. Only interior modernization is allowed.

Several landmarks give Taxco its distinctive personality. Greatest, of course, is the baroque Santa Prisca church whose twin pink towers and vivid colored dome dominate the town. Then there are fine old houses like Casa Figueroa and Humboldt House, an exquisite baroque palace. Plaza Borda, the *zocalo* lined with laurel trees, is so straight out of the 18th century you expect to see a duel in progress and ladies swooning. All this untouched colonial splendor gives Taxco its own special charm, the atmosphere of another world of yesteryear.

Mountains keep out all north winds and Taxco basks in a dry, sunny, temperate climate never too hot and never too cold. Springlike and invigorating, winters are dry and clear; summers cool and marked by late p. m. rains July through September. You'll find it healthful, restful, relaxing and almost perfect. Data: Feb. 69°, May 76°, Aug. 70°, Nov. 68°; annual average temp., 70°, rainfall 58.2".

Apart from a few minor drawbacks, Taxco offers ideal retirement at, for Mexico, medium cost. The fame of this travel folder village has drawn artists and writers, retired folk and sojourners from the ends of the earth. A trifle too touristy for some people, others enjoy its steady flow of visitors. Taxco's inner life is not visible to tourists. However, you'll meet the local residents at Paco's bar on the plaza or over a tequila lemonade during the afternoon music at Bertha's. Most residents share art interests but one and all have creative hobbies that keep them busy and occupied. Over 200 expatriates form the foreign colony and social life revolves around lunches and cocktail parties held in private homes. Although some houses are on the expensive side, unfurnished places *can* be found for as little as $60 a month. Most couples, however, prefer to buy or lease a typical old Taxco home and remodel. Best months for locating rentals are May and November. Domestic help and food are reasonably priced.

Taxco has a Presbyterian church, good water, a plaza newsstand selling American books and magazines and loads of art works. In the Sunday market you can shop for furniture and objects of precious wood, leather, *serapes,* tinware, baskets, sandals, ceramics, paintings, silverware and copper—all of which can furnish your home graciously but inexpensively. Another good buy are the smart peasant clothes tailored by chic fashion shops. Anything else you can get in Cuernavaca 90 minutes away.

Drawbacks? Taxco is one of Mexico's noisiest towns—nights are filled with barking dogs, braying burros, church bells, singing and fireworks. The place is undeniably touristed and to some extent commercialized. And you must be able to climb hills; taxis are available but your own car is useless. Last of these shortcomings is an acquired taste: Taxco has its own following of ardent admirers; others wouldn't dream of retiring here.

Heading activities is the art school, where for $10 a week or $35 a month, you can study painting, sculpture and every other kind of handicraft. The school, open all year, arranges inexpensive accommodations for students and has an excellent lending library. For prospectus, write Escuela de Bellas Artes, Taxco, Gro. You can swim at hotel pools, golf at Cuernavaca. There is one movie theater, a night club and dinner dancing at a choice of hotels. But Taxco customarily goes to bed at 10 P.M. and most residents prefer to be up early for another round of sketching, painting and photography. You'll find splendid mountain walks such as that to San Francisco Cuadra and scenic horse trails like the popular ride to Noxtopec. Then there's a choice of short bus or car trips to such places as Iguala, Tehuixtla hot springs, Cacahuamilpa Caves, Xochicalco pyramid, Cuernavaca, Cuautla, Ixtapan spa, Toluca and Acapulco. Interesting local fiestas include th spectacular Holy Week processions, the annual silver festival and the Christmas *posadas* and *Noche Buena* customs.

Best Hotel Buys: *Casa Humboldt,* I. The intellectual's guest house, good food. *Hacienda San Francisco Cuadra,* M. Fine hacienda resort 3 miles out. *Posada de La Mision,* M-E. Tourist hotel, good as a base on arrival. *Real de Taxco,* I. Small, cheerful older hotel on hill. *Hacienda El Chorillo,* M. Delightfully atmospheric, good food. *Los Arcos,* I. Older but nice, good food. *Santa Prisca.* M. One of Mexico's finest small hotels, a top buy with good food, charm, comfort and service. *Victoria,* M-E. Excellent but touristy. *Melendez,* I. An OK budget stop. Most hotels offer long term discounts.

TEHUACAN, *Pue.* Alt. 5,332', pop 32,000. In a broad valley of rolling wheat fields, this clean, pleasant resort town with its historic churches, exuberant gardens, and shady streets lined by jacaranda trees, is home of the famous Peñafiel waters which are bottled and imbibed all over Mexico. Barring a few cold days in December and January, the climate is dry, exhilarating, temperature and most healthful. Data: Feb., 62°, May 70°, Aug. 68°, Nov. 61°; annual average temp. 65°, rainfall 19".

A spa widely famed for its recuperative properties in cases of hepatitis, kidney and digestive ailments, it is site of several *balnearios* and ideal for hotel retirement. All leading hotels have pools and the largest supplies a wide choice of free activities. You can hunt, fish and ride, shop for bargains in onyx and straw, or visit nearby Zapotecan ruins.

Best Hotel Buys: *Mexico,* I. Modernized colonial hotel with two fine swimpools, roof garden and solarium. Priced for retirement. *Spa Peñafiel,* M. Large resort hotel on outskirts with landscaped grounds, very good food, nine hole golf course, tennis, swimming. Turkish baths and massages and a casino. A best buy in good living! For good economy living, try the *Monte Carlo* or *Posada de Tehuacan.*

TEPIC, *Nay.* Alt. 3,080', pop 62,500. Few tourists driving down from California stop to view this city from the Paseo de La Loma. The few who do discover it as one of Mexico's cleanest and most picturesque small towns. In a setting of hille at the foot of the extinct Sanganguey volcano, Tepic is a prosperous and modernized colonial city of broad paved streets, arcade bordered plazas and splendid old colonial homes. Half old, half new, this quiet, restful town is ideal for retirement. The climate is warm but never hot. Data: Mar. 65°, June 74°, Sept. 74°, Dec. 64°; annual average temp., 69°, rainfall 48". Though rentals are scarce, there's a small hospital and nearby are five beaches and beautiful Lake Santa Mario del Oro with good fishing and hunting. Tip: for unbelievably low living costs go to Compostela, a few miles south of Tepic.

Best Hotel Buys: *Sierra de Alica,* I. On plaza, retirement possibilities. Others: the *Palace* and *Imperial.* Tepic has a trailer park.

TEPOZTLAN, *Mor.* Alt. 5,500', pop 4,500. This serene, low priced eleven miles from Cuernavaca is almost unknown to the average American. The setting is fabulous, the village a nescapist's dream. Walled in like a Shangri-La by towering cliffs and fortress-like peaks, Tepoztlan's steep cobbled streets and quaint Old World houses are dominated by the battlements and buttresses of a massive Gothic convent. From 1,000 feet overhead, the ancient Tepozteco pryamid looks down on the town. Poinsettias grow wild and gardens are riotous. So unspoiled are the villagers that they still speak in *Nahautl* and pay their taxes with labor or corn.

Picturesque and completely unspoiled, Tepoztlan is unique among Mexican villages. Here in this sleepy community you will find true character and charm untouched by modern civilization. The village itself is still divided into eleven *barrios,* each with its own church and local chief. But predating the village's severe Spanish colonial, baroque and churrigueresque, is the rambling Tepoztlan Convent, a Dominican structure over four centuries old, built with massive walls thirteen feet thick and lacking entirely the decorative facades of the baroque period. To appreciate Tepoztlan, you must see it from the *posada* as changing patterns of light and shade bring bright sunny colors and blue sombre tones to one of Mexico's most superb panoramas. The climate is mild and delightful, similar to Cuernavaca's with a year around average of 70°.

Is Tepoztlan for you? Until recently, life here was primitive. But a minor real estate boom created by weekending Mexico City folk has changed things: pushed up land prices and brought modern amenities. But there is still no overcrowding, no big American colony to raise living costs. The bargain days are over, of course, but a few houses are generally for rent or you can build at reasonable cost. All new homes are designed in native style to harmonize with Tepoztlan's colonial past. But there is modern electricity, plumbing and even a golf course.

Painting, writing, reading and relaxing are the chief occupations. There are archeological remains galore, many unexplored. Horses are available for riding to tiny villages and there are scores of places of interest to which you can hike. Each year, Tepoztlan stages a big pagan festival in September and a three day carnival in February. Because Cuernavaca is so close at hand, Mexico City barely 90 minutes away, Tepoztlan offers simple living at medium cost with all city conveniences within easy reach. For more about the village, look up these books in your public library: *Tepoztlan* by anthropologist Redfield and *Tepoztlan Re-*

studied by Profesor Lewis. Our rating: a toprung retirement spot.

Best Hotel Buys: *Posada del Tepozteco,* M. One of the most charming small hotels in Mexico, a former colonial hacienda modernized and furnished in antiques; swimpool, 10% off by the month.

TEQUISQIAPAN, Qro. Alt. 6,000', pop 3,000. Few Americans ever run off highway 45 at San Juan Del Rio and drive eleven miles over a paved road to Tequisquiapan. Those who do discover a true bargain paradise, the cleanest, most serene and neatest little spa town in Mexico. In a countryside dotted with old haciendas, "Tequis" is a dream village of pink, blue and white houses with wrought iron balconies lining broom-swept cobbled streets. Churches, inns and pensions dot the little town. Meandering along luxurious semitropical backyards is the San Juan river, jammed with bass and trout. Old fashioned lanterns light the strets and the hotels are built like great rambling haciendas. Bubbling fountains and swimming pools are everywhere in this smiling village. At any hotel or public bath you can take the rejuvenating waters, which many swear leave you feeling ten years younger. Healing radioactive waters boil from the ground all over the village. At a constant 93°F, the waters are excellent for insomnia and a variety of ailments.

You may be relieved to find no gems of colonial architecture or touristy little gift shops. From Monday to Friday, Tequis leads a lazy life which promises a true sense of peace. Only on weekends when visitors come to take the waters does the town come to life and cars appear on the streets. At other times, you're likely to see only the hospitable Otomi Indian residents. So embarrassingly honest are they that no doors are ever locked on weekday nights. The climate is similar to San Miguel de Allende's.

Tequis is an irrefutable answer to those who claim Mexico is nowadays expensive. All costs are amazing low. Water can be drunk from the tap, all householders are responsible for sweeping the street outside and there are a good drug store, bank and bus service to nearby Queretaro. Since some Mexico City people began building weekend homes here, a handful of Americans have formed a tiny colony and houses can now occasionally be rented. Otherwise, you can live for ridiculously little in the town's atmospheric hotels. For more permanent living, you'll find two country club type retirement developments. One, Manantiales del Prado (o;ce at Havre 7-201, Mexico 6, D.F.) features plush colonial type homes with private thermal pools from $6,500.

Among Tequis' attractions are opal hunting, fishing, riding, rock hunting, swimming and visiting fiestas. Beautiful baskets, drawn work and cambaya cloth are good buys. Creamy milk, fresh meat and delicious Rancho Grande cheeses are delivered daily. But there are no movies or night life. Our rating: a barely discovered little Eden.

Best Hotel Buys: *Posada del Camino,* I. Delightful, neat small inn. *Posada Tequisquiapan,* I. Nice small older inn. *Posada San Francisco,* I. Attractive up-to-date inn. *Posada del Virrey,* I. Pleasant inn with attractive new wing. All are top buys and fine for retirement.

URUAPAN, Mich. Alt. 5,300', pop 47,000. "Michoacan Paradise" was how colonial Spaniards described this lovely semitropical resort town among the Tarascan hills near Paricutin volcano. Even the name means "where the flowers are blooming." Which is no understatement for Uruapan is a place of tall pine forests and majestic trees and beautiful parks, *quintas,* coffee and fruit plantations beside the foaming Cupatitzio River. The gay ash from Paricutin's eruption of the late 1940s was cleared away long ago and Uruapan is once again a drowsy uncommercialized town of steep cobblestoned streets, red tiled roofs and charming markets, streets and plazas. Flowers luxuriate on the recently deposited volcanic ash to such an extent that the place is now called "Flower Garden of Mexico."

For an insight into this attractive retirement spot, you should visit Gualapera, a former 17th century convent, now center of the lacquer industry sponsored by the Museum of Folk Arts. Here in a colonial setting of beamed ceilings and flagstone floors, you can witness the industrious craftsmanship of the region's Tarascan Indians. Go then to the Eduardo Ruiz National Park on the beautiful Cupatitzio River at the entrance to town. Here, among tree-embowered paths, are delightful picnic spots and bathing pools, Farther out is the lacy ninety foot cataract of Tzararacua. The climate is temperate all year, tailored for outdoor living. Data: Feb. 62°, May 72°, Aug 69°, Nov. 64°; annual average temp. 67°, rainfall 67.3".

Add it all up and you have the ingredients for a marvellous retirement spot. Yet there are few Americans here to date. All costs are low and *casas* can still be rented at prices people dream about on Lake Chapala. Moreover, this is the place to furnish your home graciously with amazingly low cost works of art. Sold at Uruapan's market is superb lacquerware of every conceivable kind, bone inlaid guitars and harps, beautiful cross-stitched embroidery, tablecloths and blouses, gold jewelry, handwoven *cambaya* peasant costumes and magnificent red, green and black glazed pattery. Tropical fruits are super abundant, the local coffee appetizing and cheap. In some cases, prices run 10% of those in Mexico City.

Activities range from sitting on the elongated plaza and watching the interesting Indian life to swimming, riding, fishing, hiking and hunting. There are Sunday evening band concerts and lots of religious fiestas and secular celebrations complete with the graceful Canacuas folk dances. Near at hand you can visit the blackened cone of Paricutin and the Tepacaltepec Dam Project. Uruapan lies at the head of the huge, undeveloped Michoacan Pacific Coast area, scheduled one day to become a vast new paradise and you can already fly down to the undeveloped beach resort of Playa Azul. Our rating: an overlooked, low cost Utopia that, with opening of the Pacific Coast will undoubtedly become a large retirement colony. Why not get in while prices still are low?

Best Hotel Buys: *Victoria,* I-M. Comfortable, central. *Hernandez,* I. Modern, pleasant. Both O.K. for retirement.

VALLE DE DRAVO, Mex. Alt. 5,700', pop 5,000. If you're seeking a cool retirement or vacation spot among hills and dales and aromatic pine forests that remind you of Scotland, turn off Highway 15 just west of Toluca and drive down to the five rocky artificial lakes created by the Miguel Aleman power project. On one of these, 4½ x 1 mile Lake Avandaro, lies the Swiss-like potters' village of Valle de Bravo—a storybook town of quaint, winding cobbled streets and tiled houses with heavy carved wooden beams, wooden balconies and whitewashed facades. From the bustling main street, gay with pottery shops, streets wind up and down with pleasing irregularity and lead out around the lake shores nestled in a beautiful northern countryside of lofty hills, hidden streams and foaming waterfalls. Quaint and pastoral and not over touristed, Valle de Bravo offers peace, rest and tranquillity among the variegated greens of sylvan bowers and gigantic evergreens.

High, cool and bracing, the climate is made for an invigorating outdoor life. Not unnaturally, it has attracted a foreign colony of Swiss, Americans and English. Nights are cool and residents customarily gather before roaring log fires. Beautiful weekend homes, many in hocienda style, dot the beautiful Avandaro subdivision where, though waterfront is not available, homes can be built with a sweeping lake view. Over fifty homes have so far been built, all sprawled in large fragrant gardens with an atmosphere of spaciousness and comfort. Two bedroom homes on 1,000 square meter lots cost approximately $4,000. Other costs are equally reasonable. Magnificent baskets and green glazed pottery sell locally for pennies and what is not available in the village can be found in Toluca nearby. Bus service is available.

You'll find excellent trout and bass fishing and sailing, watersports and riding and hiking over pleasant alpine trails. In nearby Barranca del Diablo are advanced rock paintings and there are probably others as yet undiscovered. Valle de Bravo now boasts a splendid 18-hole golf course.

Best Hotel Buys: *Refugio del Salto,* M. An alpine inn beside a waterfall, O.K. for retirement. *Golf Motel Avandaro,* M-E. Good value in a luxury golf resort.

Region 4. Tropical Savanna

THIS IS A transition zone between the jungly vegetation of Region 5 and the steppe of Region 2. It is the identical climate shared by most of India and the mean temperature in all months exceeds 64°. Vegetation consists of tall, coarse grass which withers in the dry season and scattered trees whose leaves fall in winter. Ozone flowing down from the Sierras adds stimulation to the uniform climate of the south Pacific Coast.

Starting in early October, fall is comparatively dry and comfortably warm. Winter is cool, agreeable, healthful and pleasant. On the Pacific Coast, steady offshore winds bring dry weather and from December to April, rain is rarely seen. In Vera Cruz and Yucatan, the delightful winter weather is broken only by occasional wet northers November through March which bring srtong winds, rain and brief temperatures as low as 40° at Vera Cruz and 55° in Yucatan. At other times, brief periods of cold, moist, calm, misty weather may hang for a few days over Vera Cruz and Yucatan. Spring sees a return of perfect weather, growing hot and dry after March and lasting until the first rains in June. The summer rainy season lasts from mid-June through early October: June is wettest on the Pacific Coast; Yucatan receives considerable rainfall during summer; and the trade winds bring abundant rain to Vera Cruz. Summer in northern Vera Cruz alternates between periods of hot, humid calms, frequently experienced May to July when the temperature may reach 102°, and hot northerly winds most prevalent in August. On the mountain slopes of Vera Cruz, the trade winds occasionally deposit the tedious, drizzling *chipi-chipi* rains. By and large, however, the summer climate is no hotter or more humid than that of southern Florida and the winters are infinitely preferable.

On the Pacific Coast, despite some cloudiness in summer and early fall, skies are surprisingly clear. Cloudiness varies from 66% at Manzanillo to only 38% at Salina Cruz and increases inland to 58% at Comitan. Acapulco boasts an excellent record of 159 clear days annually compared to only 75 that are cloudy. Fog decreases southward from 20 days annually at Manzanillo to 16 at Tapachula. Frost is unknown in Region 4, the temperature varying only 5°-15° between summer and winter. On the Pacific Coast the annual average temperature is 73° (80° on the coast, 66° inland), the average high temperature varies from 76°-90° and the average low 52°-86°. Rainfall averages 36"-54" on the coast and is highest around Acapulco and also in the extreme south around Tapachula, which receives an average of 94". Rainy days vary from 52 annually at Manzanillo to 152 at Tapachula, thunder storms occur on 10-36 days along the coast, more frequently inland. Humidity is oppressive only during the rainy season. The annual average relative humidity is 70% raising to 77% on the northern Pacific Coast and decreasing around Tehuantepec to 67%. It increases again on the cooler interior mountain slopes of extreme south Mexico, rising to a high of 85% at Comitan.

The coastal strip of northern Vera Cruz enjoys a languid tropical climate with an annual average temperature of 75°, an annual average high of 82° and an annual average low of 70°. Rainfall totals 60" and falls on approximately 145 days each year, mostly after dark. Here, too, the humidity is high only in the rainy season, comparatively dry and agreeable at other times. The annual average relative humidity is 82%. Trade wind cloud brings the total cloudiness to 62% and while days entirely clear of cloud number only 36 per pear, only one day in three can actually be called cloudy. Early morning fogs appear on 56 days annually at Vera Cruz, on 108 days at Tuxpan and thunder occurs on some 18 days each year.

On the Yucatan peninsula, the trade winds bring more heat and humidity to the Caribbean coast than to the Gulf of Mexico side. Example: Cozumel on the Caribbean has 74" of rain on 140 days with thunder storms on 56 days and a relative humidity of 86%; Campeche on the Gulf has 35" of rain on 91 days with thunder storms on 15 days and a relative humidity of 75%. However, the effect of steady trade winds on the Caribbean ameliorates the heat and humidity to where, in reality, there is little to choose between the two coasts. The annual temperature averages 78° with an average high of 84° and a low of 72°. Campeche reports fog on 9 days annually and out of the year, 106 days are entirely free of cloud, only 70 obscured by cloud.

Conclusion: in most respects, this is the climate of south Florida, warmer in winter and perhaps slightly warmer in summer. For those who enjoy Miami in summer, the coastal regions have much to offer. Between mid-October and early May, the climate is ideal for beach vacations and outdoor sports. For a winter vacation, the Pacific side has the more reliable weather.

ACAPULCO, Gro. Alt 23', pop 85,000. On an almost landlocked turquoise bay ringed by brilliant green mountains, Acapulco is a polychrome paradise of terraced hotels set on dramatic red cliffs above sparkling strips of white beach. Boulevards, luxury hotels and modern shops rim the twisted contours of its majestic harbor. There are 23 beaches and a glittering array of every kind of fleshpot imaginable. To Hollywood stars and wealthy American executives this heavenly spot is a millionaire's playground. But Acapulco is not Miami Beach, rather it is *a pot pourri* of tropical Mexico and Florida. Four times as many Mexicans vacation here as do Americans. And to most, Acapulco is their dream of a poor man's paradise.

This glamour city is such a byword we need waste no more space on its description. Suffice it to say it resembles Miami Beach but has infinitely more charm and beauty. There are fishing and a sailfish rodeo in April, an eighteen hole golf course and country club, sailboat and glass bottom boat trips, a ski club and water skiing, organized skin diving, lots of dinner dance spots and night clubs of every description, jai alai, bullfights in season, numerous celebrations and festivals, a summer school, tennis, wide screen movies and even an archeological zone. But despite some, which like Caleta are highly commercialized, the beaches are the big draw. Traditional routine is to spend the morning in the calm waters of curving Caleta Beach and the afternoon either promenading or enjoying the livelier surf at Los Hornos. To avoid crowds, though, we suggest taking an early morning dip at Caletilla, spending the morning out at lighthouse-capped Roqueta Island beach reached by ferry, the afternoon at Cobana near Hornos and viewing the sunset from either the *zocalo* or Pie de La Cuesta, eight miles out, where you lie in a hammock while beach boys dive through the raging surf. Other good beaches are Revolcadero, beyond Puerto Marques with surf, and Encontada, still farther out but often rough.

A study of climate shows that winter is the best season. Data: Feb. 78°, May 83°, Aug. 83°, Nov. 81°; annual average temp. 81°, maximum 88°, minimum 73°. Relative humidity 79%, rainfall 54.3", cloudiness 39%. Days with rain 80, cloud 75, fog 10, strong winds 2.1, thunder 10.7. From mid-April till mid-December, however, hotels cut rates by 10%-50%. Is this season a good buy? By and large, summer temperatures run only 7°-8° above those in winter and Acapulco in summer is no more hot or humid than is Miami. Moreover, if you choose a breeze fanned hotel on the slopes, you *can* enjoy a comparatively cool vacation at bargain rates. Good uncrowded months are April to June and in fall.

Rents are high, hence for a longer sojourn or even retirement, you'll probably do best to locate a comfortable pension or pension-hotel. Nevertheless, there are bungalows and apartments for rent, usually advertised in newspapers or available through real estate agents. Seafood is inexpensive, Acapulco has a good hospital and doctors, good shops and all modern facilities. But for year around living, most people find the climate rather warm.

Beach and boulevard hotels are fine in winter but in summer, despite the added taxi fare to the beaches, you'll be better off higher up. Notwithstanding the advertising of deluxe hotels which would have you think Acapulco is expensive, you'll find excellent hotels in every price bracket. There are loads of superior second class hotels offering economical living and many are cooler and quieter than the big luxury palaces located on noisy boulevards. The hills are dotted with delightful pensions which will do you proud for $5-$6 a day, meals, terrace and view thrown in.

Discounts, customary for longer stays, can reduce your costs to $4.50-$5.50—and remember, we're talking about clean, comfortable hotels and pensions, not slums. Thus below, you will not find the usual tourist traps listed. Instead, these are the hotels patronized by better class Mexicans who demand cleanliness, comfort, good food and service at sensible prices and they make sure they get them. Even at the most expensive, your total daily expenses should not exceed $15 including taxis, drinks, beach chairs and nightclubbing. Reservations are advised in winter and summer. If you have difficulty locating any hotel, write the Acapulco Information Bureau. Don't forget, too, that though you may stay at an economical hotel, you can freely enter and make use of the pools, lounges and other swank facilities of the most luxurious.

Best Hotel Buys: *Aloha,* I. Downtown near Caleta, quiet, restful, small. *Belmar,* M. Low location, suite type rooms, pool, gardens. *Del Pacifico,* I. Central, near Caleta Beach. *De La Playa,* M. Downtown with own beach and night club. *El Pozo del Rey,* E. Small, breezy, on peninsula, pool, a best buy in comfort! *Helvetia,* I. Small, breezy, balconies on sea, home cooking. *Las Anclas,* I. Excellent Danish run pension hotel. *Mallorca,* I.M. Near Caleta, breezy, rooms with terraces and view. *Papagayo,* M-E. Big, older Hornos Beach hotel, a good buy! *Puerto Arturo,* I-M. Breezy downtown hotel. *Riviera,* M. Low location downtown, pool. *Santa Clara,* I. Well run with German cuisine. *Siete Mares,* I. Breezy, quiet hotel on peninsula, excellent food. *Miami,* I. Near beach, good food. *Quinta Maria,* I. Economy pension at Hornos Beach.

BARRA DE NAVIDAD, *Jal.* Alt. 10', pop 1,000. Primitive and lovely, this South Seas like village straddles a sandbar between a green lagoon and the great sweep of beach lining the shimmering Bay of Barra de Navidad. All around, on mountains and headlands, a luxuriant jungle presses in upon this gem. Poor roads and isolation have kept this beautiful Pacific beach resort unturisted and uncommercialized. But new roads are going through and already a new canal type subdivision is planned.

Twenty miles north of B de N and accessible only by boat or jeep is an even more paradisical spot, Tenacatita. Here the primitive village flanks an indescribably lovely beach bounded by overwhelming rock formations. Fishing is not organized at either but small boats or *canuas* can be chartered, the fishing is superb, the skin diving unbelievably good and birdwatching in the lagoons most rewarding. Bathing is unsurpassed. Our rating: both AAA1 escapist spots.

Best Hotel Buys: *Melaque,* M. Modern resort hotel on beach, nice rooms, pool. Five miles north at Cuastecomate Bay is the *Motel El Dorado,* M; and at Tenacatita, the primitive but pleasant *Bungalows Tenacatita.*

CAMPECHE, *Camp.* Alt. 30', pop 45,000. Surrounded by the remains of an ancient fortified wall and studded with crumbling fortresses, this old colonial city climbs a hill above the turquoise Gulf of Mexico. Little known but nonetheless a delightful seashore vacation spot, it offers both beaches and an historical colonial background. Built of Italian marble shipped in as ballast are the statues, stairways, fountains and verandahs which abound among the city's churches, colonial monuments and fine old pastel colored homes. In spite of the damp, musty tropical air—due as much to Campeche's antiquity as to climate—the weather in spring, fall and winter is superior to Florida's Data: Feb. 74°, May 81°, Aug. 81°, Nov. 76°; annual average temp. 78°, maximum 83°, minimum 73°. Relative humidity 75%, rainfall 35.5". Days with rain 91, unclouded skies 106, partly cloudy 189, dense fog 9, strong winds 5.4, thunder 14.7.

Although Campeche has no retirement colony, the town offers attractive living conditions. There are bargains in every type of seafood and in venison, alligator and jaguar skins and gold filigree jewelry. Besides swimming and fishing, you can explore the numerous forts, visit the historical museum and enjoy the pre-Lenten carnival.

Best Hotel Buys: *Castelmar,* I. Old but attractive with god food and private beach. *Lopez,* I-M. First rate with excellent restaurant and service. *Baluartes.* I-M. New, modern, multi-story beachfront hotel, spotless, comfortable and excellent value!

COZUMEL, Q.R. Alt 15', pop 3,000. The regular airline service from Merida is the only practical way to reach this lush, oblong island twelve miles off the Yucatan peninsula in the Caribbean. Flying in, one notes the creamy golden beaches backed by coconut palms lining the island's western shore and the scores of still lagoons and isolated coves which rim this lovely isle. From the airstrip, a station wagon takes you over a grassy road lined by staring iguanas to the thatched roof, pastel toned village of San Miguel. White hulled sloops and schooners are anchored in the harbor and half the town seems built of shells. On the outskirts are the familiar round, thatched Mayan houses and beyond, a luxuriant jungle full of parrots, orchids and weird air plants.

Time was when Cozumel could be called a bargain paradise. That was before big national magazines began writing it up. Nowadays, prices are almost as high as Acapulco's and sleek cars have replaced the bicycle and burro of yesteryear. Even so, costs are far less than those of St. Thomas or Nassau and for escapists, Cozumel is infinitely superior. Barring a few brief northers, November through April is perfect and fresh ocean breezes blow throughout the year. Data: Average annual temp. 78°, maximum 85°, minimum 71°. Relative humidity 86%, rainfall 75". Days with rain 140, thunder 56.

Most of Cozumel is straight out of the 16th century when roistering pirates anchored offshore. The people are delightfully friendly and the indolent tropical air creates an inescapable flavor of leisure and timelessness. Occasional houses may be rented from $100 a month (mostly more). Venison, seafood and pineapples are excellent and abundant and local tailors do marvellously cheap work. You can swim from San Juan or San Francis-

co beaches, snorkel in clear Chancanab Lagoon, prog lobsters or go shelling and visit Mayan ruins on the island or the adjoining mainland. Both fishing and skin diving are outstanding.

Best Hotel Buys: the *Plaza* and *Isleno,* both M, give good value. For budget accommodation, inquire about family style pensions like *Casa Martin* or *Casa Ribera, Casa Lopez, Posada Yoli,* etc.

ISLA MUJERES, Q.R. Like Cozumel, this low limestone island six miles off the Yucatan peninsula is an alluring Caribbean retreat. To get there at all involves a day long ride by jolting second class bus from Merida to Puerto Juarez, where you transfer to the launch *Carmita* for the six mile run out to the island. Isla Mujeres is worth a far more arduous trip. On this long, narrow island with sandy beaches rimmed by rainbow seas, a village of brightly painted houses meanders along narrow sand lanes almost entirely free of traffic. The island has a climate similar to that of Cozumel and at least as much charm and the few people who have been here consider it one of the Caribbean's loveliest gems. Fishing, shelling and skin diving are superb and skin divers have brought up relics from sunken treasure galleons. You'll find a ruined Mayan observatory and there are sailboats for rent. Our rating: for a simple, unhurried island vacation Isla Mujeres is a real discovery.

Best Hotel Buys: *Rios,* I. Modest. *Posada del Mar,* E. Small beach resort. *Zacil-Ha,* E. Flavorful beach resort. *Super Manzana,* M-E. Modern housekeeping cottages.

JALAPA, Ver. Alt. 4,381'. pop 70,000. Built on a mountain slope overlooking an exuberant scene of terraced garden slopes, this partly modernized colonial city is encircled by a mountainous land of orchids, rivers and waterfalls. In its winding, hilly, colonial streets, life has hardly changed in a hundred years. Jalapa is famed for its overhanging, flower covered balconies and its beautiful women. But the new sections provide every convenience in the way of wide streets and handsome modern buildings. Untouristed and quiet, this charming old town has lots to recommend it for retirement.

The semi-tropical climate is marred only by the soft *chipi-chipi* rains and sometimes by fog. Data: Feb. 60°, May 68°, Aug. 66°, Nov. 60°; annual average temp. 54°, rainfall

63.5". Proof of the area's mild climate and fertility are the beautiful Lecuona Gardens at nearby Banderilla, home of more than 200 varieties of orchids, and azaleas and gardenias.

The smallest of expatriate colonies keeps Jalapa unspoiled and costs low. After exploring Mexico with an edition of Harian's *Bargain Paradises of the World*, novelist Edward Godwin chose the Jalapa area as the most beautiful in all of Mexico—perfect for retirement in every way. The city has its own symphony orchestra and there are interesting trips to nearby plantations while all the attractions of the garden state of Vera Cruz are close at hand.

Best Hotel Buys: *Del Pardo*, I. Good food, best here.

MANZANILLO, Col. Alt. 15', pop 20,000. In an amphitheater of jungle-clad hills forming a picturesque natural harbor, Manzanillo is a lusty tropical seaport that reminds you of Rio. A peninsula splits the coast into two bays, each in turn dotted with smaller bays and beaches, many deserted. Santiago Bay, with its golden sands streaked with black, is for still water bathing. Beaches on Manzanillo Bay incline towards surf and Cuyutlan, a few miles south, is famed for its terrifying green waves. Manzanillo Bay—a languid, atmospheric town of narrow streets and a tree shaded plaza with a do-nothing air. Bus services link the town with the Santiago peninsula, resort location of hotels and modern beach homes.

At its best November to May and rather hot in summer, Manzanillo is nonetheless a popular summer resort for Guadalajarans. Data: average annual temperature 79°, maximum 87°, minimum 72°. Relative humidity 77%, rainfall 36", cloudiness 66%. Days with rain 52, fog 20, gales 16, thunder 21.

For those who enjoy Florida living, Manzanillo offers similar conditions year around. Homes at Santiago Beach can sometimes be rented and excluding resort facilities, all costs are low. The plethora of seafood is bargain priced. Fishing is unparalleled and there are excellent skin diving, hunting, birdwatching and riding. But Manzanillo has no night life. Our rating: a comparatively unknown and unspoiled beach resort with excellent water sports and lots of atmosphere and charm. Recommended for an inexpensive winter sojourn.

Beautiful homesites are available on hilltops overlooking the bays and also at Bahia de Santiago Yacht and Country Club development, at which memberships, including lot, cost $2,500-$3,950. *Caution:* invest in nothing here, including memberships, until it has been thoroughly investigated by an experienced Mexican lawyer in your employ.

Best Hotel Buys: *Colonial*, I. Pleasant downtown hotel. *Playa Santiago*, I-M. Cottage style hotel on hill above sea, discount to retirees. *La Posada*, M. Small American run inn on beach near town, hospitable.

PUERTO VALLARTA, Jal. Alt. 100', pop 7,500. Accessible only by air from Guadalajara or Mazatlan, or by dry season bus, this loveliest of Mexico's fishing villages overlooks the wide, forty mile sweep of Banderas Bay. To north and south, great headlands and clusters of arched rocks break the coast into innumerable coves and beaches. Resembling a terraced Italian fishing village, Puerto Vallarta's quaint cobbled streets lead downhill to the *malecon* and shore where, due to its isolation, supplies must still be landed by freighter. A clear river divides the town in two. All is tranquil, uncommercialized and utterly delightful.

With perhaps the best climate on Mexico's Pacific Coast, Puerto Vallarta is mild and dry October to June and cooled by ocean breezes in summer. Data: Mar. 64°-84°, June 77°-91°, Sept. 79°-91°, Dec. 60°-86°.

The far away charm of this sultry Eden has lured several hundred Americans to settle in its lush tropic beauty. The houses of writers and artists line Gringo Gulch, as the river is called. And a rash of new homes, rental apartments and a supermarket and movie theater have appeared among the steeply tilted, cobbled streets and pastel colored houses that cling to the hillsides. Thus far, however, only a handful of cabs, trucks and jeeps has been imported and the Puerto remains unexploited and inexpensive. A low cost station wagon service links all hotels to Los Muertos Beach, an easy walk south of town, and you can live in Puerto Vallarta very well without a car. Other beaches, including Los Tules to the north, are all steep with deep water close in and free of undertow. There are few bothersome insects and the water supply, though mercurial, is satisfactory. English language films are shown every second night at the open air movie. But there are no phones yet.

Come here in midwinter and you'll pay $120-$300 a month for one of the furnished resort apartments that come equipped with maid, cook and utilities. But at other seasons, rates drop 10% (at hotels also). Long term rentals are cheaper and with a bank trust arranged, you can build an attractive home for $5,000-$20,000. A building boom is already far advanced and you'll find a real estate office and several club type lease developments.

Fishing and skin diving are both outstanding and there are rental sailboats and horses, a Sunday *serenata,* popular cocktail gatherings attended by everyone and one or two cafes where dancing goes on till the wee hours. Among several interesting trips is the day-long launch cruise to Yelapa, an isolated village twelve miles south set in an indescribably beautiful valley below a waterfall. Here a small American escapist colony makes its headquarters and lives in South Seas style. A primitive but surprisingly comfortable hotel of thatched bungalows supplies satisfactory accommodations at rather steep prices. Our rating: Puerto Vallarta is *the* best small resort on Mexico's Pacific Coast. Ideal for a long winter sojourn. Several hotels are priced right for retirement.

Best Hotel Buys: *Oceano,* I-M. Older well run seafront hotel, good food. *Rio,* M. At town edge on river facing sea, modern, pool, hospitable. *Rosita,* I. Popular, older hotel with new wing; old wing offers good value. *Tropicana,* M. Small, at Los Muertos Beach, good food and swimming. *Posada de La Selva,* M. Across river, very good terraced cottage resort in jungle setting. Others include the beachside *Playa de Oro* to the north; *Las Campanos,* a new hillside cottage resort; and the *Chula Vista,* and *Posada de Pedregal,* both I or I-M.

SAN BLAS, *Nay.* Alt. 25', pop 1,800. If you're seeking a sleepy fishing village with thatched huts and tropical vegetation that looks like Polynesia, turn off Highway #15 just north of Tepic and drive down through dense forests of gigantic coco palms to San Blas. Crowned by a crumbling Spanish fort, San Blas is a tranquil tropical village of thatch and wattle houses on cobbled streets grouped around an old customs house. Back of the village, dark, mysterious, mangrove lined rivers wind off through the jungle. In front are several of the finest uncommercialized beaches in Mexico. The sands

are hand and can be driven over; the surf is light.

Though hot and humid in summer and subject at all times to rather bothersome insects, San Blas is one of the most overlooked yet easily accessible beach Utopias in Mexico. Inexpensive houses are occasionally for rent or you can park your trailer right on the beach. All costs are low, fishing is excellent and boats cheap. With a rented boat, you can cruise up jungle estuaries haunted by alligators and brightly plumaged birds. And with a full day to spare, boats will take you to the unique island of Mexcaltitlan and back. A small colony of Americans-in-the-know spends the winter here each year at budget prices.

Best Hotel Buys: *Bucanero,* I-M. Modest town hostelry with pool. *Casino Colon,* I-M. Modern Mexican resort hotel on Bay of Matanchen. *Playa Hermosa,* I. Modest, three story resort hotel on Borrego Beach.

TECOLUTLA, *Ver.* Alt. 10', pop 800. In tropical northern Vera Cruz, among the lagoons at the mouth of the Tecolutla River, you'll find this little paradise of flawless white sand beach rimmed by murmuring coconut palms. Vacation interest centers not upon the village, an uninteresting collection of shacks on a river flat, but upon Tecolutla's two beach hotels. Bathing from the long, straight, gently sloping beach ranks among the best on the entire Gulf of Mexico.

With a climate marred only by occasional winter northers, Tecolutla's data reads thus: Feb. 70°, May 77°, Aug. 77°, Oct. 72°; annual average temp. 73°, rainfall 57.2". Insects are bothersome at times but are never serious. Weekending Mexicans are Tecolutla's principal clientele and this resort continues untouristed, unexploited and inexpensive. It's a fine spot to spend the winter at low cost. Fishing is excellent, the beach is littered with shells and driftwood, you can stalk crocodiles along the jungly river and nearby is the interesting pyramid of Tajin and the unique town of Papantla, home of the thrilling Volador or Flying Men ceremony.

Best Hotel Buys: *Balneario Tecolutla,* I-M. White three story resort hotel with sea views, garden and pool. *Marsol,* I. Pleasant beach hotel with balconies, pool, gardens and good food. Both are slightly time worn but are priced right.

TUXPAN, Ver. Alt. 46', pop 25,000. For a completely relaxing vacation at an off-the-beaten-track, do-nothing resort, Tuxpan is hard to beat. A tanker and pineapple port, Tuxpan is a typical Mexican town of hilly, narrow streets, parks, plazas and a river promenade, all aflame with orange blooms. On the opposite bank of the wide Rio Pantepec, and linked by bridge, is the village of Santiago de La Peña. And to the north, hard, easy to drive over and sweeping far out of sight, is the immense white beach of La Barra Norte, longest and finest beach on the Gulf of Mexico.

Rather hot in summer and subject to brief winter northers, Tuxpan is at its best in spring and fall. Data: Mar. 72°, June 83°, Sept. 81°, Dec. 68°; annual average temp. 76°, maximum 84°, minimum 67°. Relative humidity 84%, rainfall 52.7". Days with rain 161, cloud 145, gales 1.6, dense fog 108, thunder 16.

There are plush residential sections and houses may be rented inexpensively. Fishing, boating and bathing are superb, La Barra is lined with driftwood and shells, and at rustic beach restaurants like Chita's, the seafood is delicious. But this serene, sunny seashore town has few other distractions.

Best Hotel Buys. *Florida,* I. Fairly comfortable town hotel. *Los Mangos,* M. Pleasant motel in riverside garden; trailer space.

VILLA JUAREZ, Pue. Alt. 3,900', pop 9,300. Also called Xocotepec de Juarez, this colorful mountain town lies in a garden setting of fruit trees, flowers and orchids. For those who prefer a quiet country environment and rural activities, this area is attractive for a longer stay or for retirement.

Best Hotel Buys: *Mi Ranchito,* I. At Km. 213 on outskirts, a delightful and typical Mexican country resort in 30 acres of gardens; swimming pool; good food; OK for retirement.

ZIHUATANEJO, Gro. Alt. 15' pop 1,800. If you're seeking a really idyllic Pacific beach resort that is virtually undiscovered, undeveloped, unspoiled, uncrowded, unpolished, uncomplicated and uncostly, this is it! By air or bus, it's 150 miles northwest of Acapulco, a haphazard fishing village on an almost landlocked bay with miles of velvety beach split by six rugged headlands. For its main street, the village has a banyan shaded beach lined with upturned log *canuas.*

These same *canuas* ferry you to other beaches like Moderno, La Ropa and amazingly beautiful Las Gatas and to islands like Ixtapa inhabited by crowds of chattering parrakeets. Needless to say, you'll soon fall under the spell of Zihuatanejo's tropic beauty and there are no neon signs, fashionable hotels or other Gold Coast trappings.

Climatically, Zihuatanejo enjoys the identical climate of Acapulco, which is to say it's 75°-83° all year with light breezes to cool the sticky summer days. To date, lack of a good road has kept Zihuatanejo an escapist's lotus land but Mexicans are beginning to put up weekend houses, there is electricity from 6-11 P.M. and an abundance of low cost lobsters, oysters and other succulent seafoods. Skin diving, snorkeling and fishing are out of this world, the atmosphere relaxing, night life nil.

Best Hotel Buys: *Belmar* and *Casa Arcadia,* I. Both on town beach, not strong on luxury but passable and clean. *Catalina,* M-E. Comfortable resort hotel on terraces above La Ropa Beach a mile from village, closed in summer. *Irma,* I. Small, modern inn on cliff above beach.

Region 5.
Tropical Rainy Trade Wind Climate

STRICTLY SPORTSMEN'S country and, with one exception, unsuited for retirement, this jungly terrain includes Mexico's only true rain forests. Due to its proximity to the sea and trade wind breezes (plus northers in winter) it is not so entirely tropical as, say, the Amazon jungle. Nor is it so continuously humid and oppressive as many people believe. There is seasonal variation in both humidity and rainfall and also in temperature. On the other hand, there is neither winter nor frost and the temperature in all months remains above 64°.

Fall is warm and cloudy until November and cloudiness continues through the winter when northers bring lower temperatures November through February. Spring sees strong, southerly *surada* winds which bring hot, sultry weather bad for asthmatics, rheumatic and cardiac sufferers. Summer is hot and humid. In the south, May is hottest, in the north July. After July, the skies are continually obscured by cloud. In fact, this is Mexico's cloudiest region with an average cloudiness of 66%. The mean annual temperature is 76°-80°.

Climatic data for Coatzacoalcos demonstrates the overall pattern: Coatzacoalcos, V.C., 46'. Average temperatures: annual 77°, annual maximum 83°, annual minimum 70°. Relative humidity 87%, cloudiness 66%. Rainfall 115" annually falling on 211 days with a 24-hour record maximum of 8.5". Prevailing wind northeast, maximum velocity recorded 74 knots. Days per year with clear skies 67, cloudy skies 122 (most July to November), thunder 28.2. (Foggy days at Ciudad del Carmen 1, Villa Hermosa 26.)

Conclusion: an interesting region best visited December to April when its beach resorts also have some merit.

ISLA AGUADA, Camp. Located on fish-jammed Terminos Lagoon, this sleepy village is site of El Tarpon Tropical, a bungalow fishing resort which for something like $38 a day provides room, meals, boat and guide— not *too* expensive for what is undoubtedly some of the finest tarpon and lagoon fishing on earth.

ISLA DEL CARMEN, Camp. Alt. 10', pop 15,000. A stepping stone on the Gulf Highway to Yucatan and linked to the mainland by ferries at either end, Carmen Island is 30 x 3 miles of exotic coconut plantations ringed by flawless beaches. The inshore side faces Laguna de Termino, site of the most fabulous tarpon fishing on earth. And Ciudad del Carmen, the pastel-tinted shrimping port at the island's western tip, is one of the most picturesque ports on the Gulf of Mexico. During the 1950s, a shrimp boom transformed Ciudad del Carmen into a boom town. But things have quieted down and today you can make your headquarters at a surprisingly comfortable hostelry and enjoy god meals built around seafood and the superlative Campeche shrimp. Though Ciudad del Carmen still is somewhat primitive, the population is all white and completely literate. You make your own amusements here but the fishing is stupendous and now that the boom seems to have subsided, the island seems inevitably destined to regain its Eden-like qualities.

Best Hotel Buys: *Fernandez,* I. Modest but hospitable and very pleasant with good food. Located at Calle 22#123. *Hotel Las Campanas,* M. In flavorful villa at Calle 36#100. *Motel Lino,* M. Best here.

CATEMACO, Ver. Alt 1,000'. A couple of hours' drive south of Vera Cruz city lies Mexico's loveliest lake, Catemaco. Cradled in a volcano crater and surrounded by twisted vines and roots and tropical trees, the rapidly changing colors of the water make Catemaco a place of enchantment. There are boating, fishing and water skiing and interesting villages and waterfalls to visit. This region is also outstanding for its prolific bird life. Our rating: a rustic but utterly delightful region for a real rest in the tropics.

Best Hotel Buys: *Plaza Azul,* I-M. A hideaway resort hotel with bungalows on lake. Almost completely unknown to American tourists.

TLACOTALPAN, Ver. Alt. 20', pop 11,000. Reached by ferry from Paso Nacional near Veracruz, this charming old resort overlooks the landlocked delta of the Papaloapan and San Juan Rivers. For generations, Tlacotalpan served as a private retreat for the wealthy families of Veracruz and vivid trees and flowers still arch over streets lined by handsome old houses. Two pink and blue churches loom over the plaza and green lawns border the town's broad thorofares. Apart from a small factory on the north side of town the booming progress of the Papaloapan River seems to have by-passed Tlacotalpan. No permanent American colony has settled here yet. The town's great Fiesta de Candelaria, held February 2-8 and famed for its lusty *bamba* dances, ranks as one of Mexico's most spirited folkloric events. Meanwhile, Tlacotalpan dozes in its luxuriant riverbank setting—an ideal yet undiscovered Utopia for a sojourn or retirement.

Best Hotel Buys: *Viajero,* I. Very modest. Private homes offer superior accommodation.

VERA CRUZ, Ver. Alt. 10', pop 165,000. For a low cost beach vacation in the Queen City of the Gulf tropics, head for this historic seaport where guitar music fills the air and a carnival spirit reigns all winter. Viewed in the early morning from the lichen encrusted Spanish fort of San Juan de Ulua on an island in the harbor, this sun bleached port begins with a broad harbor-side *malecon* lined by palms and strikingly contemporary buildings, then plunges back into an old colonial city of ancient walls and narrow cobbled streets surrounding the arcaded Plaza de Armas. To the south, gently sloping beaches of hand packed dark sand run for miles. First there's Villa del Mar, two miles south, with its gaily colored beach umbrellas; the Mocambo with its big resort hotel; and finally Boca del Rio at the rivermouth, a ramshackle but picturesque fishing village with a smart, modern clubhouse. It's true the beaches can't compare with those of the Pacific and sharks discurage bathers at times . . . but Vera Cruz remains an interesting colonial city with that paradoxical combination of vivacity and indolence so common in the tropics. In Vera Cruz you'll find a lighthearted Caribbean mood that expresses itself in the slow, easy manana tempo and bursts out after dark in the sensuous La Bamba and the passionate *huapangos* at which the Parichos are so adept.

On the edge of Region 4 and with strong overtones of this region's climate, Vera Cruz is lazy and tropical in summer when there is considerable rain, and warm the rest of the year with occasional brief winter northers. Data: Mar. 73°, June 81°, Sept. 81°, Dec. 72°; annual average temp. 77°, maximum 81°, minimum 72°, Relative humidity 80%, rainfall 64", cloudiness 60%. Days with rain 133, fog 56.4, strong winds 119, thunder 21.3. Rain, however, rarely falls in the daytime and northers are always followed by delightful weather.

With trim new subdivisions, excellent and inexpensive seafood and cigars and its gay plaza life and water sports, Vera Cruz has considerable attributes as a place to retire. In fact, several Americans have already retired here. Away from the city's noise, conditions are splendid; air conditioning can be had; and almost all costs are low. Streetcars and buses run everywhere and a car is far from essential. Water sports, including astoundingly good tarpon fishing, take top place among activities but there is also rewarding birdwatching on the nearby Papaloapan River, an interesting historical museum in town, a major carnival prior to Lent, and easy trips to such places as Cempoala ruins and the beautiful beaches of Chachalaca and Sacrifios Island. Almost everyone dines on the plaza during the twice weekly *serenatas*. Just south of Vera Cruz and within an hour's drive is the picturesque fishing village of Alvarado, starting point for a scenic riverboat trip up the jungly Papaloapan River to Tlacotalpan. And if you prefer a spa, Vera Cruz has that too: the Balneario Puente Nacional twenty minutes out on the Jalapa highway.

Best Hotel Buys: *Balneario Puente Nacional* (at Puente Nacional), 1. A comfortable, Mexican style spa hotel surrounded by mountains with thermal swimpool, riding, fishing, etc. Discount to retirees, a best buy! *Mocambo* (at Mocambo Beach), I-M. An older but attractive white terraced beach resort hotel with Olympic sized swimpool. Discount to retirees. The best hotel in Veracruz is the *Veracruz*, E; the second best is the *Emporio*, I-M. A good budget hotel is the *Braña*. The *Diligencia, Colonial* and *Villa del Mar* are pleasant and reasonably priced.

Odds and Ends

Mexico is a land of longevity: a recent census revealed that the Republic had 84,474 persons aged over 85 and eighty-five persons aged 100 or over.

Under latest regulations, applicants for *inmigrante* permits who receive social security or other income which is under the required amount may qualify by making a proportionate annual deposit in Nacional Financiera. Although a couple applying for *inmigrante* permits require a monthly income of $320, a couple with only $220 can qualify by depositing $1,200 annually in Nacional Financiera to make up the deficit. Once in Mexico, they would receive this sum back in twelve equal annual installments but without any interest. The following year, they would again deposit $1,200 and so on each year until they become *inmigrados*.

OTHER HARIAN BOOKS

AROUND THE WORLD FOR $1500
—Norman Ford's world-wide travel guide

■ ■ the complete guide to see all the world or any part of it

■ ■ via MEDIUM-CLASS travel, the way that cuts travel costs

His book is an encyclopedia of cost-cutting "know-how" for the traveler everywhere. Of course, it details what to see in each country you might visit. And it goes on to show **how** to see it: the low-cost local tours you might want to take, when it is advisable to go on your own, what it costs to rent an auto, the touring centers for seeing the back country, the sight-filled ways to journey from one city to another. You'll like the hotels which he names —all first-rate yet charging much below the ornate tourist palaces down the street. Always, too, he shows how to meet the local people and thus find the color and depth of the inner life of the countries you visit.

Around the World for $1500 describes, as well, the low cost, interesting ways to reach the lands that fascinate you. It tells you about the steamships that offer more travel and lower costs; the often-unknown airplane routings that give you more cities and countries; the land routings that take you across Europe or South America or the storied Middle East or India. It names the travel reductions you might be entitled to; what you must know about local trains, buses, ferries, taxis, etc.; the seasons to travel, tipping, how to plan your trip and choose the cities and countries you can do in the time you have available.

With this book you have the "know-how" for seeing the world or any part of it. With it you can circle the globe or do a smaller area; take the Grand Tour of Europe, perhaps, which means Switzerland, the shores of the Mediterranean, Italy, Rome, Paris, London, and a dozen other places. With it, you can journey from the high Inca Lands down to the Chilean lakes and on to Rio. Or do Mandalay and its pagodas and temples. Or Israel, India, Tahiti, Hongkong, Japan, or a score or more of other lands.

Always, **Around the World for $1500** shows that with "know-how" travel anywhere can be inexpensive. So why not let it open the world to you? It costs only $2.

HOW TO TRAVEL—
AND GET PAID FOR IT

There's a job waiting for you somewhere: on a ship, with an airline, in overseas branches of American firms, in foreign farms overseas—even exploring if you're adventurous.

The full story of what job you can fill is in Norman Ford's big book **How to Travel and Get Paid for It**. Whether you're male or female, young or old, whether you want a lifetime of paid traveling or just hanker to roam the world for a short year or so, here are the facts you want, complete with names and addresses and full details about the preparations to make, the cautions to observe, the countries to head for.

You learn about jobs in travel agencies (and as tour conductors), in importing and exporting concerns, with mining and construction companies. Here's the story of jobs in the Red Cross and the UN organizations, how doctors get jobs on ships, the way for a young girl to land a job as airline hostess, the wonderful travel opportunities if you will teach English to foreigners, and the fabulous travel possibilities for those who know stenography.

"Can a man or woman still work his or her way around the world today?" Norman Ford asks in his book as you might ask today. He replies in 75,000 words of facts, "The answer is still a very definite yes!" $1.50.

ALL OF EUROPE
AT LOW COST

The Guide that rates Europe's choice hotels by price.

With this book, it takes only a glance to make a real discovery night after night. Because every hotel (and restaurant, too) is rated by price, you will never overspend, but you will always get the top values on the budget you've allotted yourself (which can be as little as $6 a day for hotels and meals). **At all times, this is the complete guide to seeing Europe at low cost.**

From one end of Europe to the other, it leads you to the towns and cities that have fascinated generations of travelers. It details what to see, the most interesting routings if you're going by rail, bus, or plane. For every stop it names the choice hotels and restaurants at the price you want to pay.

For still more help in see Europe well, there's also a COMPLETE guide to motoring through Europe (and you'll use this whether you drive all the way or merely rent an auto now and then for local excursions).

This is the only guide to low cost travel in Europe which Time Magazine found "thorough, realistic" and gives top rating for its "excellent coverage" of hotels and restaurants throughout Europe. Price, $2.50.

IT'S CHEAPER TO TRAVEL—

when you go on your own

The ONLY way to travel without overspending and get close to the lands and people you visit is to travel on your own. Never forget that when you travel, you spend $1000 on transportation, hotels, meals, etc. in order to take $35 or $40 worth of sightseeing buses.

Well planned travel on your own puts the emphasis on cutting the $1000 and saving most of the $35-$40 in order to get the depth and color that never exists for the average tourist, while you have the opportunity to explore a city at leisure, seeing, smelling, tasting, hearing, and feeling its inner life.

This book helps you get the utmost out of the lands and places you visit, out of their history, culture, peoples. In its 175 pages, it details everything about planning and executing your trip, taking you all through the ramifications of the travel business and showing that in travel it seldom follows that the more you spend, the more you see or the more you get. Instead, it shows that the more you do know about hotels, restaurants, guides, car rentals, sightseeing, rail, bus, plane, etc., the more enjoyably you travel, the richer is your travel experience, while you dramatically lower your costs.

Because the way to get close to the lands you want to see is to travel like the educated medium and upper classes in these countries, this book stresses the same MEDIUM-class travel they use. Here, then, are the guide-lines for whatever part of the world interests you: Europe or Mexico, Hongkong or Paris, the West Indies or South America. Here is the "know-how" for seeing one or all like the man who's been there a dozen times before.

With **It's Cheaper to Travel**, it is cheaper to travel, often cheaper than staying at home. So, to travel well, while getting the rich experience which travel should give you, get this book. $1.50.